FROM NOW ON

MALACHI WARD

Alternative Comics

Stargazer was originally published in *Study Group Magazine 3D*, Henix in *Elfworld #3*, Divination in *Sundays #5*, Negative Space in *Milk and Carrots #2*, Excerpt and Hero of Science in *Mome 22,* The Oviraptor in *Study Group Magazine #1*, Beasts of Kay-7 in *Top Shelf 2.0*, Sweet Dreams in *Smoke Signal #5*, and The Scout in *Hive #3*

Thanks to Erik Aucoin, Marc Arsenault, Dave Pifer, David Ritchie, Julie Pearson, Sean Ford, Jeff Lemire, Farel Dalrymple, Rob Clough, Charles Forsman, Gabe Fowler, Brian Herrick, Alex Kim, Joe Lambert, Eric Reynolds, Jordan Shiveley, Zack Soto, François Vigneault, Leigh Walton, Mom, Dad, Sam, Paul, and of course, Keiko, for being a role model in ways she doesn't know.

Published by **Alternative Comics**
21607B Stevens Creek Blvd.
Cupertino, California 95014
IndyWorld.com

Marc Arsenault, General Manager
David Nuss, Associate Publisher
Erik Aucoin, Commissioning Editor
Laura Susong, Assistant Editor

Printed in the United States of America

ISBN: 978-1-934460-91-7

MalachiWard.com | malachi.ward@gmail.com

TABLE OF CONTENTS

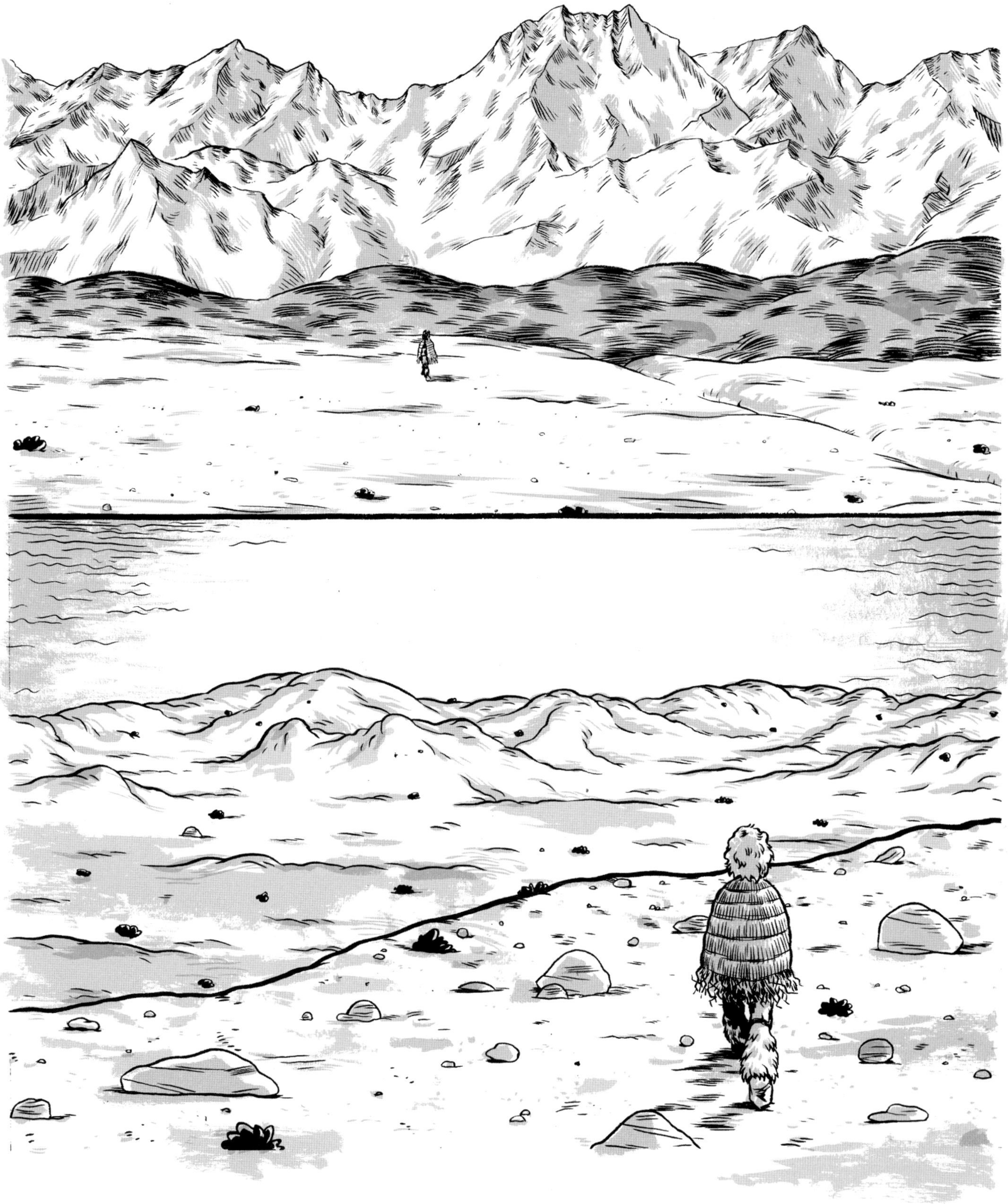

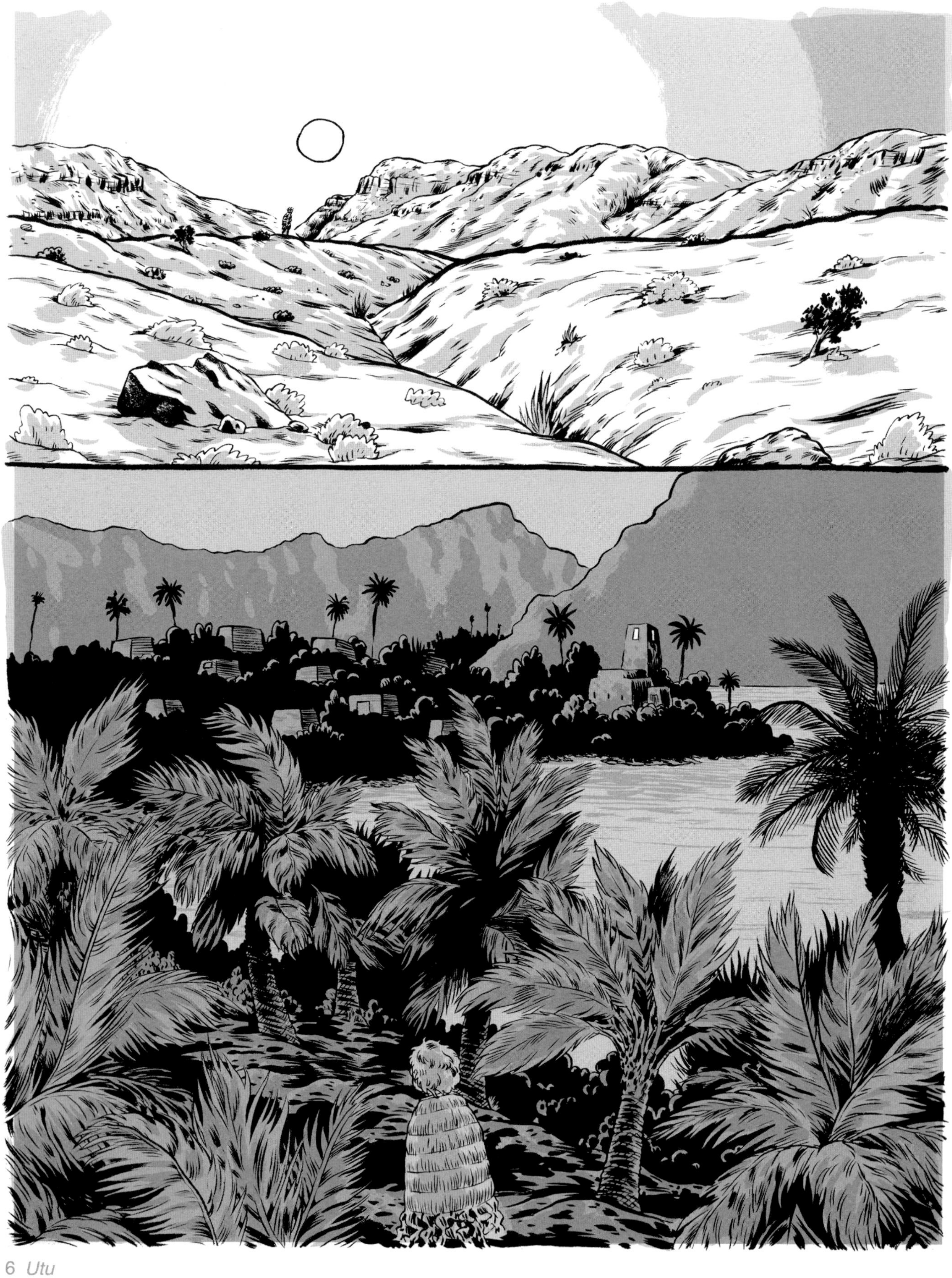

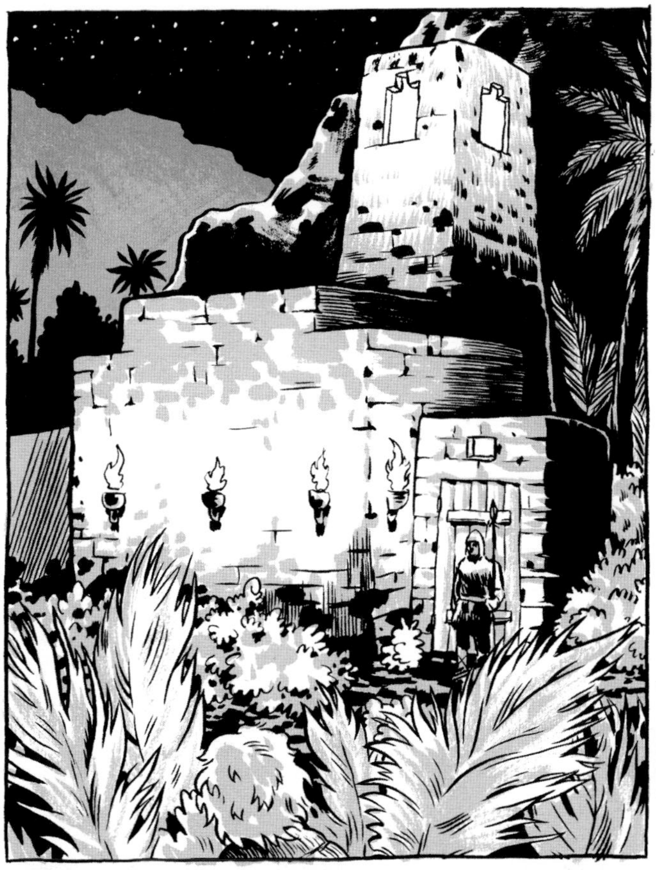

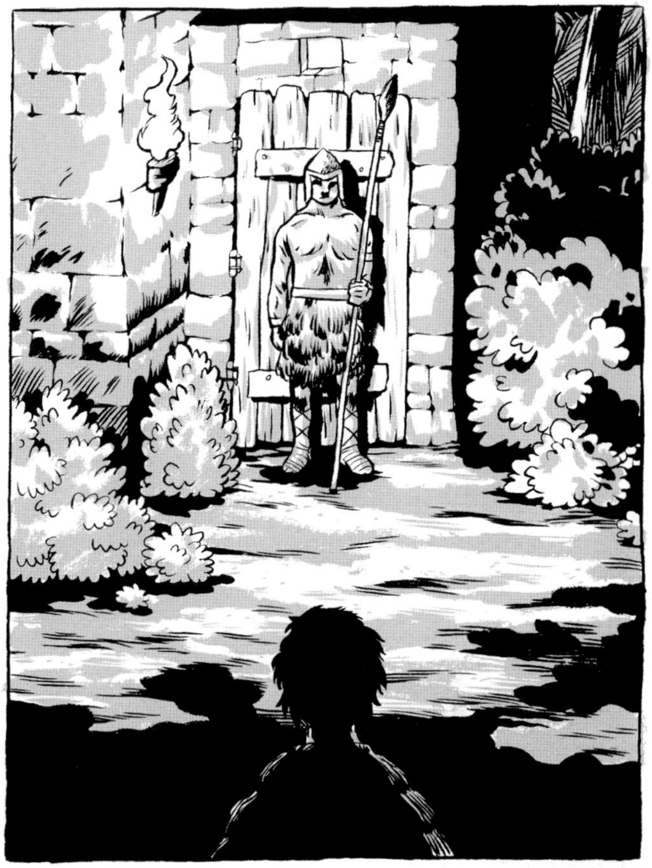

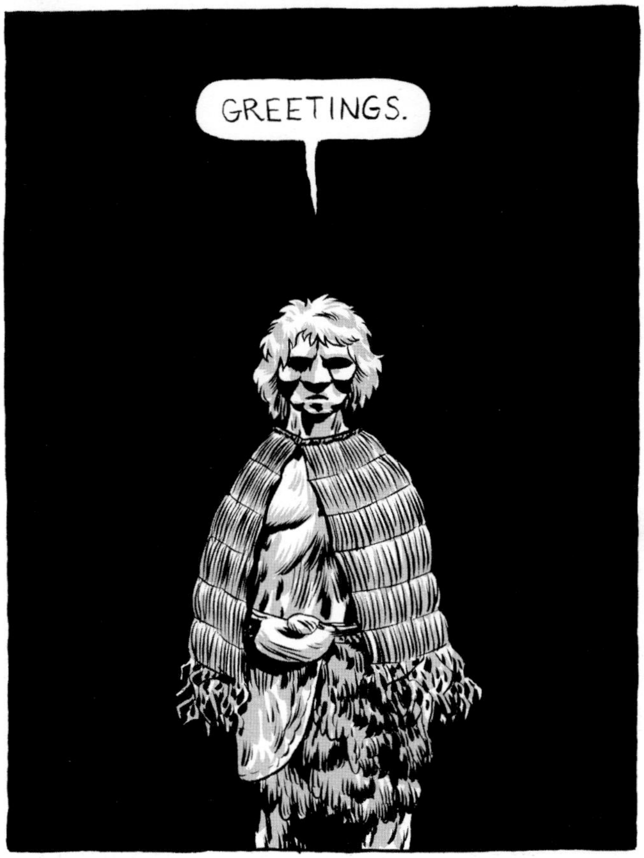
GREETINGS.

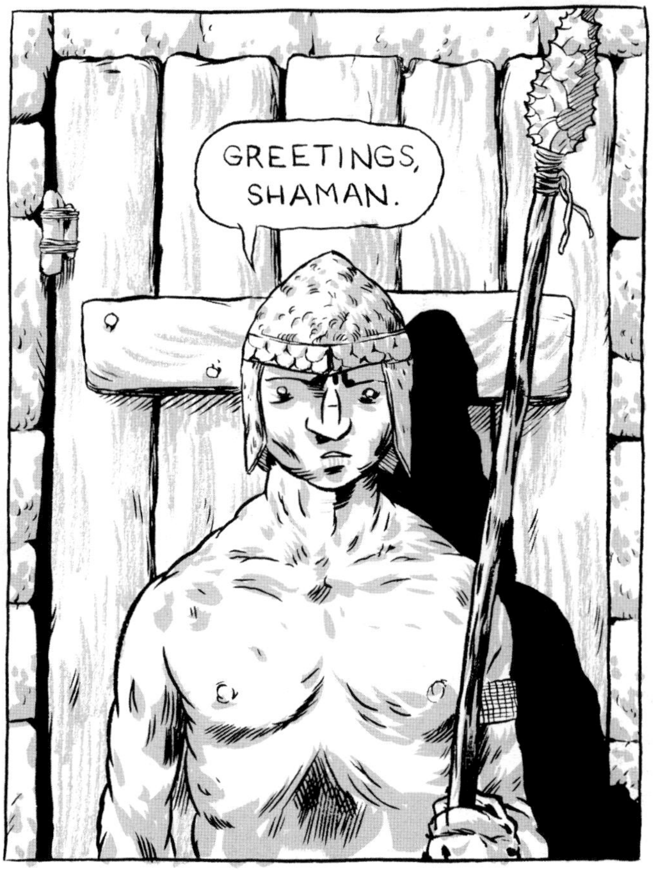
GREETINGS, SHAMAN.

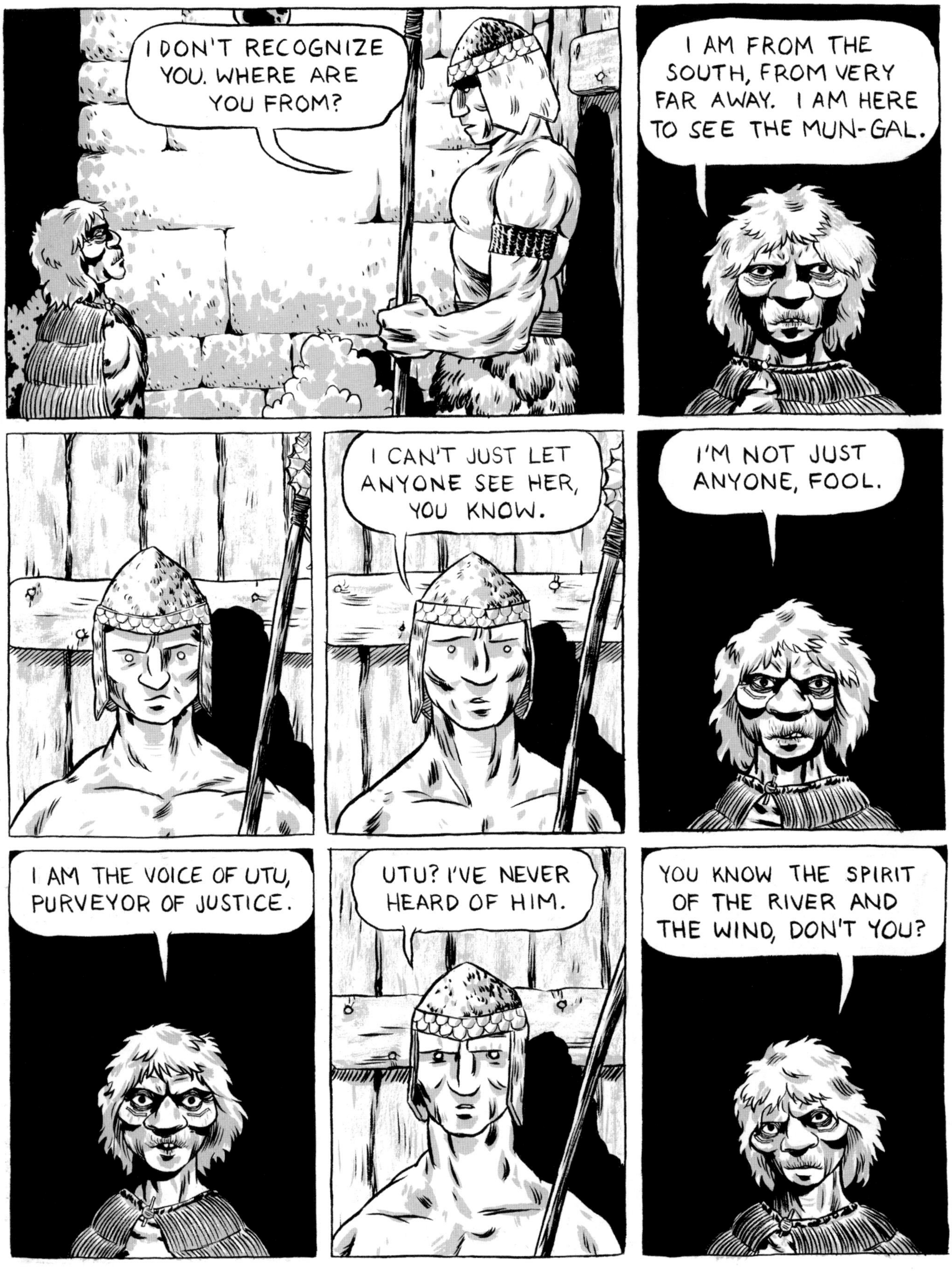
I DON'T RECOGNIZE YOU. WHERE ARE YOU FROM?
I AM FROM THE SOUTH, FROM VERY FAR AWAY. I AM HERE TO SEE THE MUN-GAL.
I CAN'T JUST LET ANYONE SEE HER, YOU KNOW.
I'M NOT JUST ANYONE, FOOL.
I AM THE VOICE OF UTU, PURVEYOR OF JUSTICE.
UTU? I'VE NEVER HEARD OF HIM.
YOU KNOW THE SPIRIT OF THE RIVER AND THE WIND, DON'T YOU?

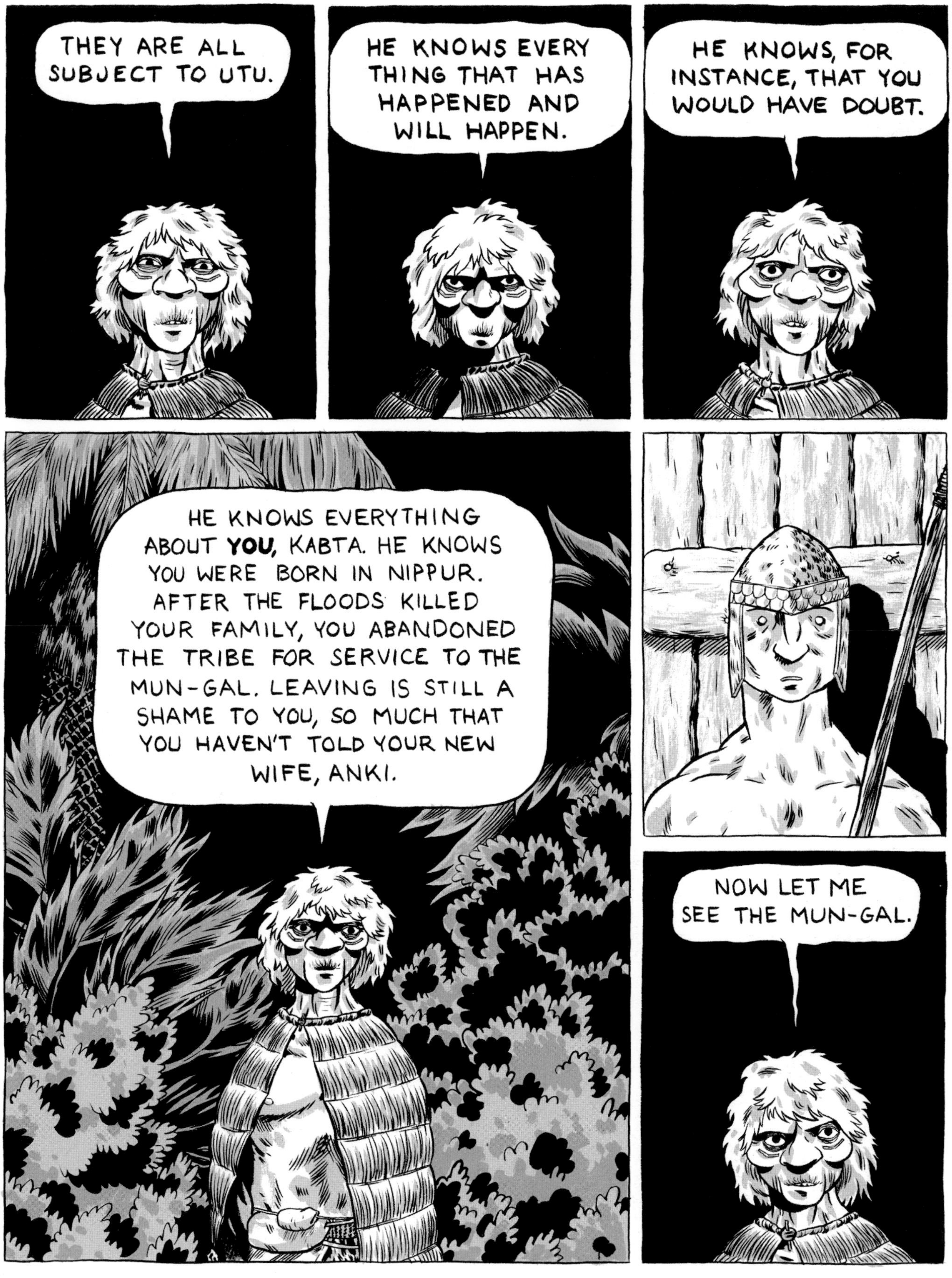
THEY ARE ALL SUBJECT TO UTU.
HE KNOWS EVERY THING THAT HAS HAPPENED AND WILL HAPPEN.
HE KNOWS, FOR INSTANCE, THAT YOU WOULD HAVE DOUBT.
HE KNOWS EVERYTHING ABOUT YOU, KABTA. HE KNOWS YOU WERE BORN IN NIPPUR. AFTER THE FLOODS KILLED YOUR FAMILY, YOU ABANDONED THE TRIBE FOR SERVICE TO THE MUN-GAL. LEAVING IS STILL A SHAME TO YOU, SO MUCH THAT YOU HAVEN'T TOLD YOUR NEW WIFE, ANKI.
NOW LET ME SEE THE MUN-GAL.

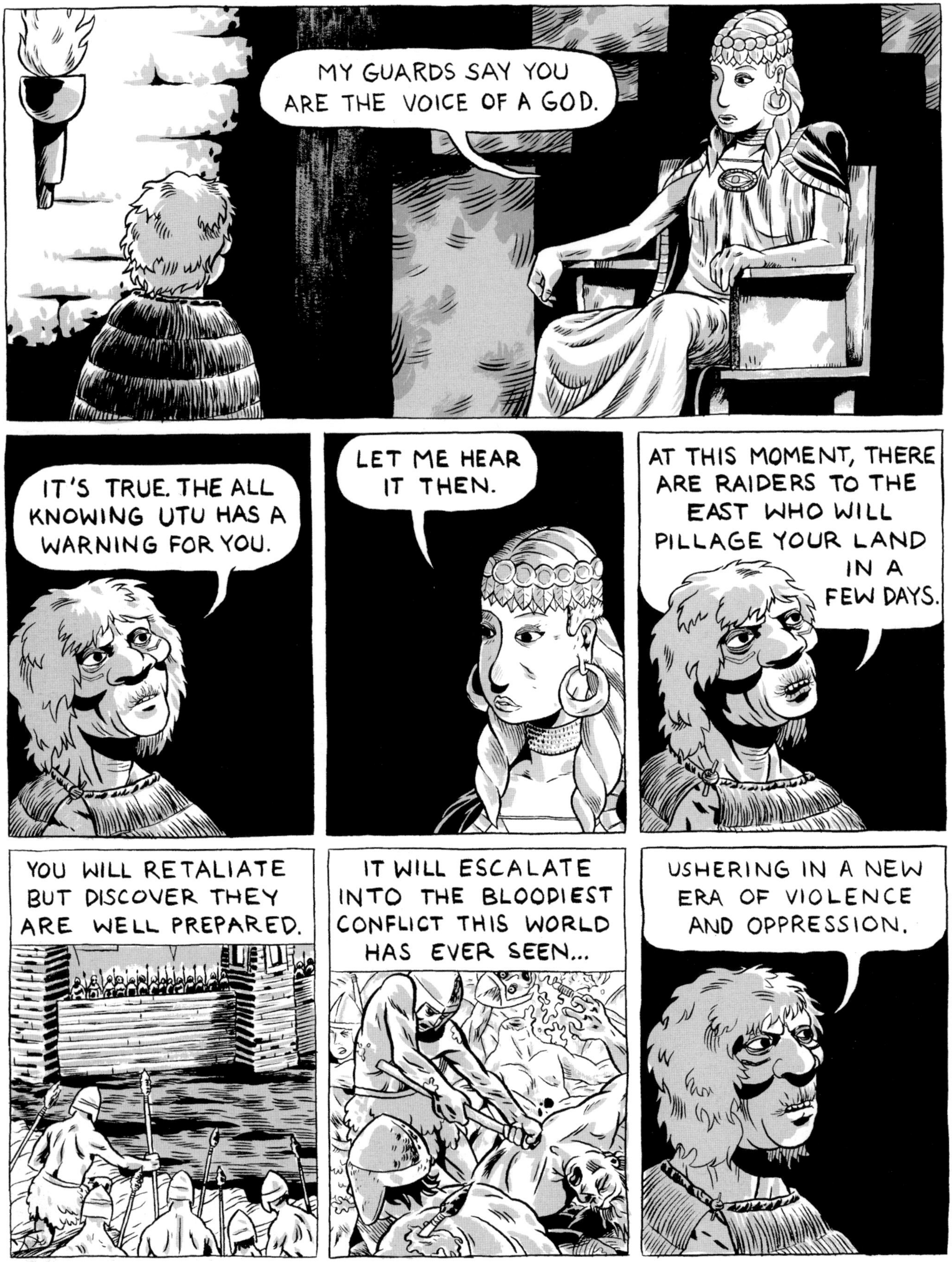
MY GUARDS SAY YOU ARE THE VOICE OF A GOD.
IT'S TRUE. THE ALL KNOWING UTU HAS A WARNING FOR YOU.
LET ME HEAR IT THEN.
AT THIS MOMENT, THERE ARE RAIDERS TO THE EAST WHO WILL PILLAGE YOUR LAND IN A FEW DAYS.
YOU WILL RETALIATE BUT DISCOVER THEY ARE WELL PREPARED.
IT WILL ESCALATE INTO THE BLOODIEST CONFLICT THIS WORLD HAS EVER SEEN...
USHERING IN A NEW ERA OF VIOLENCE AND OPPRESSION.

WHAT ABOUT ERIDU AND UR? WON'T THEY AID ME IN THE CONFLICT?

THEY WILL, AND EVENTUALLY YOU WILL CONQUER THE PEOPLE OF THE EAST, BUT THE PRECEDENT SET BY THESE BATTLES WILL POISON THE WORLD.

WHAT IS OUR ALTERNATIVE, PROPHET?

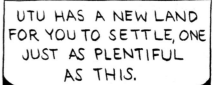

UTU HAS A NEW LAND FOR YOU TO SETTLE, ONE JUST AS PLENTIFUL AS THIS.

AND WHEN THE CLANS IN THE EAST REACH OUR NEW HOME, WHAT WILL WE DO? MOVE AGAIN?

UTU IS A GOD OF JUSTICE. YOU WILL BE PROVIDED FOR.

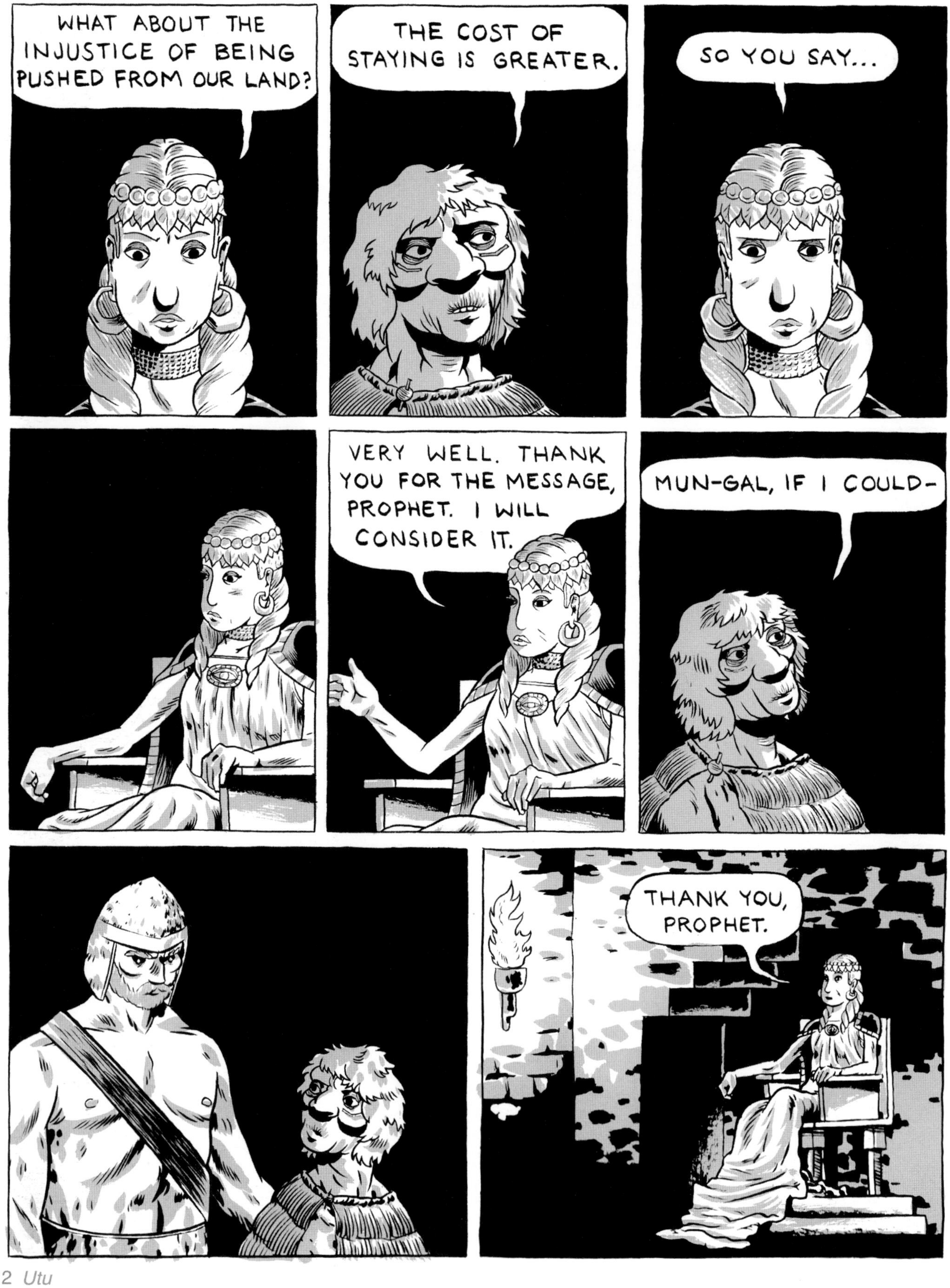
WHAT ABOUT THE INJUSTICE OF BEING PUSHED FROM OUR LAND?
THE COST OF STAYING IS GREATER.
SO YOU SAY...
VERY WELL. THANK YOU FOR THE MESSAGE, PROPHET. I WILL CONSIDER IT.
MUN-GAL, IF I COULD-
THANK YOU, PROPHET.

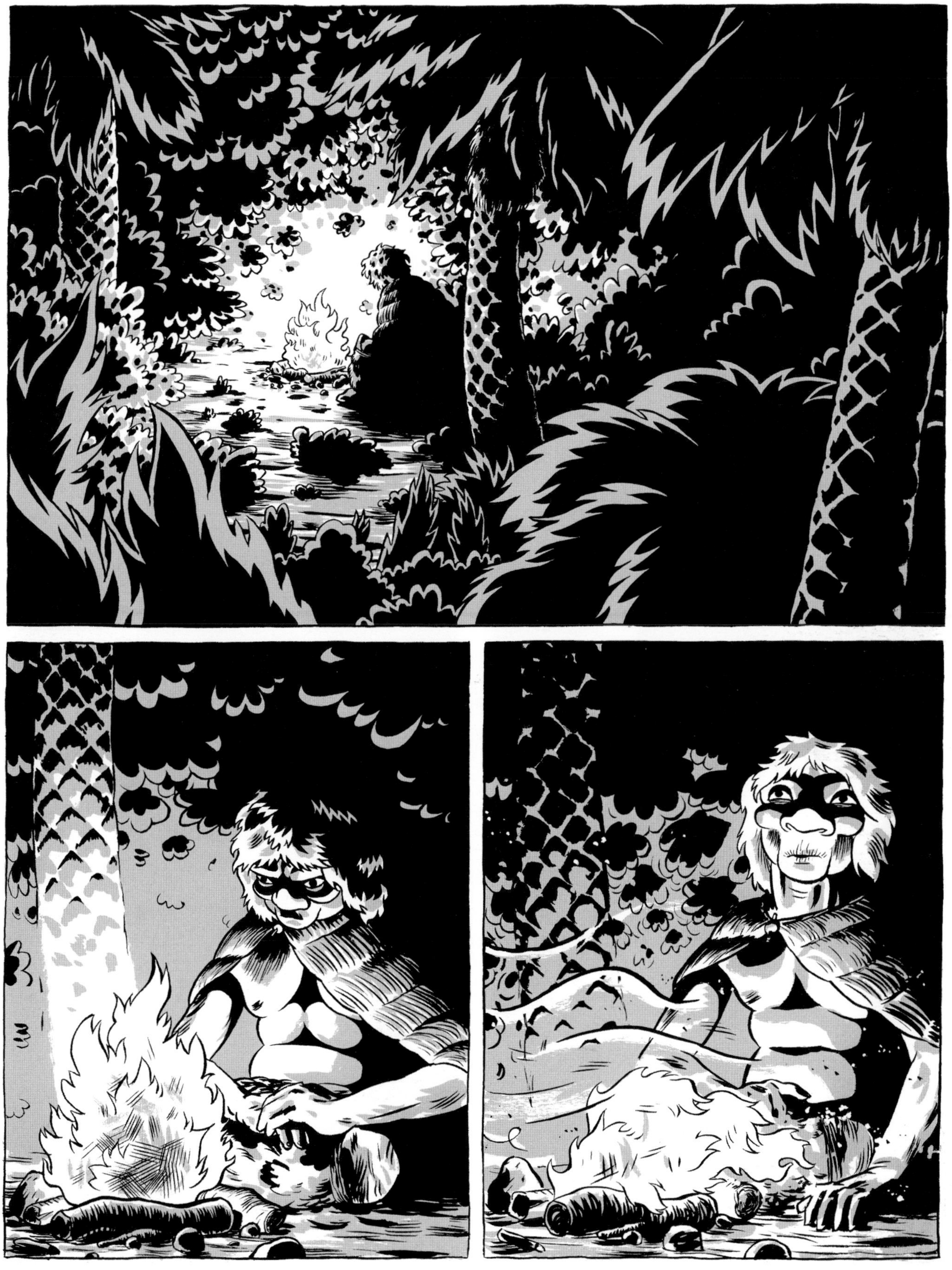

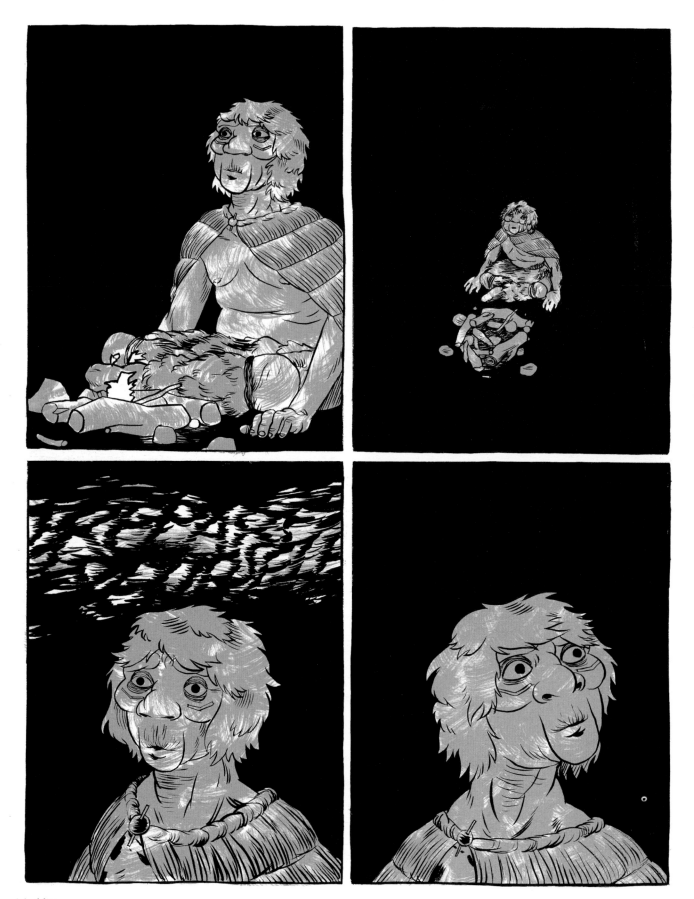

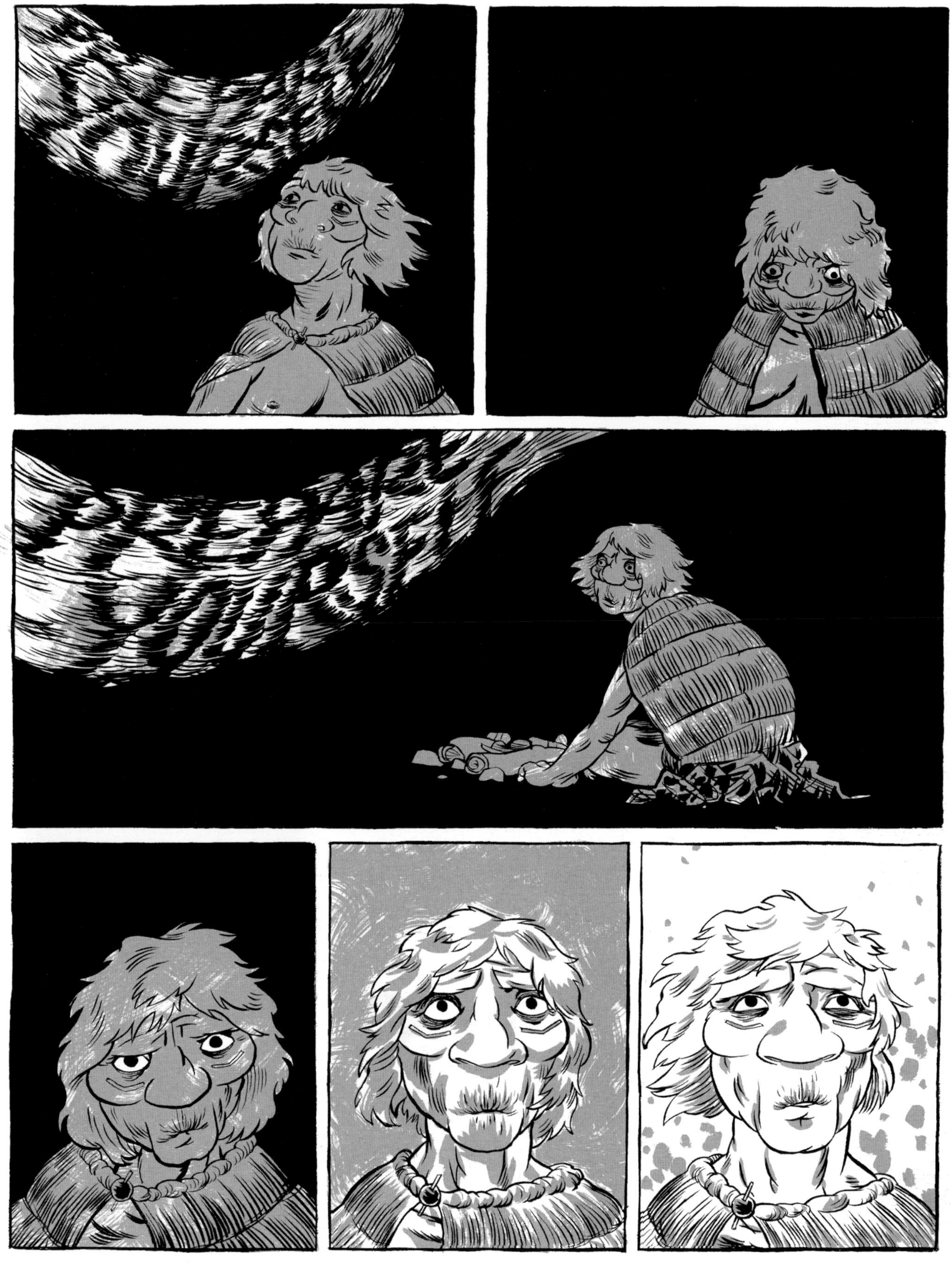

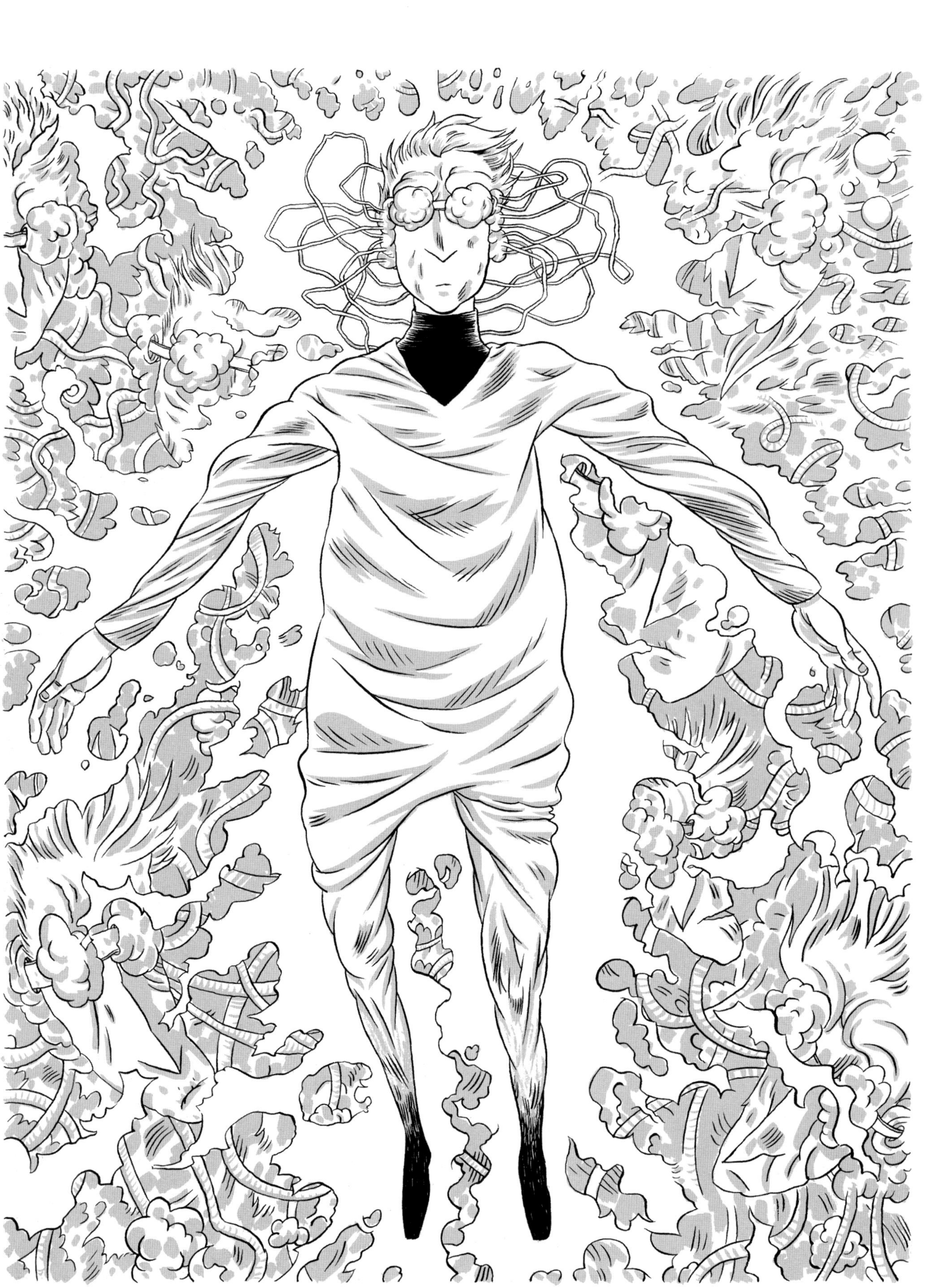

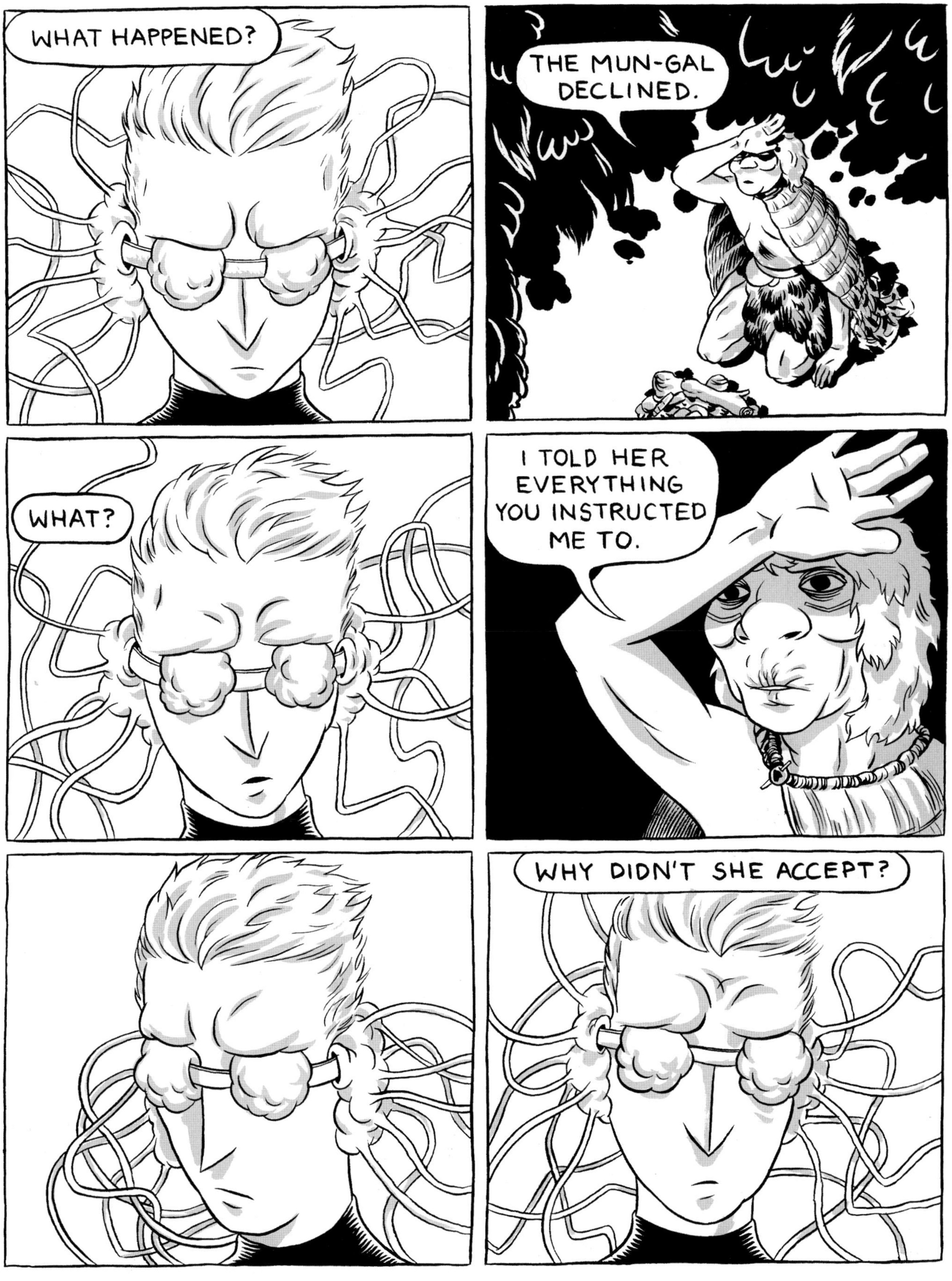
WHAT HAPPENED?
THE MUN-GAL DECLINED.
WHAT?
I TOLD HER EVERYTHING YOU INSTRUCTED ME TO.
WHY DIDN'T SHE ACCEPT?

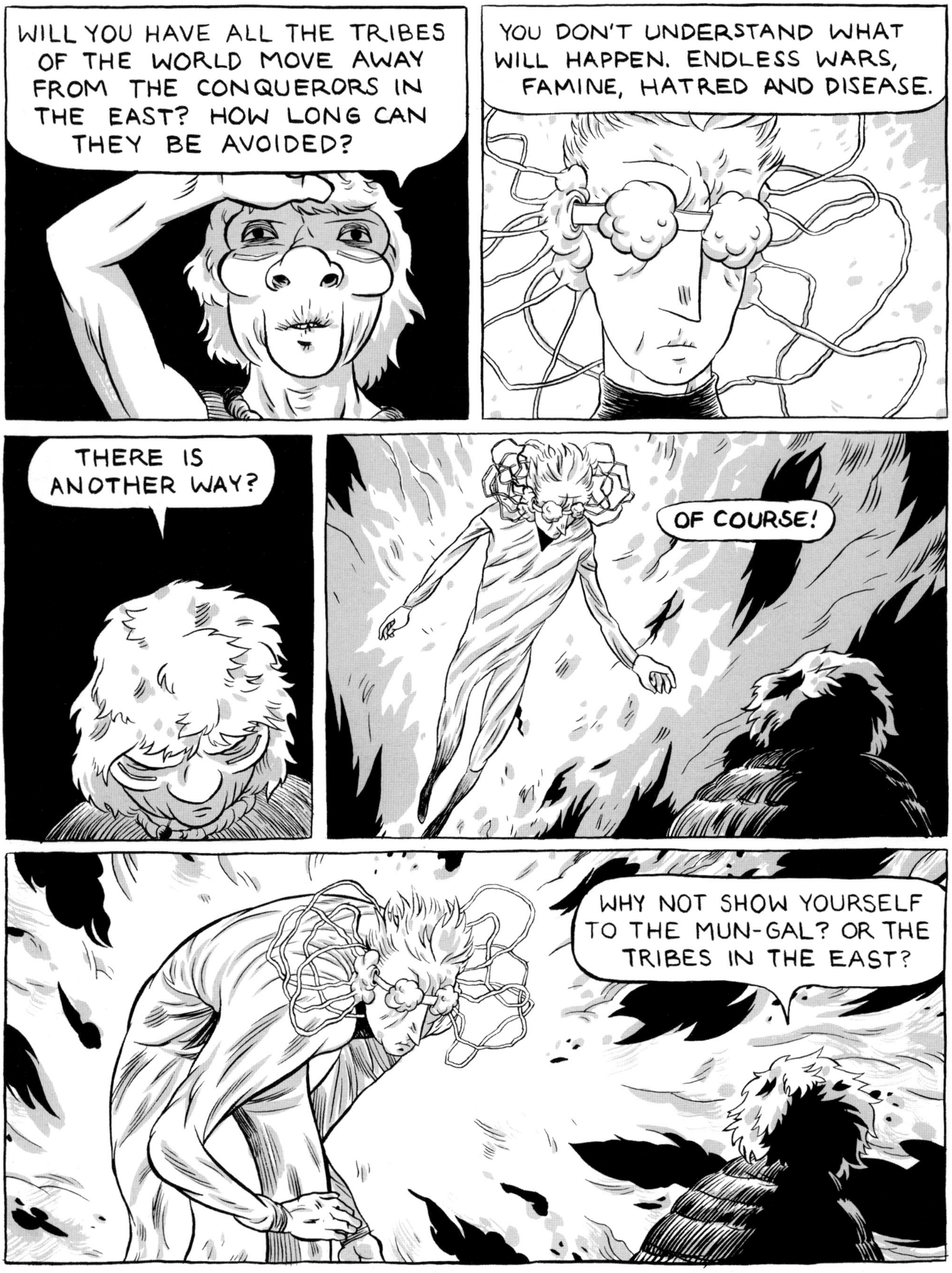
WILL YOU HAVE ALL THE TRIBES OF THE WORLD MOVE AWAY FROM THE CONQUERORS IN THE EAST? HOW LONG CAN THEY BE AVOIDED?
YOU DON'T UNDERSTAND WHAT WILL HAPPEN. ENDLESS WARS, FAMINE, HATRED AND DISEASE.
THERE IS ANOTHER WAY?
OF COURSE!
WHY NOT SHOW YOURSELF TO THE MUN-GAL? OR THE TRIBES IN THE EAST?

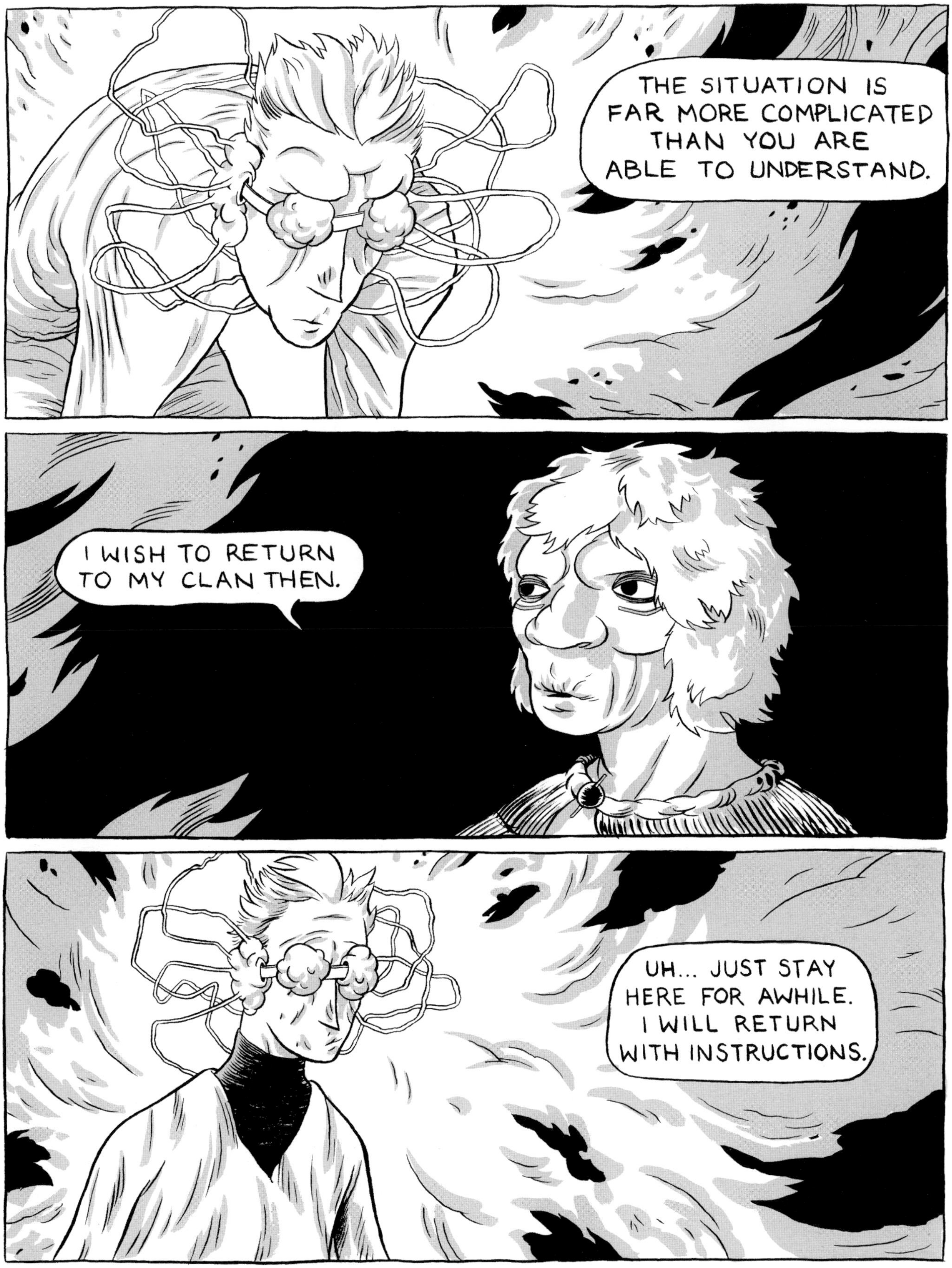
THE SITUATION IS FAR MORE COMPLICATED THAN YOU ARE ABLE TO UNDERSTAND.
I WISH TO RETURN TO MY CLAN THEN.
UH... JUST STAY HERE FOR AWHILE. I WILL RETURN WITH INSTRUCTIONS.

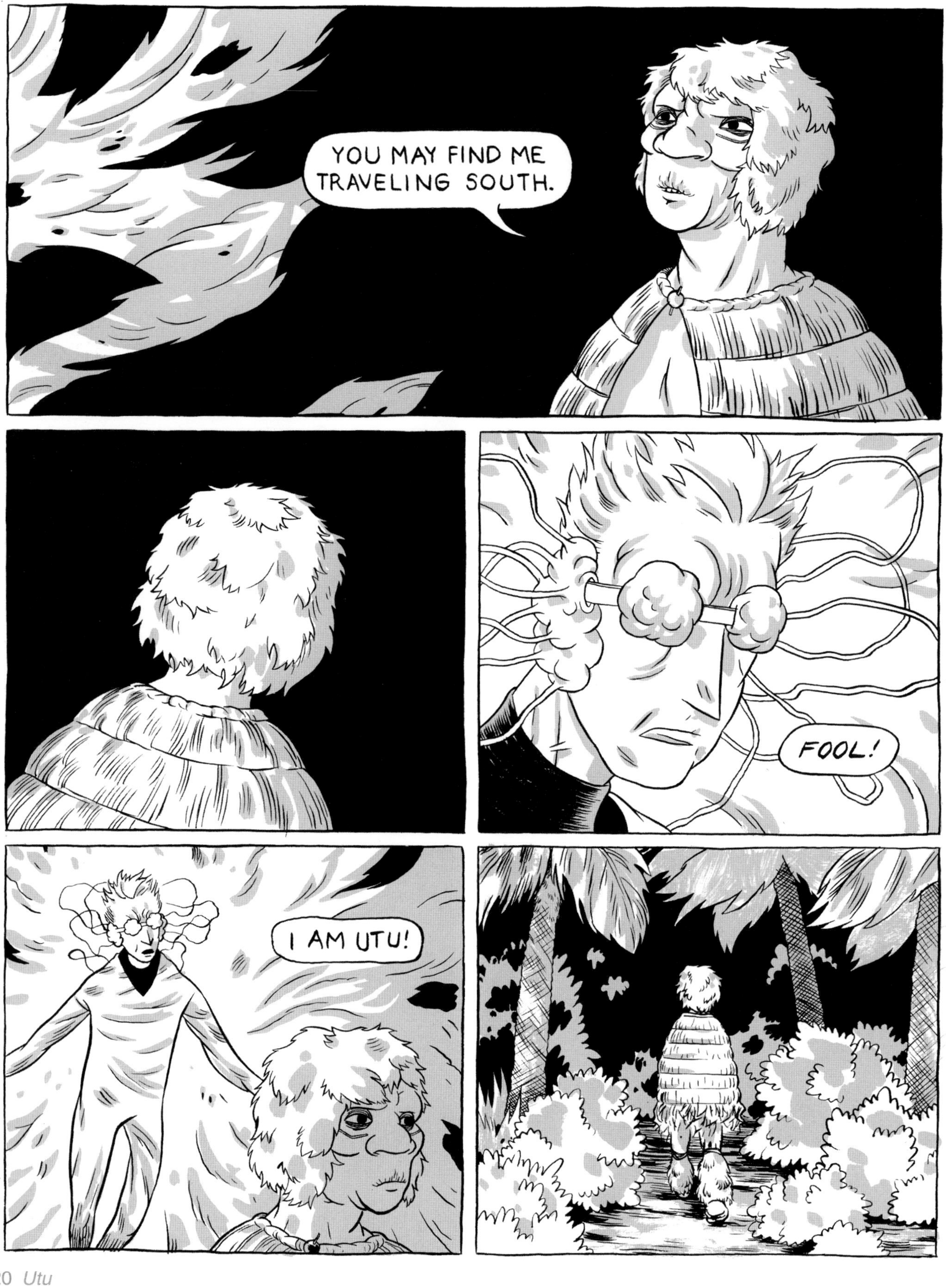
YOU MAY FIND ME TRAVELING SOUTH.
FOOL!
I AM UTU!

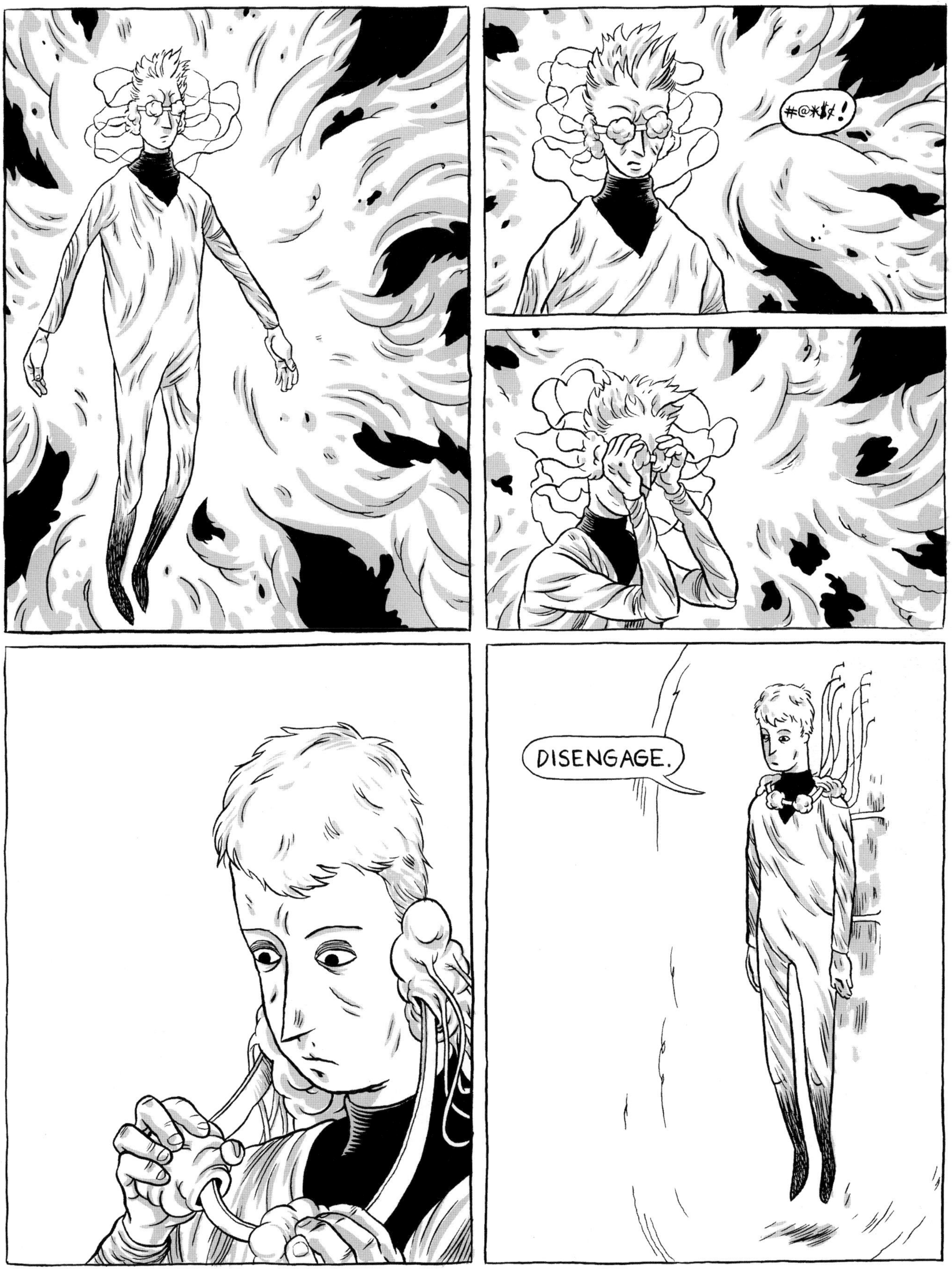
#@✱$✗!
DISENGAGE.

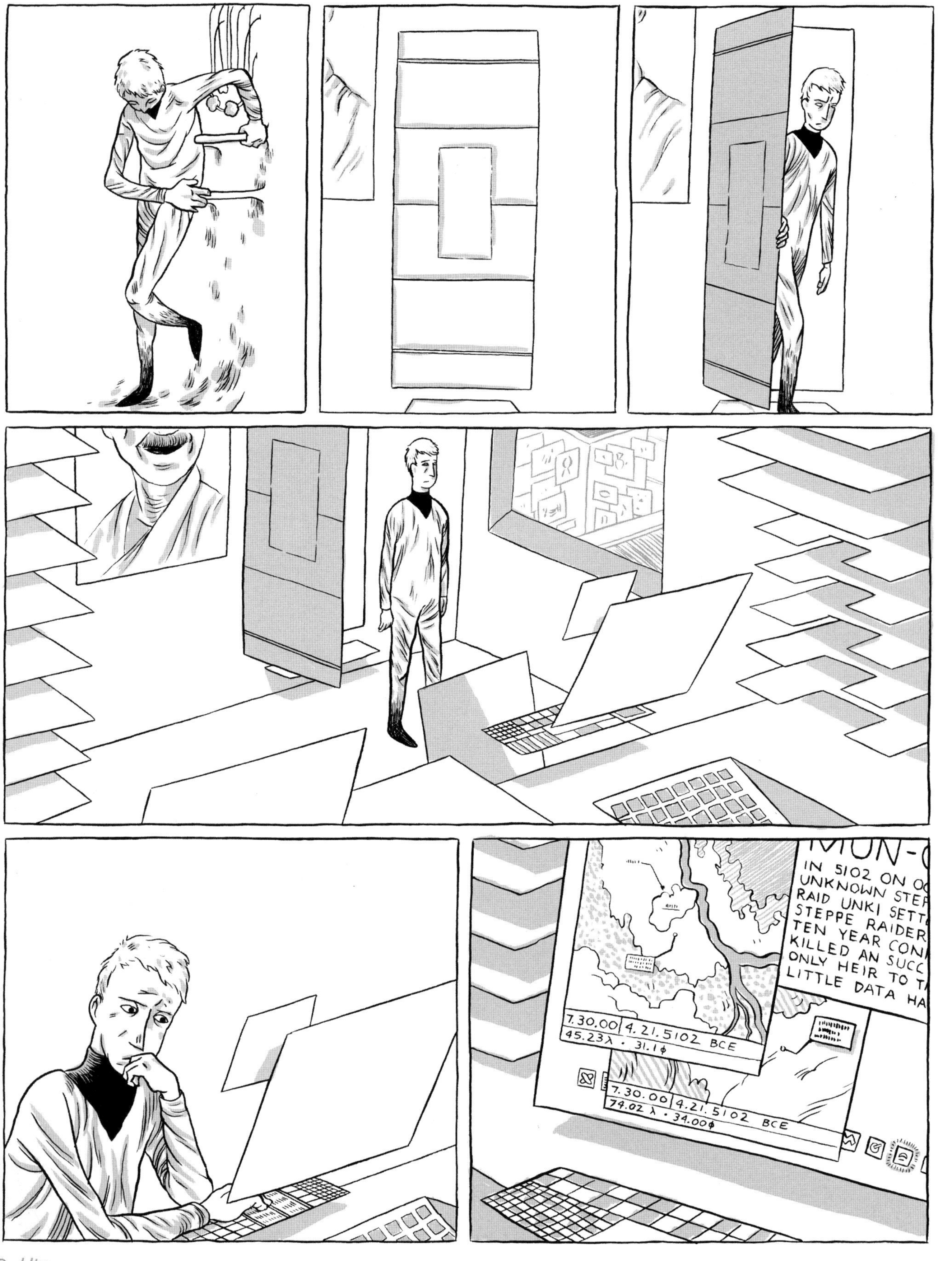

MUN-
IN 5102 ON
UNKNOWN
RAID UNKI
STEPPE
TEN YEAR
KILLED AN
ONLY HEIR TO
LITTLE DATA
7.30.00
4.21.5102 BCE
45.23λ · 31.1φ
7.30.00
4.21.5102 BCE
74.02 λ · 34.00φ

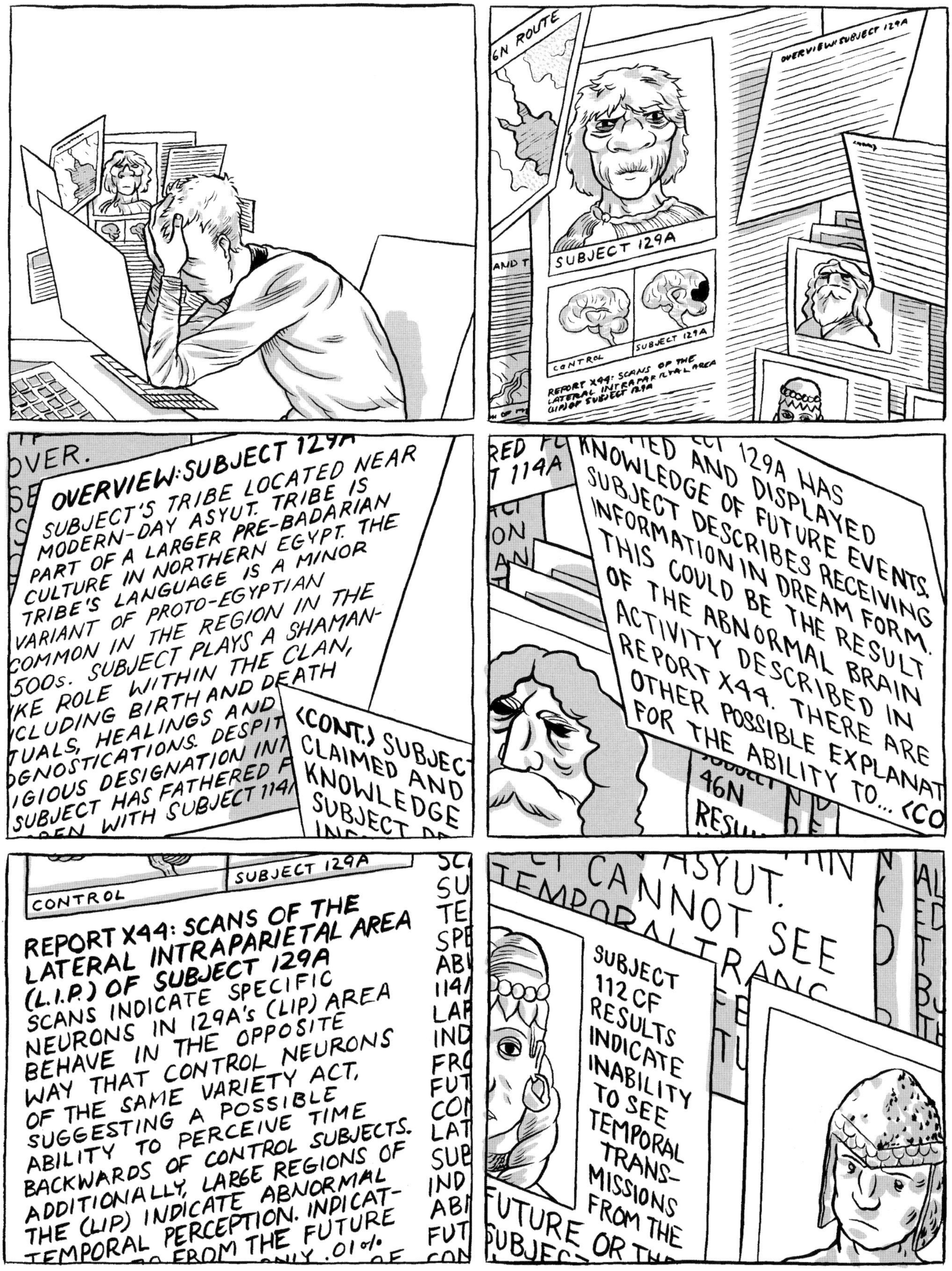
6N ROUTE
OVERVIEW: SUBJECT 129A
SUBJECT 129A
CONTROL
SUBJECT 129A
OVER.
OVERVIEW: SUBJECT 129A
OVERVIEW: SUBJECT'S TRIBE LOCATED NEAR MODERN-DAY ASYUT. TRIBE IS PART OF A LARGER PRE-BADARIAN CULTURE IN NORTHERN EGYPT. THE TRIBE'S LANGUAGE IS A MINOR VARIANT OF PROTO-EGYPTIAN COMMON IN THE REGION IN THE 500s. SUBJECT PLAYS A SHAMAN-IKE ROLE WITHIN THE CLAN, CLUDING BIRTH AND DEATH TUALS, HEALINGS AND OGNOSTICATIONS. DESPIT IGIOUS DESIGNATION INT SUBJECT HAS FATHERED F WITH SUBJECT 114A
(CONT.) SUBJEC CLAIMED AND KNOWLEDGE SUBJECT
RED 114A
CT 129A HAS IED AND DISPLAYED KNOWLEDGE OF FUTURE EVENTS. SUBJECT DESCRIBES RECEIVING INFORMATION IN DREAM FORM. THIS COULD BE THE RESULT OF THE ABNORMAL BRAIN ACTIVITY DESCRIBED IN REPORT X44. THERE ARE OTHER POSSIBLE EXPLANAT FOR THE ABILITY TO... (CO
46N
CONTROL
SUBJECT 129A
REPORT X44: SCANS OF THE LATERAL INTRAPARIETAL AREA (L.I.P.) OF SUBJECT 129A
SCANS INDICATE SPECIFIC NEURONS IN 129A's (LIP) AREA BEHAVE IN THE OPPOSITE WAY THAT CONTROL NEURONS OF THE SAME VARIETY ACT, SUGGESTING A POSSIBLE ABILITY TO PERCEIVE TIME BACKWARDS OF CONTROL SUBJECTS. ADDITIONALLY, LARGE REGIONS OF THE (LIP) INDICATE ABNORMAL TEMPORAL PERCEPTION. INDICAT- FROM THE FUTURE .01%
ASYUT.
CANNOT SEE
TEMPORAL TRANS
SUBJECT 112CF RESULTS INDICATE INABILITY TO SEE TEMPORAL TRANS-MISSIONS FROM THE FUTURE OR TH
FUTURE
SUBJECT

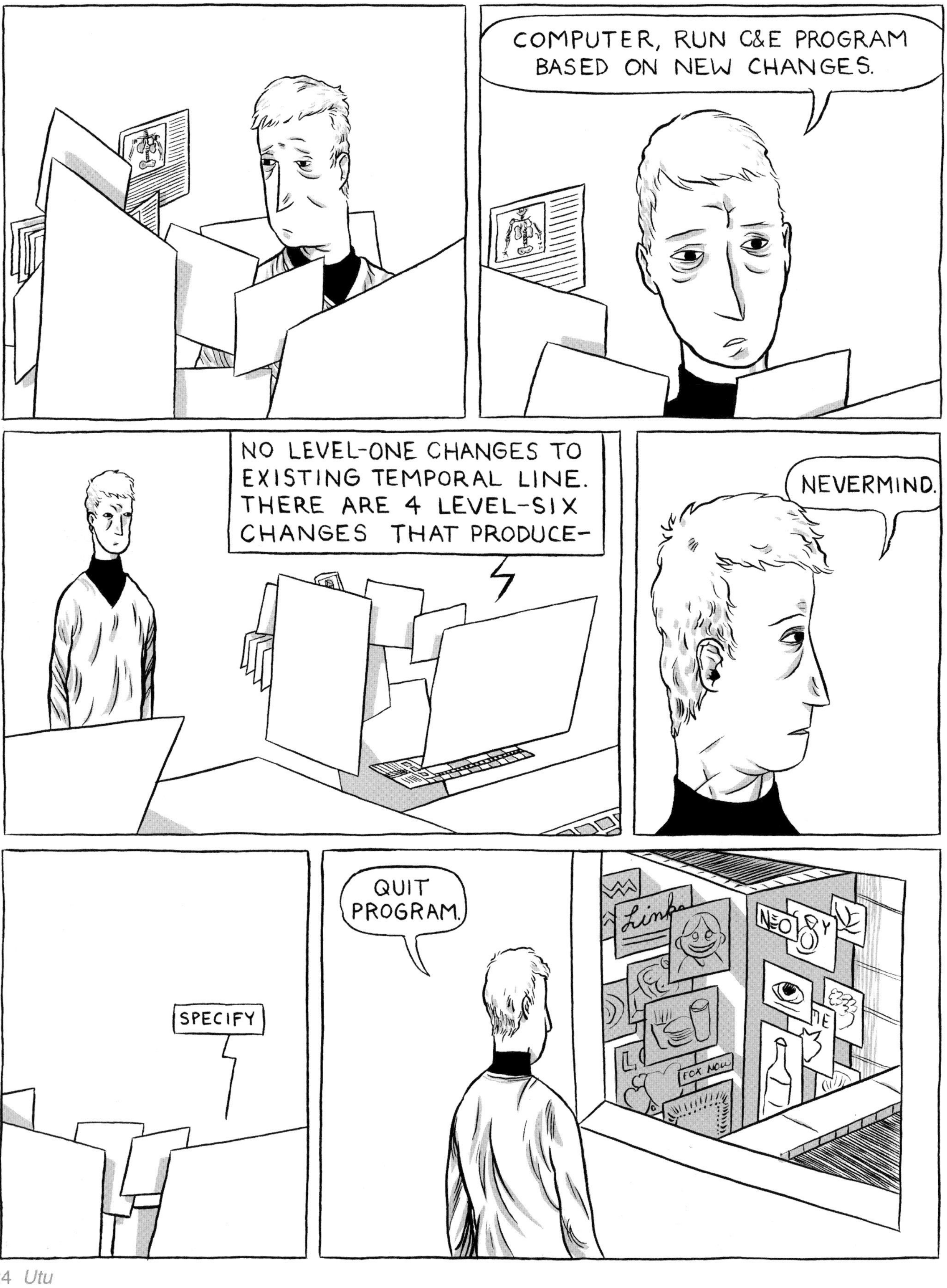
COMPUTER, RUN C&E PROGRAM BASED ON NEW CHANGES.
NO LEVEL-ONE CHANGES TO EXISTING TEMPORAL LINE. THERE ARE 4 LEVEL-SIX CHANGES THAT PRODUCE-
NEVERMIND.
SPECIFY
QUIT PROGRAM.

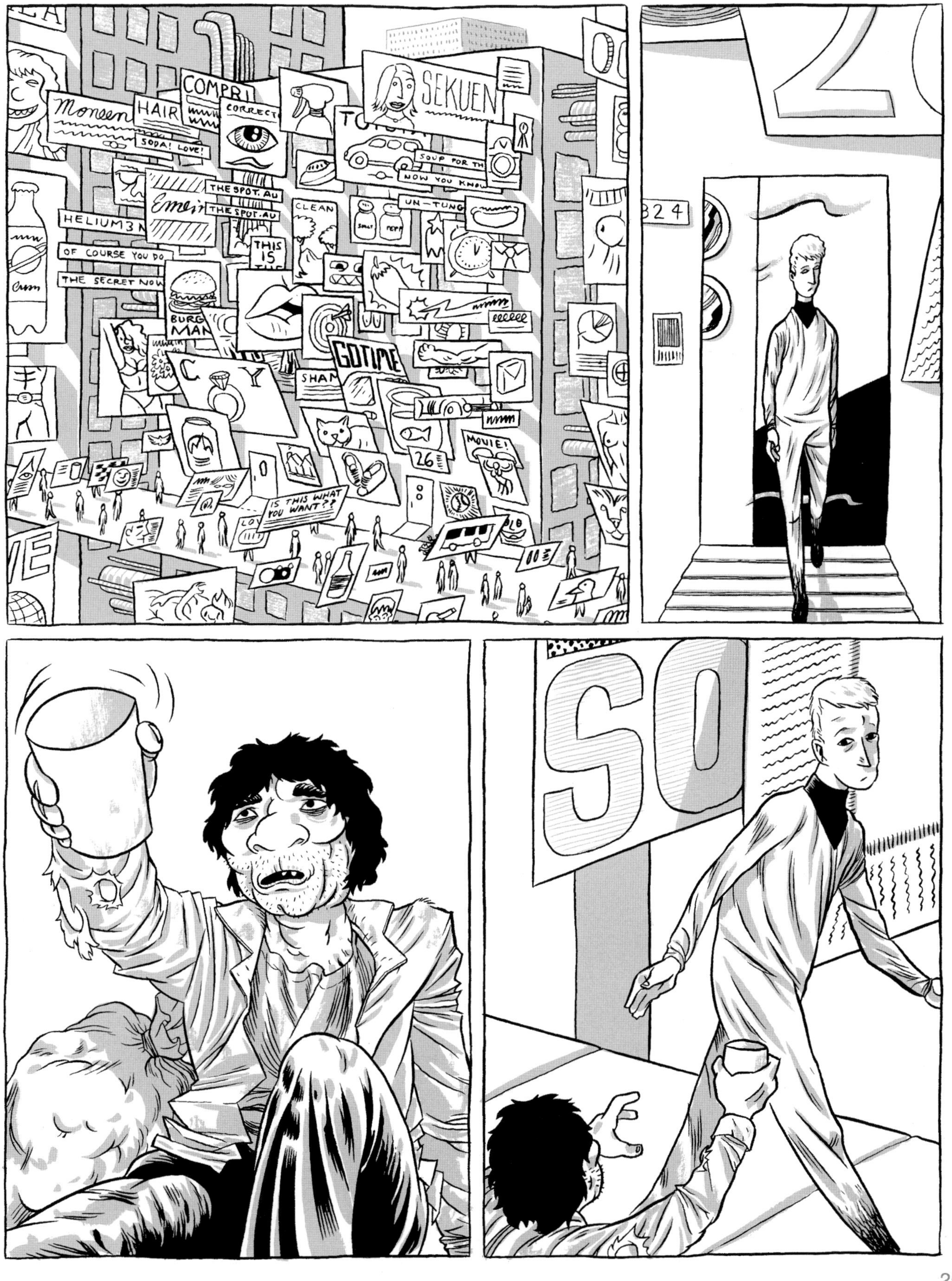
Moneen
HAIR
COMPRI
CORRECT
SEKUEN
SODA! LOVE!
SOUP FOR TH
NOW YOU KNOW
THE SPOT. AU
THE SPOT. AU
HELIUM3
OF COURSE YOU DO
THE SECRET NOW
CLEAN
UN-TUNG
THIS IS
BURG MAN
GOTIME
SHAM
MOVIE!
26
IS THIS WHAT YOU WANT??
324
SO

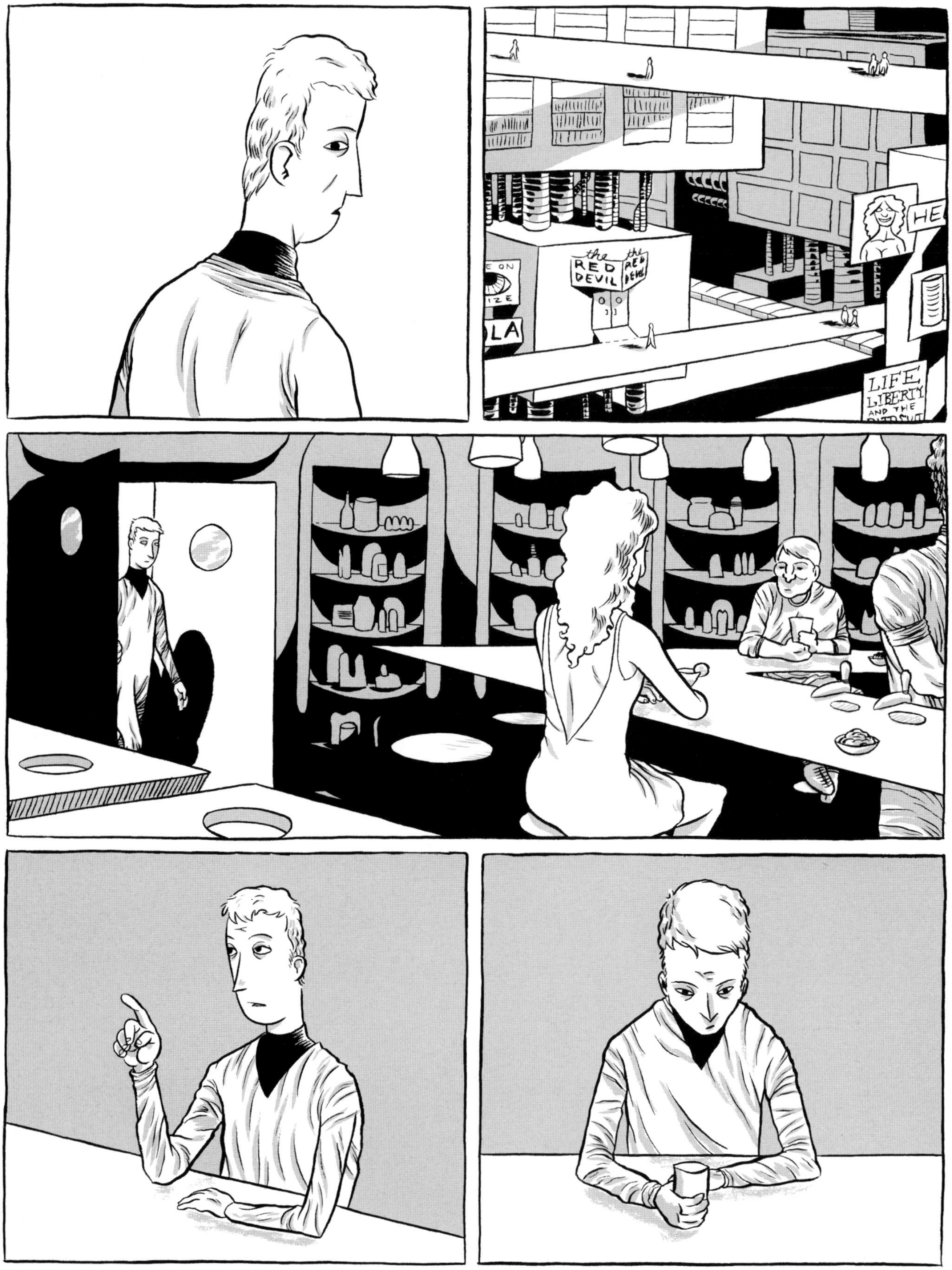
the RED DEVIL
the RED DEVIL
LIFE, LIBERTY AND THE

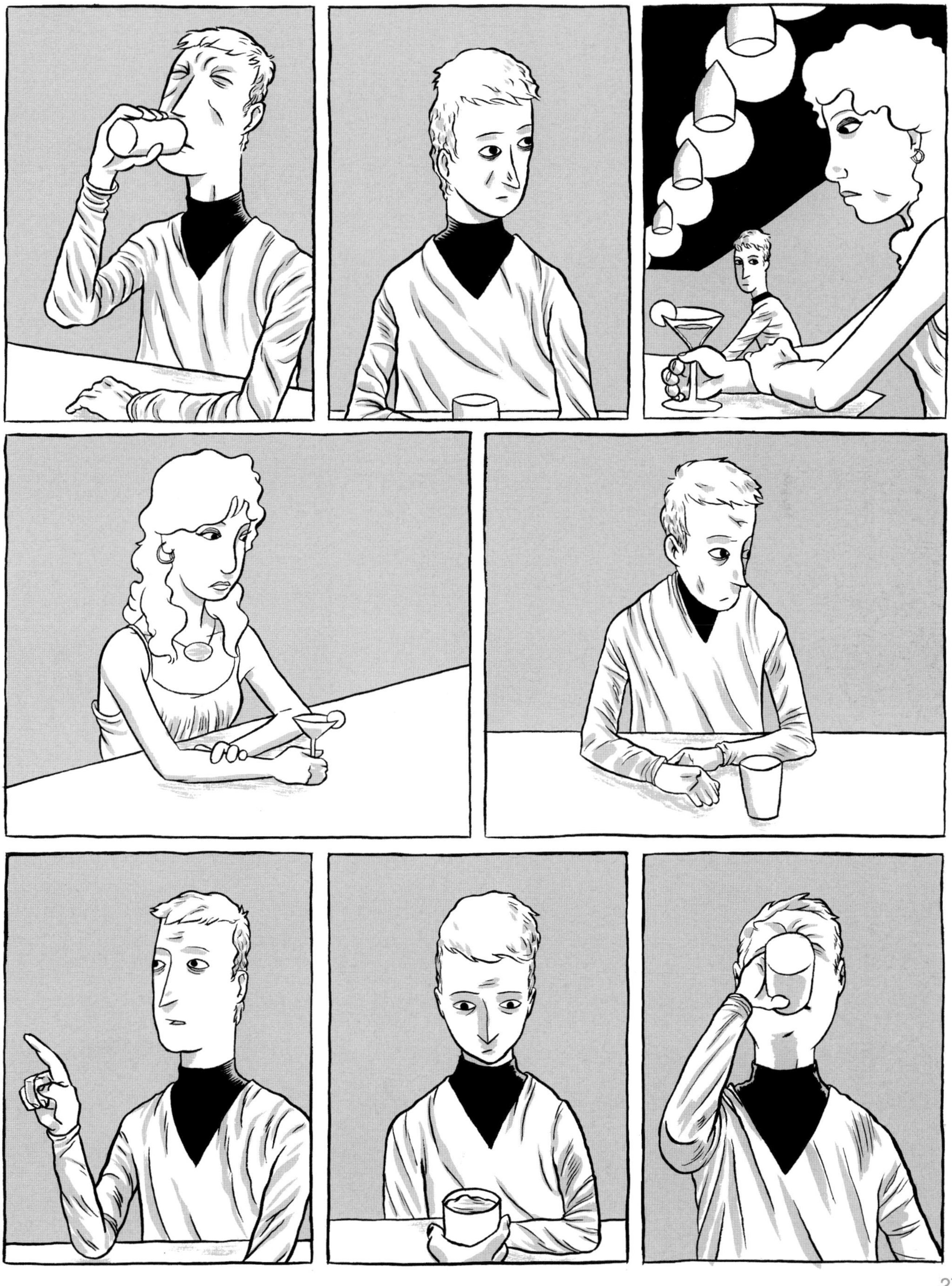

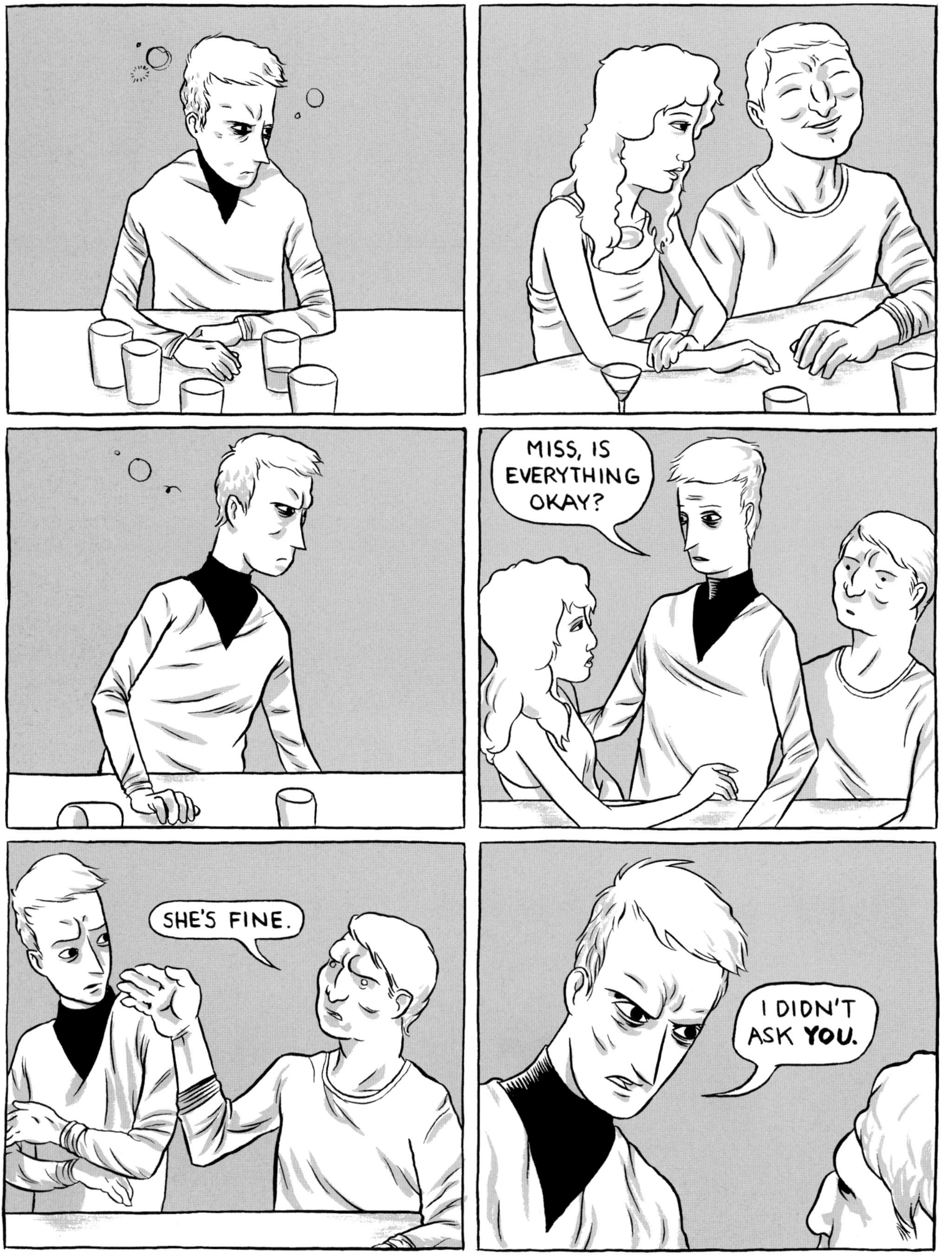
MISS, IS EVERYTHING OKAY?
SHE'S FINE.
I DIDN'T ASK **YOU.**

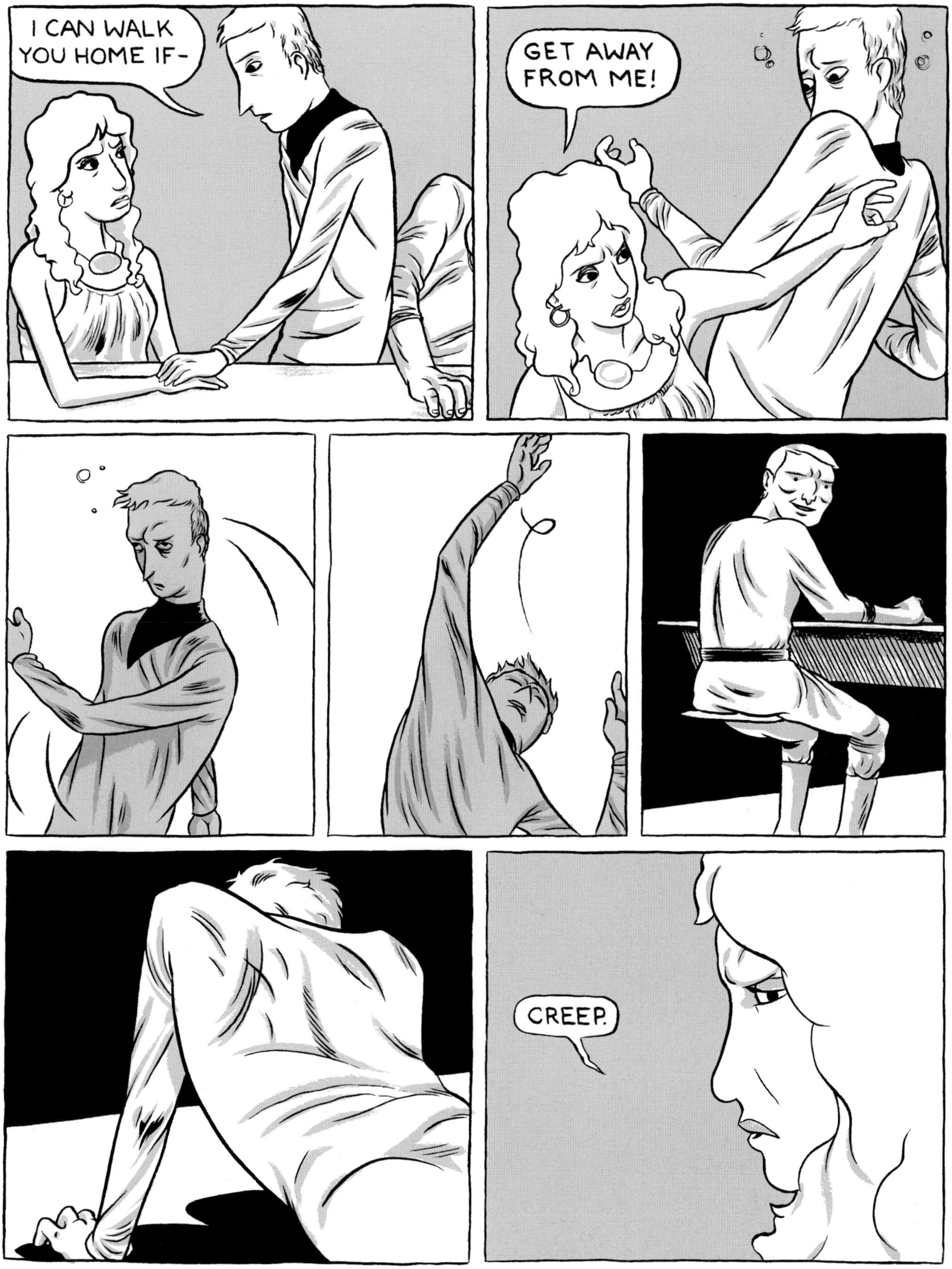
I CAN WALK YOU HOME IF-
GET AWAY FROM ME!
CREEP.

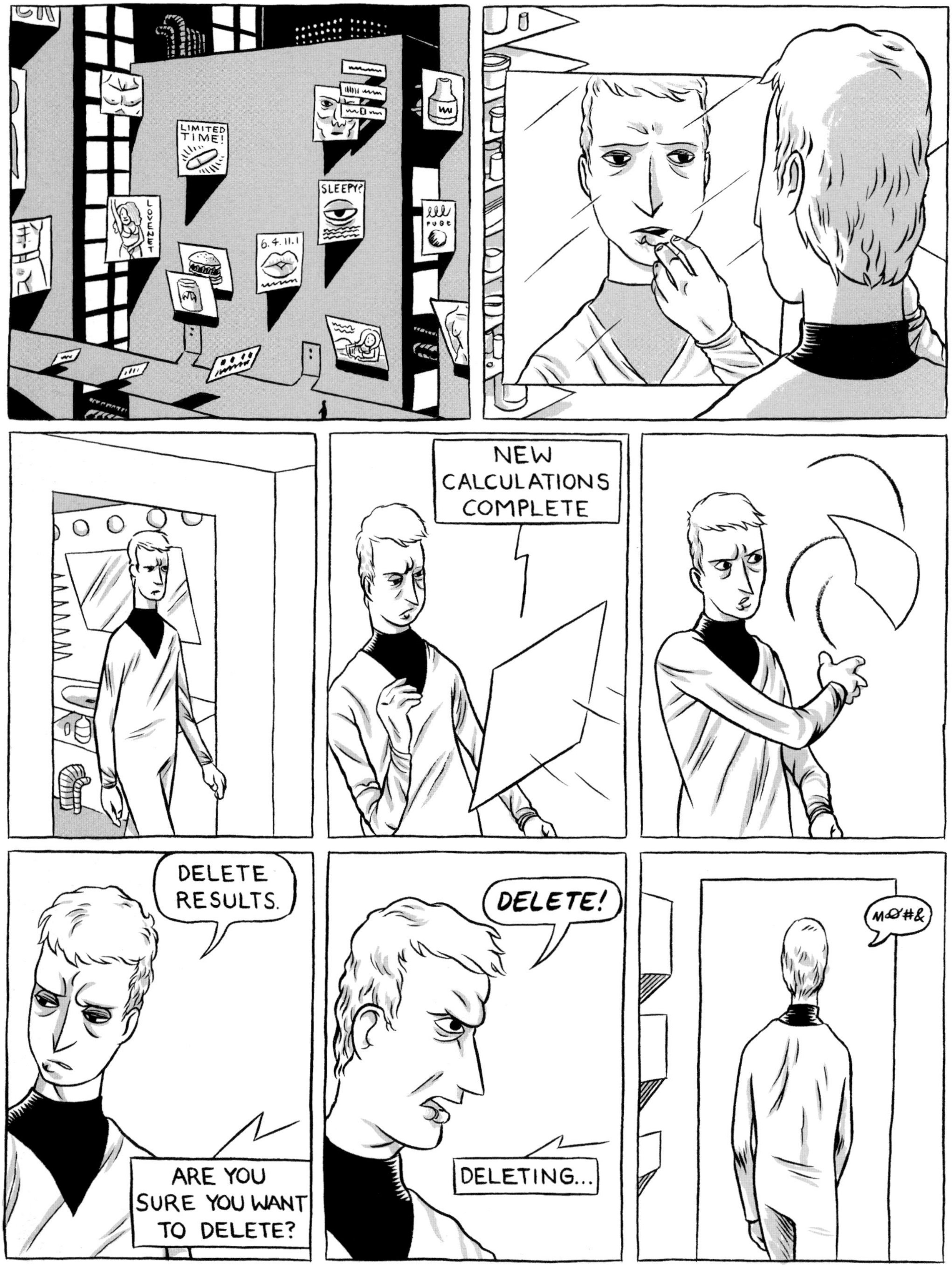
LIMITED TIME!
LOVENET
SLEEPY?
6.4.11.1
NEW CALCULATIONS COMPLETE
DELETE RESULTS.
ARE YOU SURE YOU WANT TO DELETE?
DELETE!
DELETING...

TURN OFF THE LIGHTS.

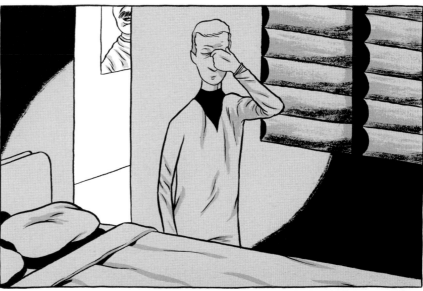

THE END

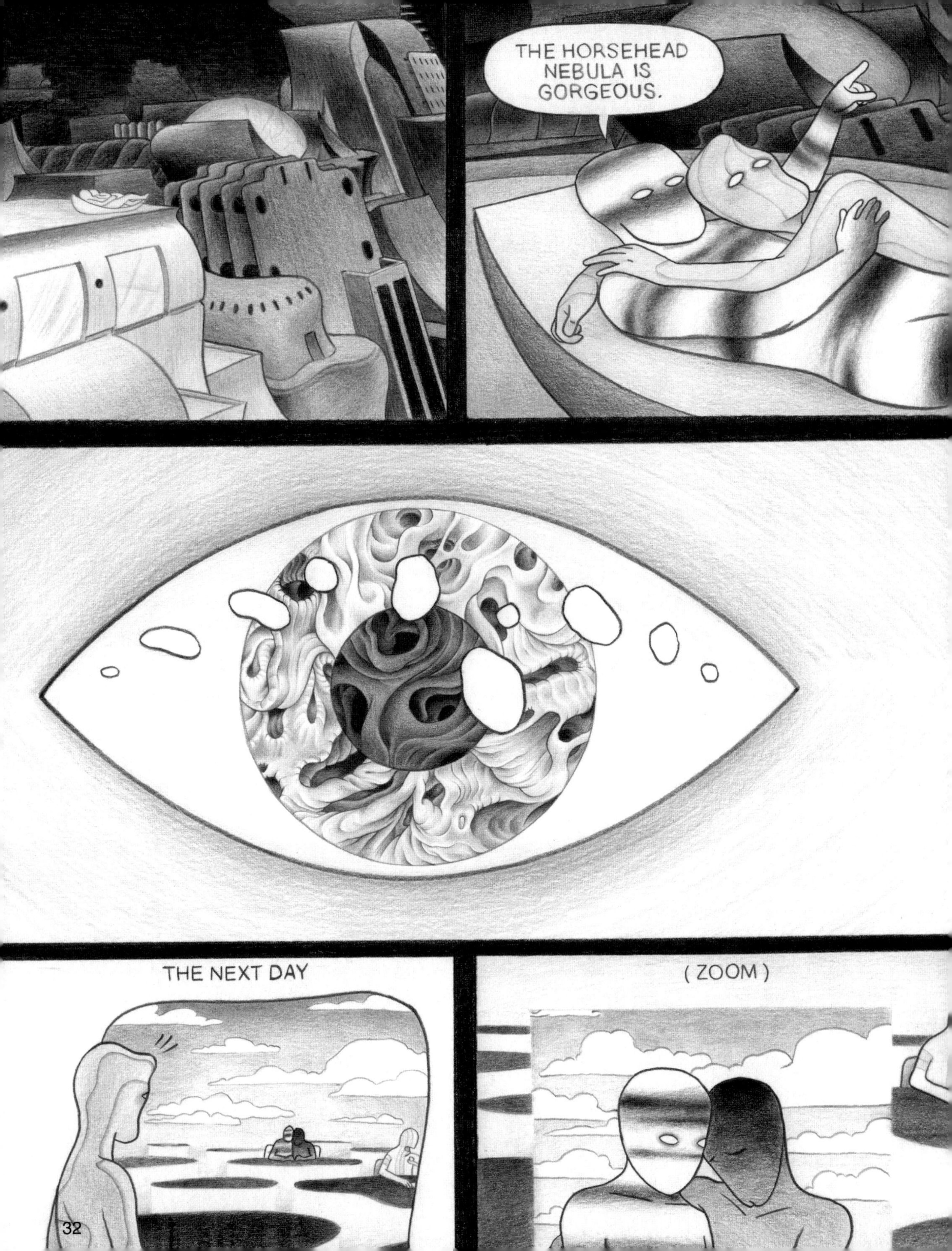
THE HORSEHEAD NEBULA IS GORGEOUS.
THE NEXT DAY
(ZOOM)

I DON'T SEE IT...
ADJUST YOUR VISION TO DETECT INFRARED.
OK-
BLINK
BLINK

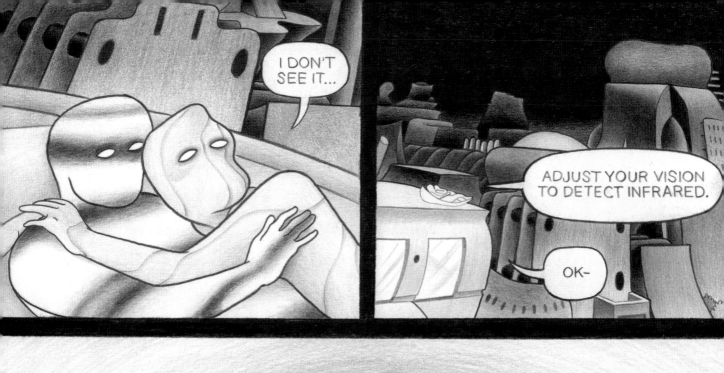

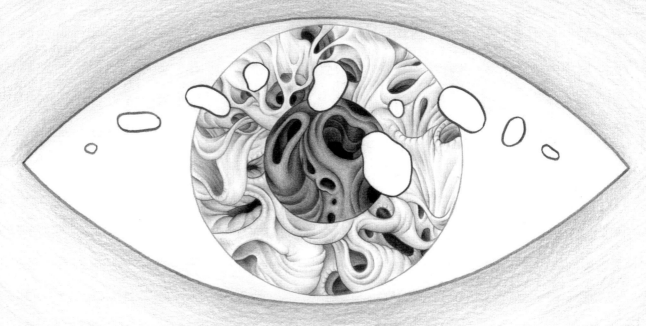

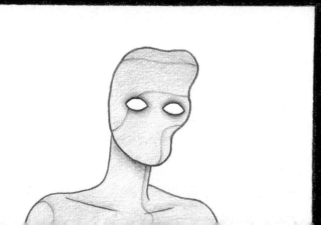

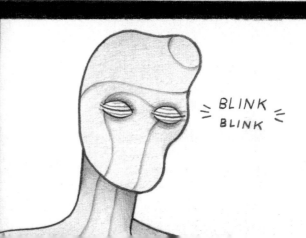

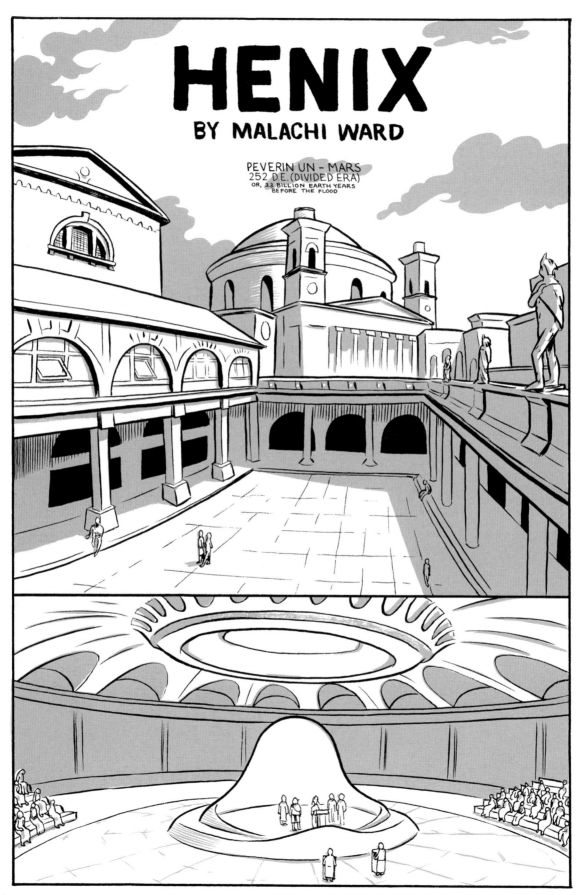

HENIX

BY MALACHI WARD

PEVERIN UN – MARS
252 D.E. (DIVIDED ERA)
OR, 3.3 BILLION EARTH YEARS
BEFORE THE FLOOD

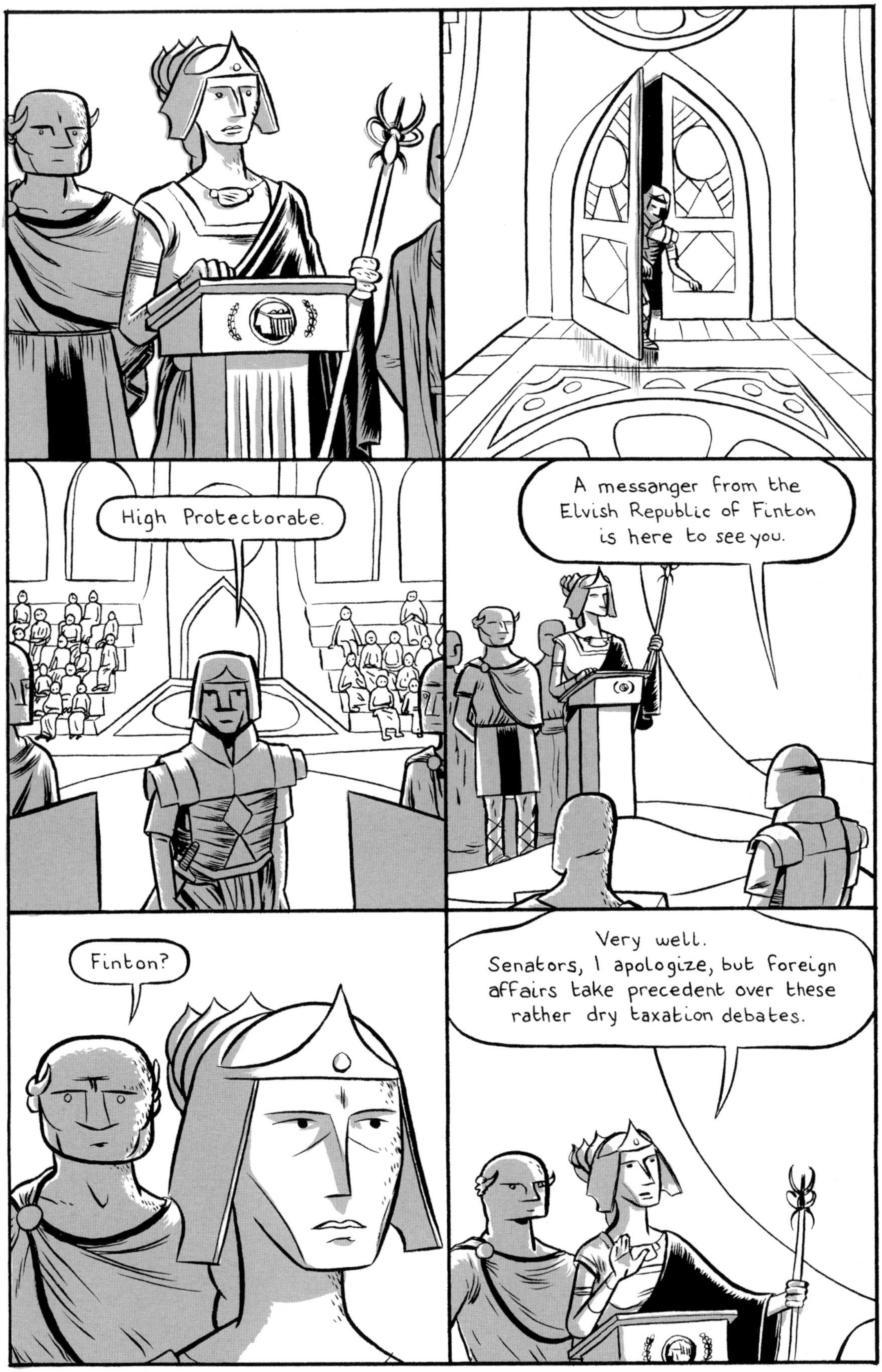
High Protectorate.
A messanger from the Elvish Republic of Finton is here to see you.
Finton?
Very well. Senators, I apologize, but foreign affairs take precedent over these rather dry taxation debates.

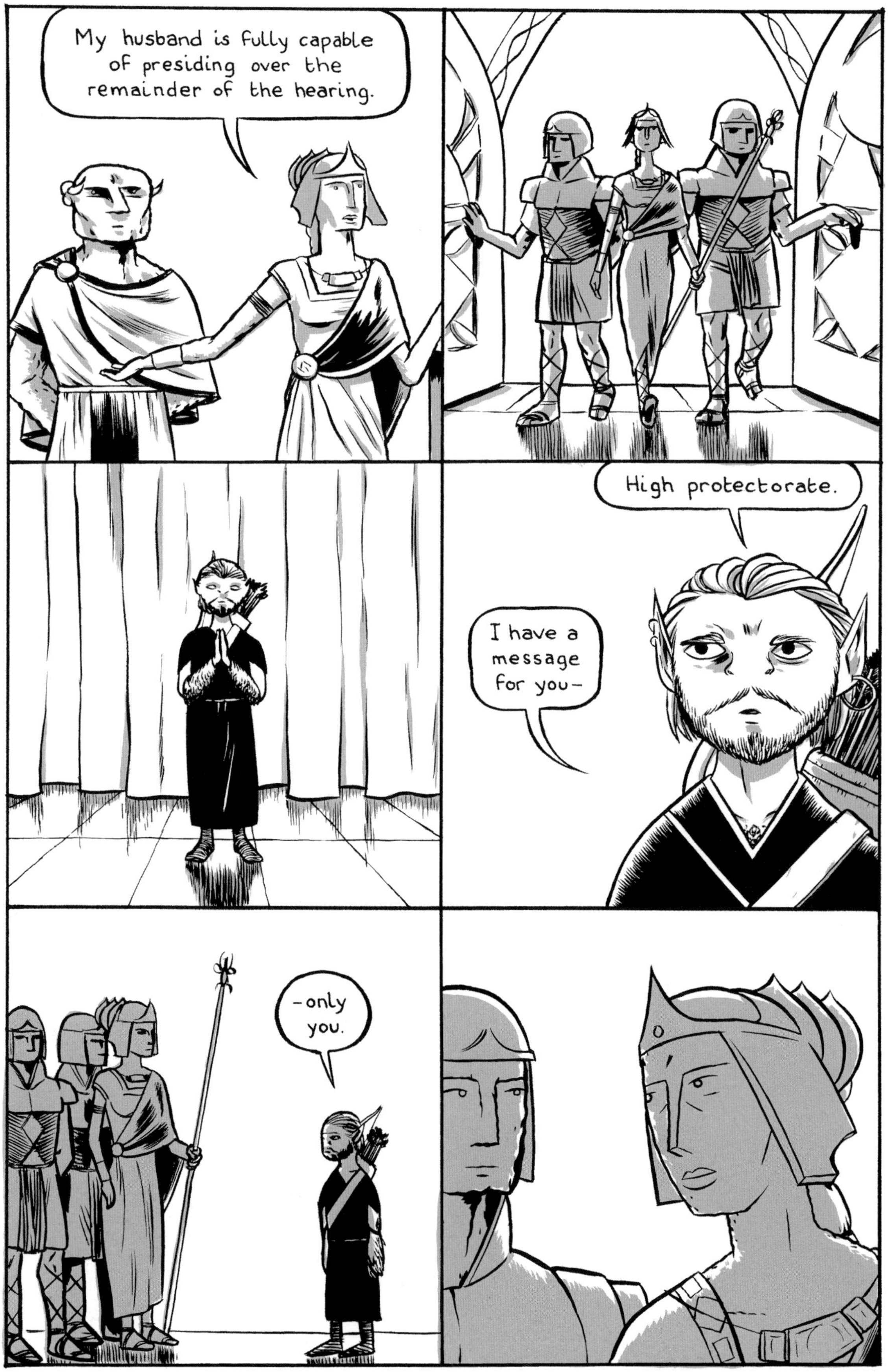
My husband is fully capable of presiding over the remainder of the hearing.
High protectorate.
I have a message for you-
-only you.

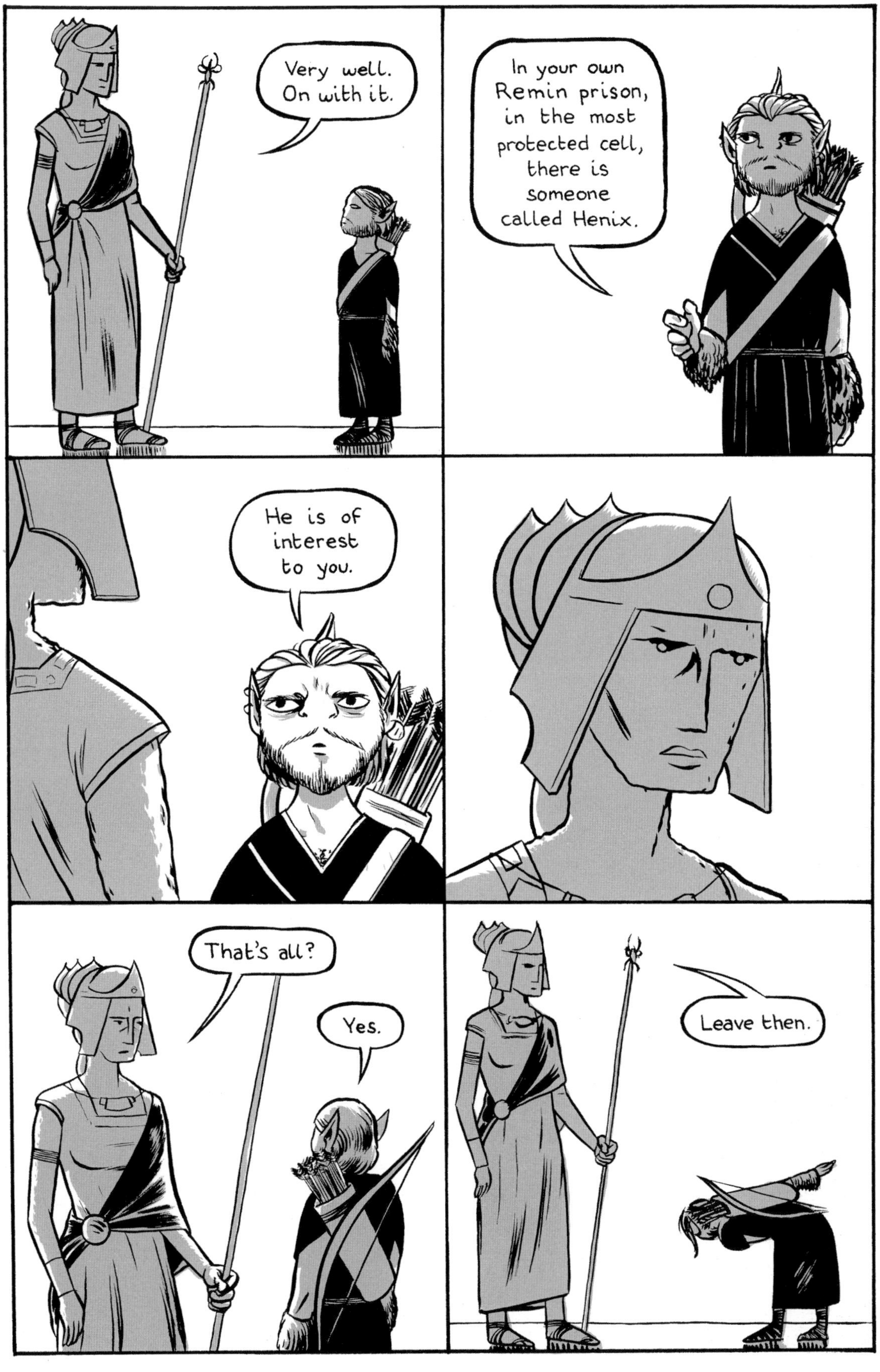
Very well. On with it.
In your own Remin prison, in the most protected cell, there is someone called Henix.
He is of interest to you.
That's all?
Yes.
Leave then.

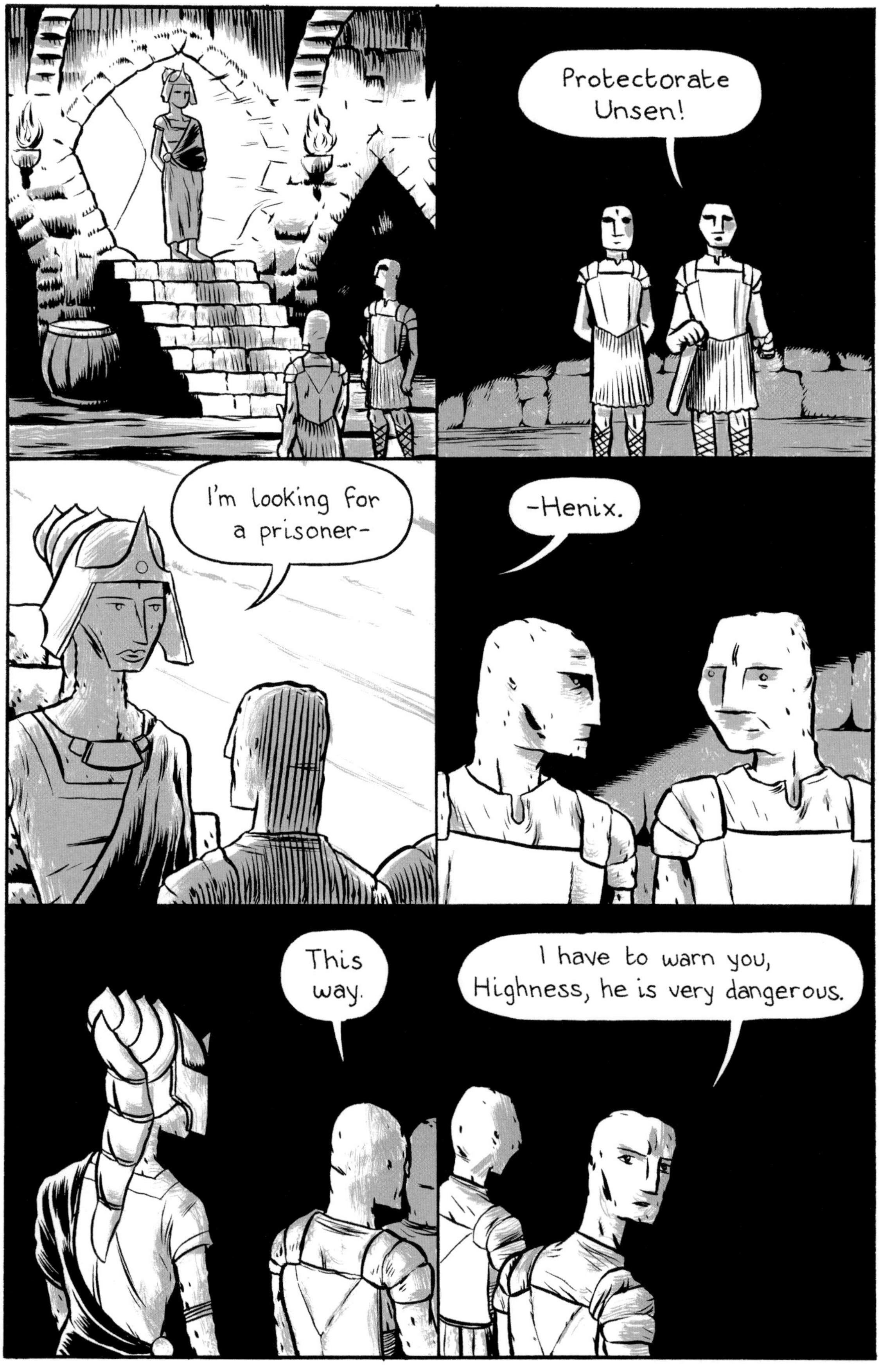
Protectorate Unsen!
I'm looking for a prisoner-
-Henix.
This way.
I have to warn you, Highness, he is very dangerous.

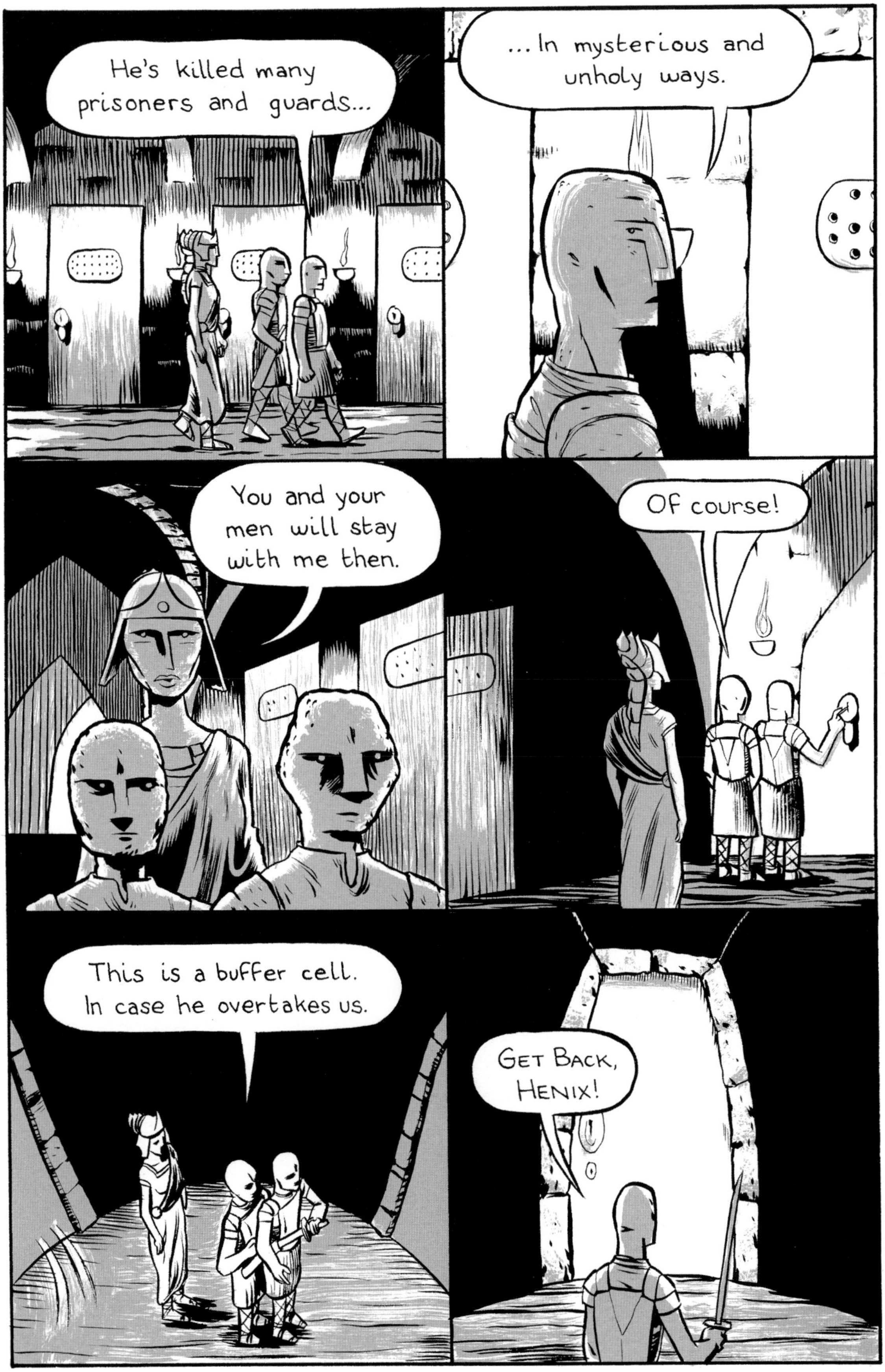
He's killed many prisoners and guards...
...In mysterious and unholy ways.
You and your men will stay with me then.
Of course!
This is a buffer cell. In case he overtakes us.
GET BACK, HENIX!

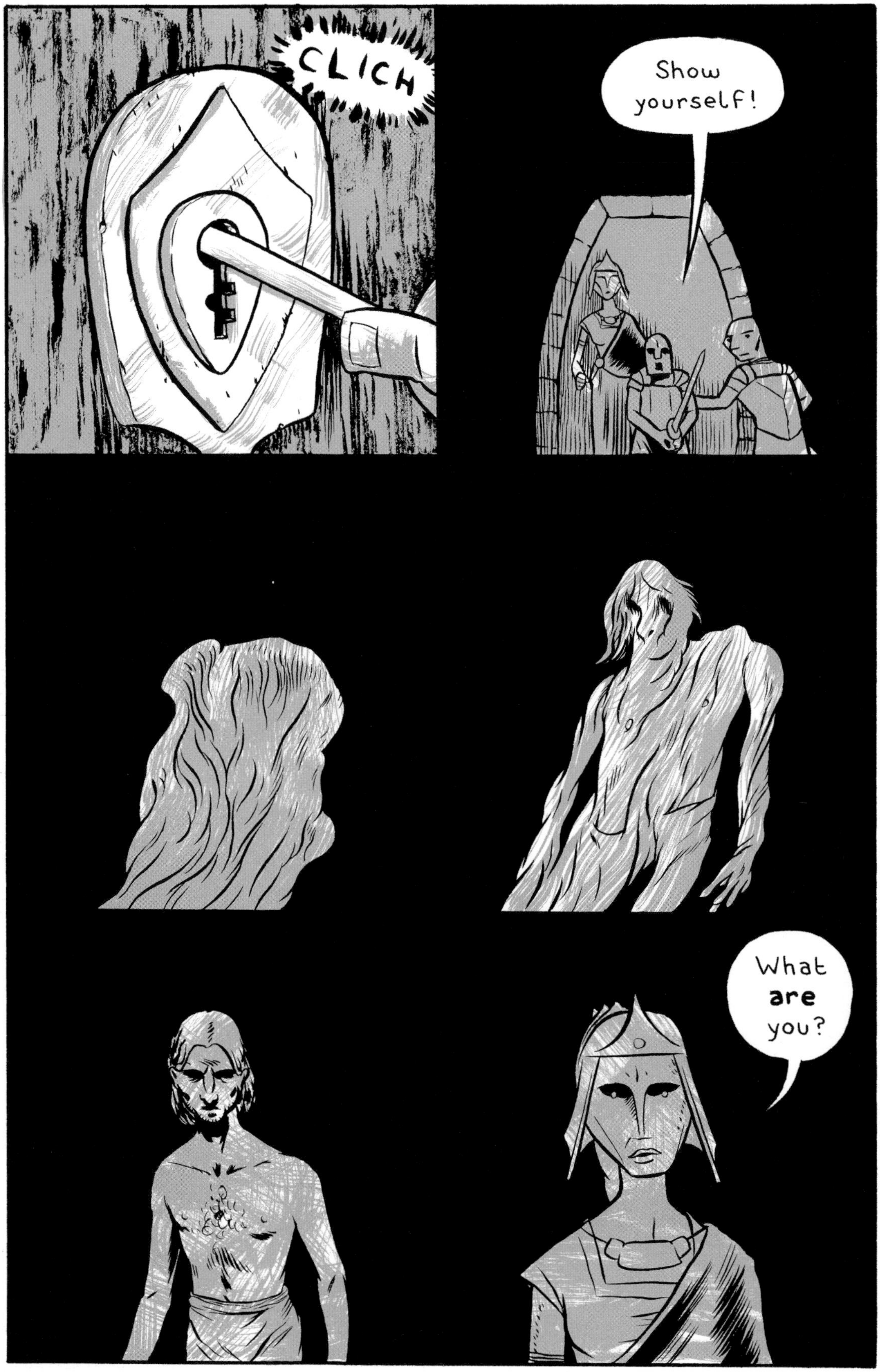
CLICH
Show yourself!
What **are** you?

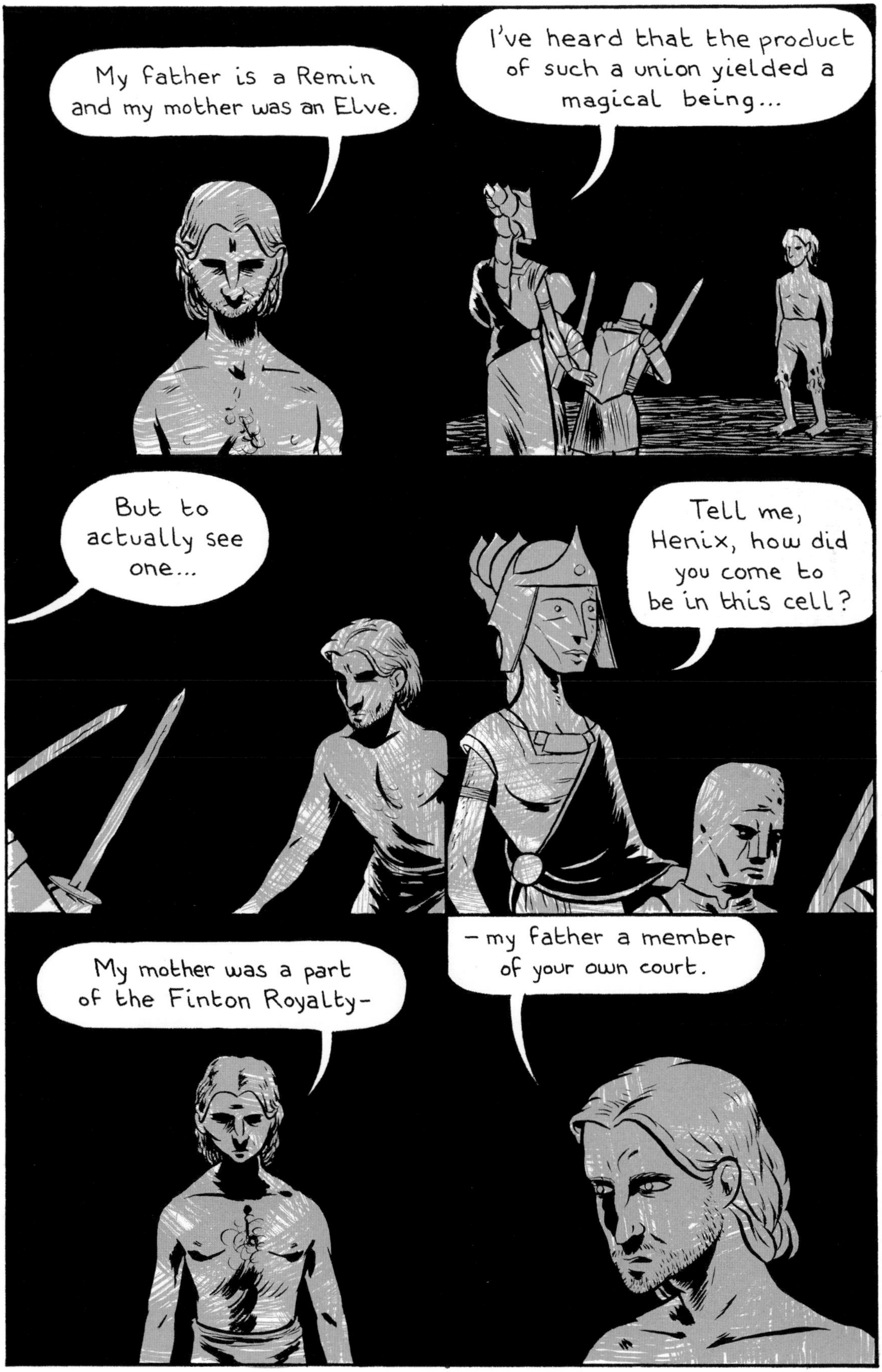
My father is a Remin and my mother was an Elve.
I've heard that the product of such a union yielded a magical being...
But to actually see one...
Tell me, Henix, how did you come to be in this cell?
My mother was a part of the Finton Royalty-
- my father a member of your own court.

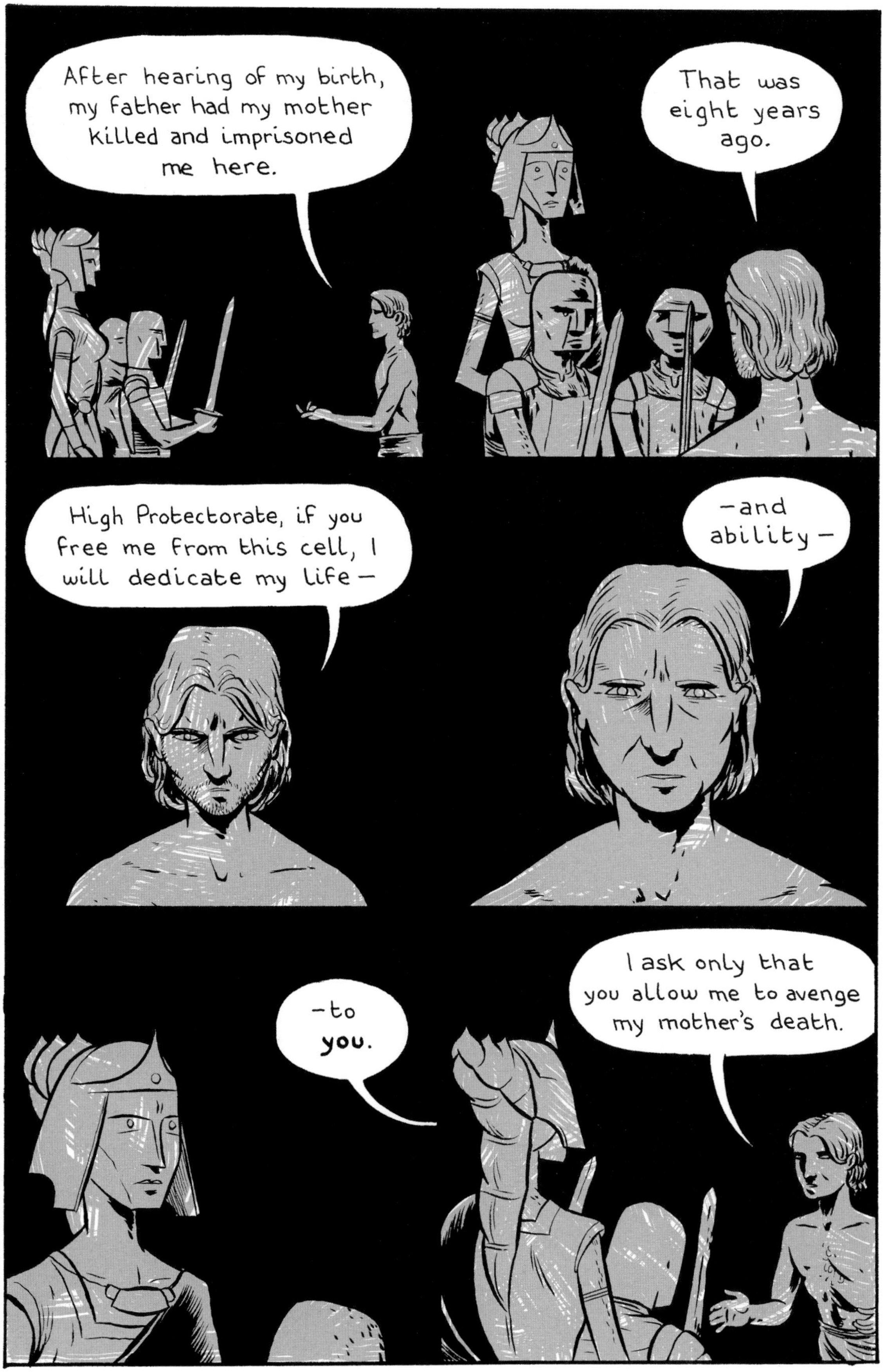
After hearing of my birth, my father had my mother killed and imprisoned me here.
That was eight years ago.
High Protectorate, if you free me from this cell, I will dedicate my life—
—and ability—
—to you.
I ask only that you allow me to avenge my mother's death.

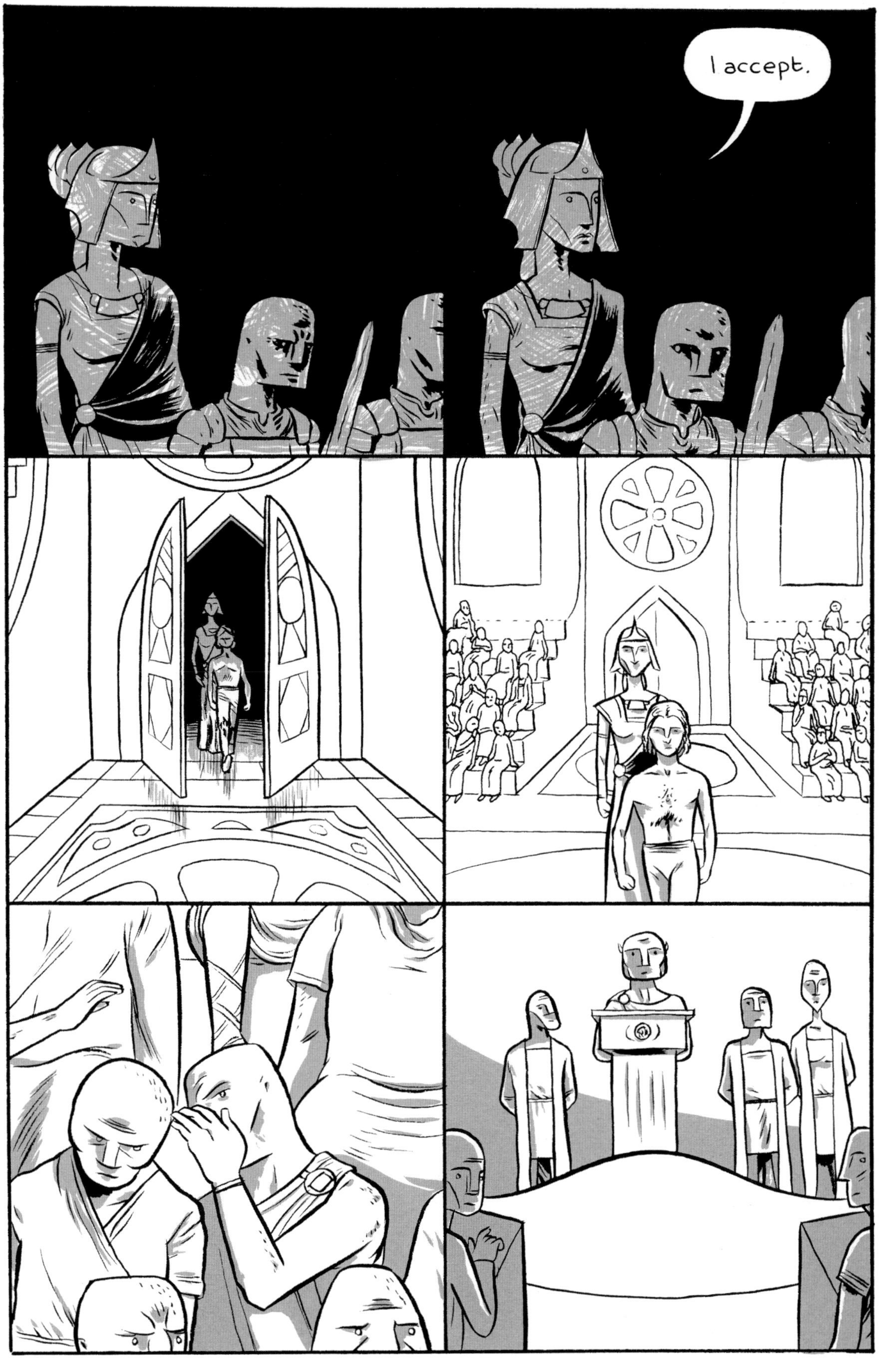
I accept.

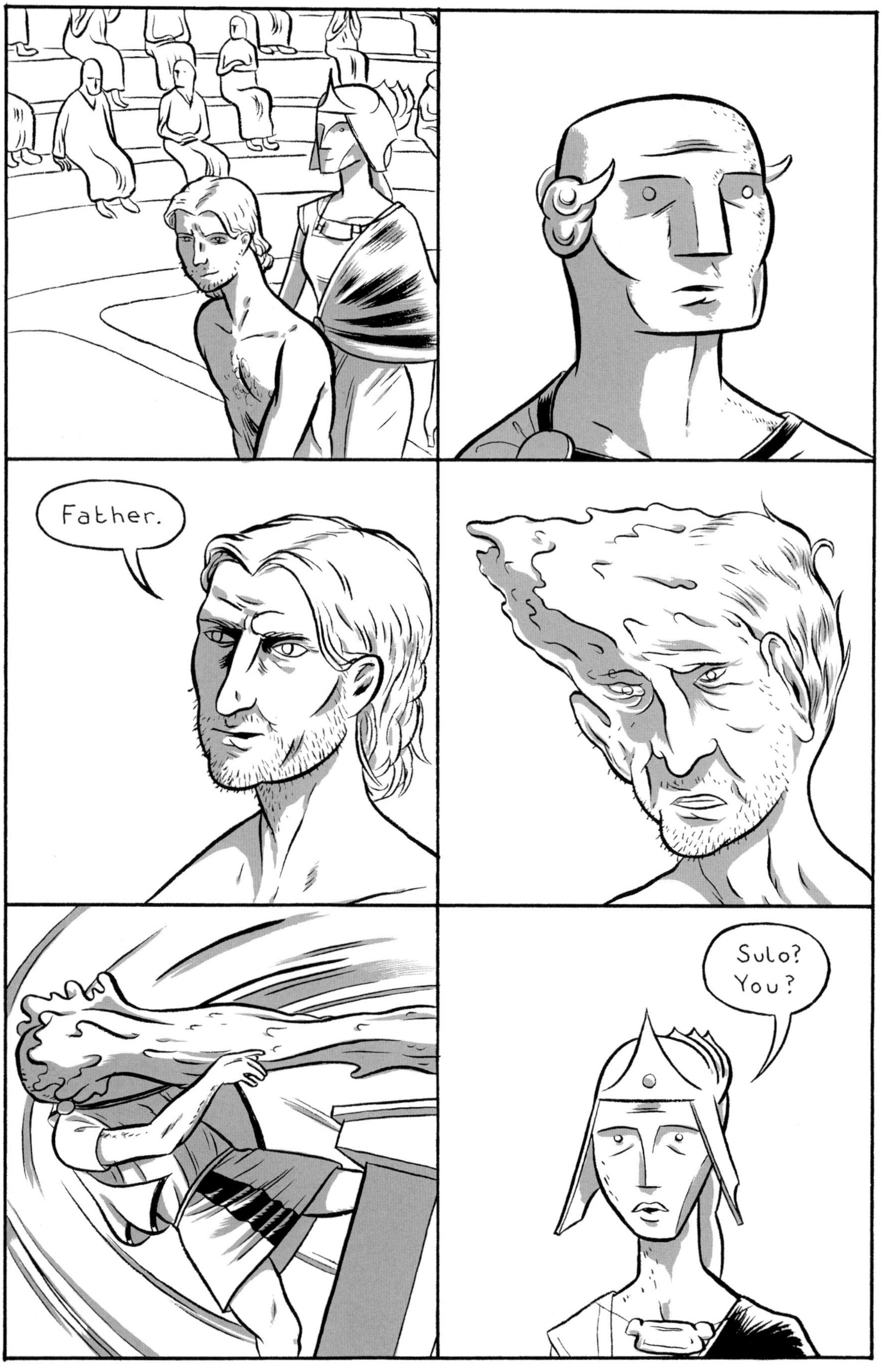
Father.
Sulo? You?

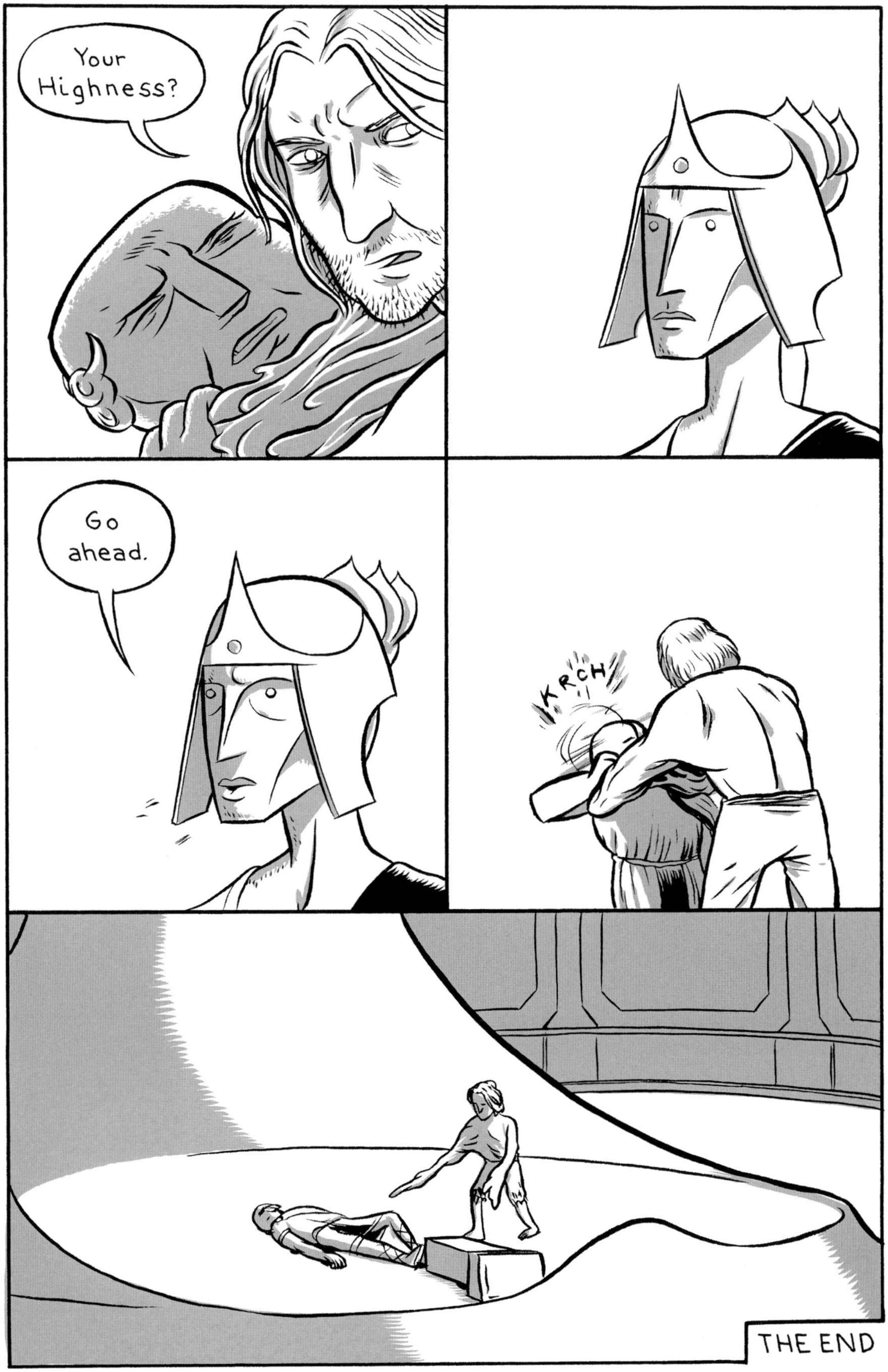
Your Highness?
Go ahead.
KRCH
THE END

Divination
by Malachi Ward

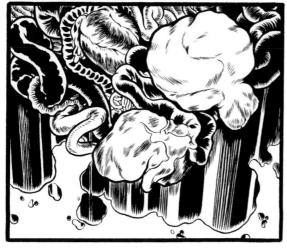

NEGATIVE SPACE

MALACHI · 2012

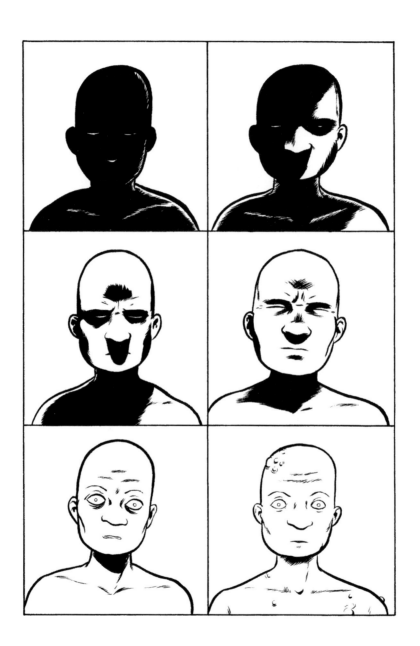

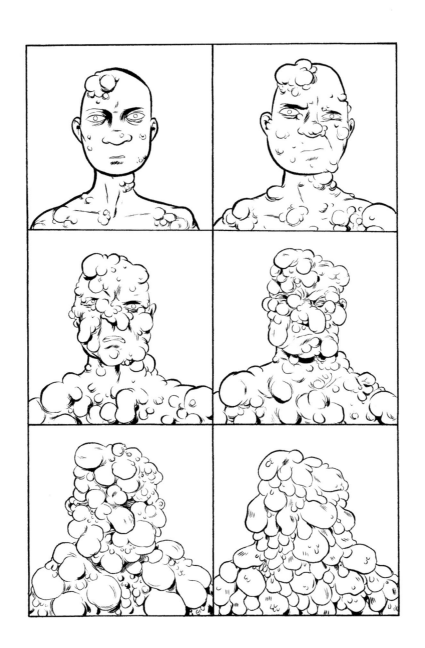

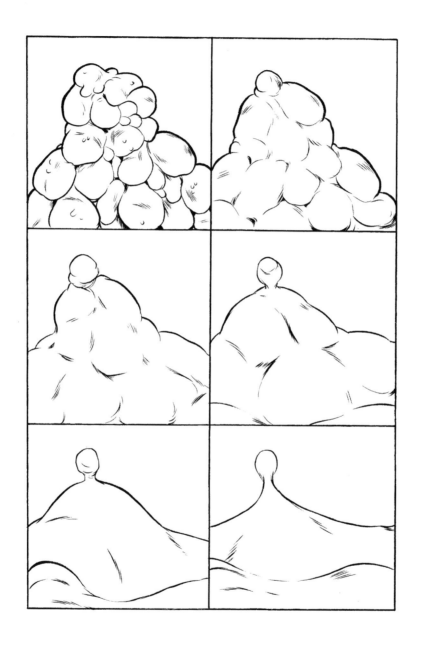

"EXCERPT FROM SENTI'S LETTER TO RELA" BY MALACHI WARD, JANUARY 2011

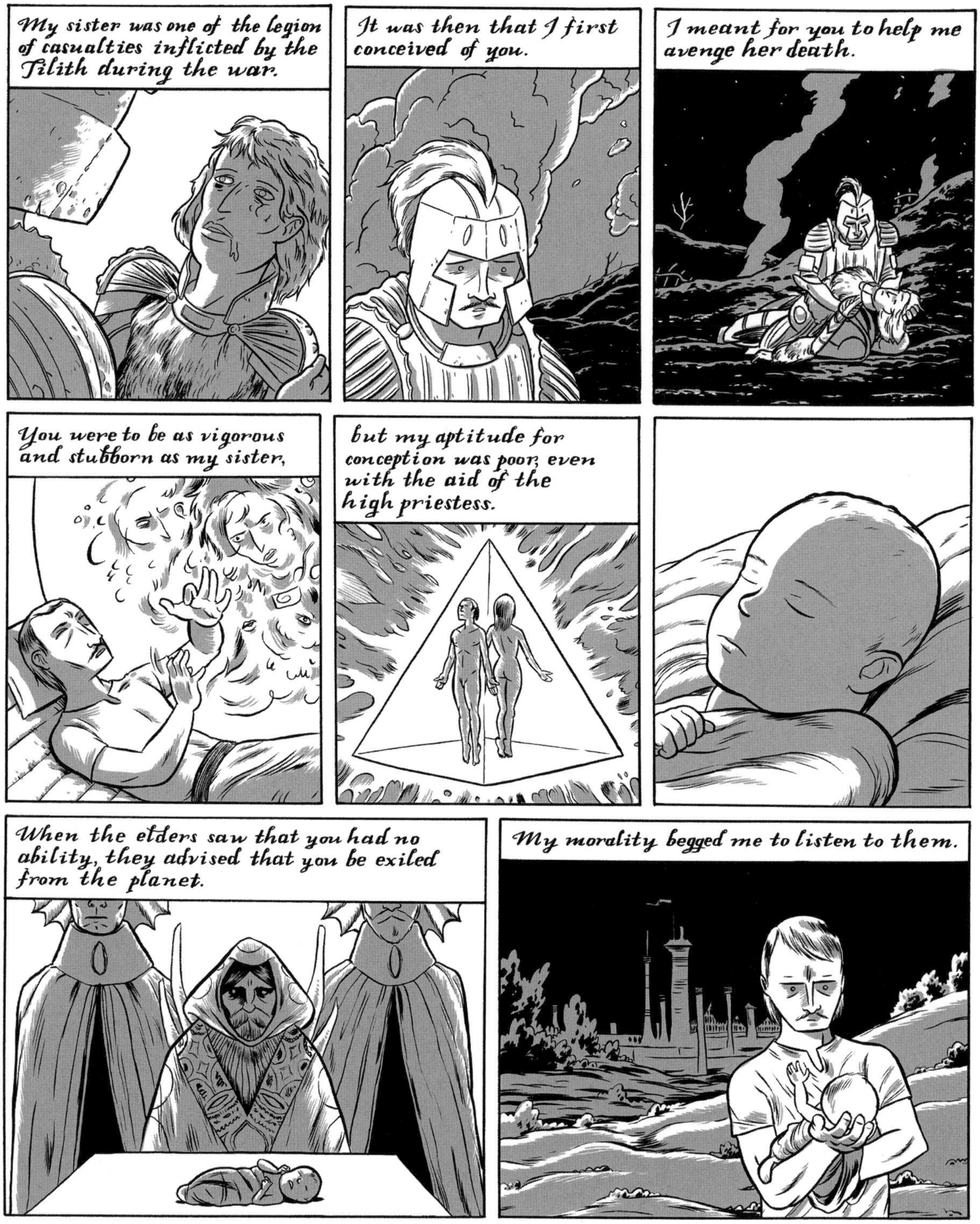
My sister was one of the legion of casualties inflicted by the Tilith during the war.
It was then that I first conceived of you.
I meant for you to help me avenge her death.
You were to be as vigorous and stubborn as my sister,
but my aptitude for conception was poor, even with the aid of the high priestess.
When the elders saw that you had no ability, they advised that you be exiled from the planet.
My morality begged me to listen to them.

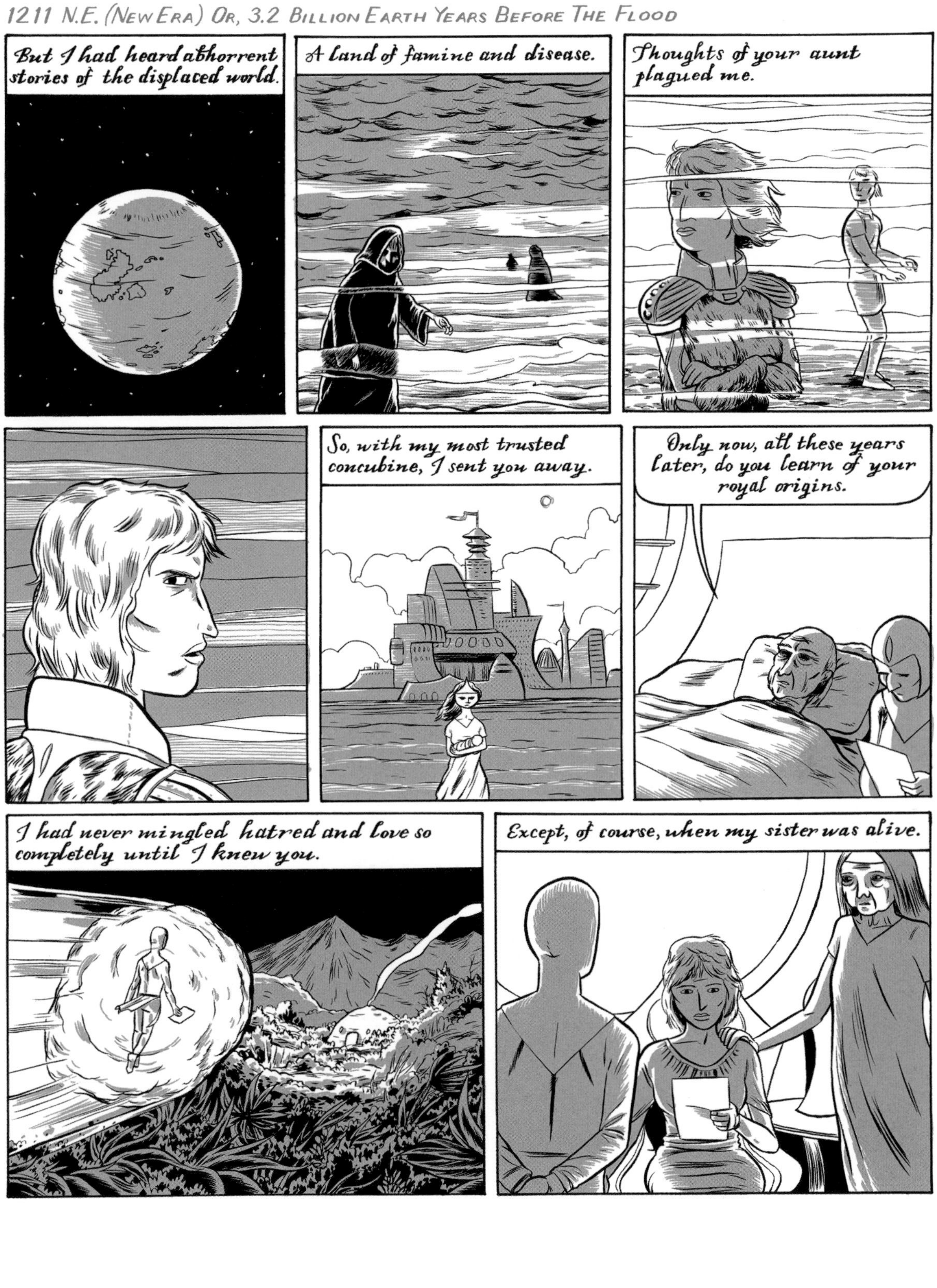
1211 N.E. (New Era) Or, 3.2 Billion Earth Years Before The Flood
But I had heard abhorrent stories of the displaced world.
A land of famine and disease.
Thoughts of your aunt plagued me.
So, with my most trusted concubine, I sent you away.
Only now, all these years later, do you learn of your royal origins.
I had never mingled hatred and love so completely until I knew you.
Except, of course, when my sister was alive.

I COULD USE A TRICORDER RIGHT ABOUT NOW. IT'D HELP MAKE SOME SENSE OF THIS THING.

AS LONG AS I'M WISHING, I GUESS A TRANSPORTER WOULD BE BETTER.

OR A TIME MACHINE THAT WON'T LEAVE ME STRANDED IN THIS FORSAKEN JUNGLE.

I GUESS THEY DIDN'T REALLY HAVE TIME MACHINES IN STAR TREK.

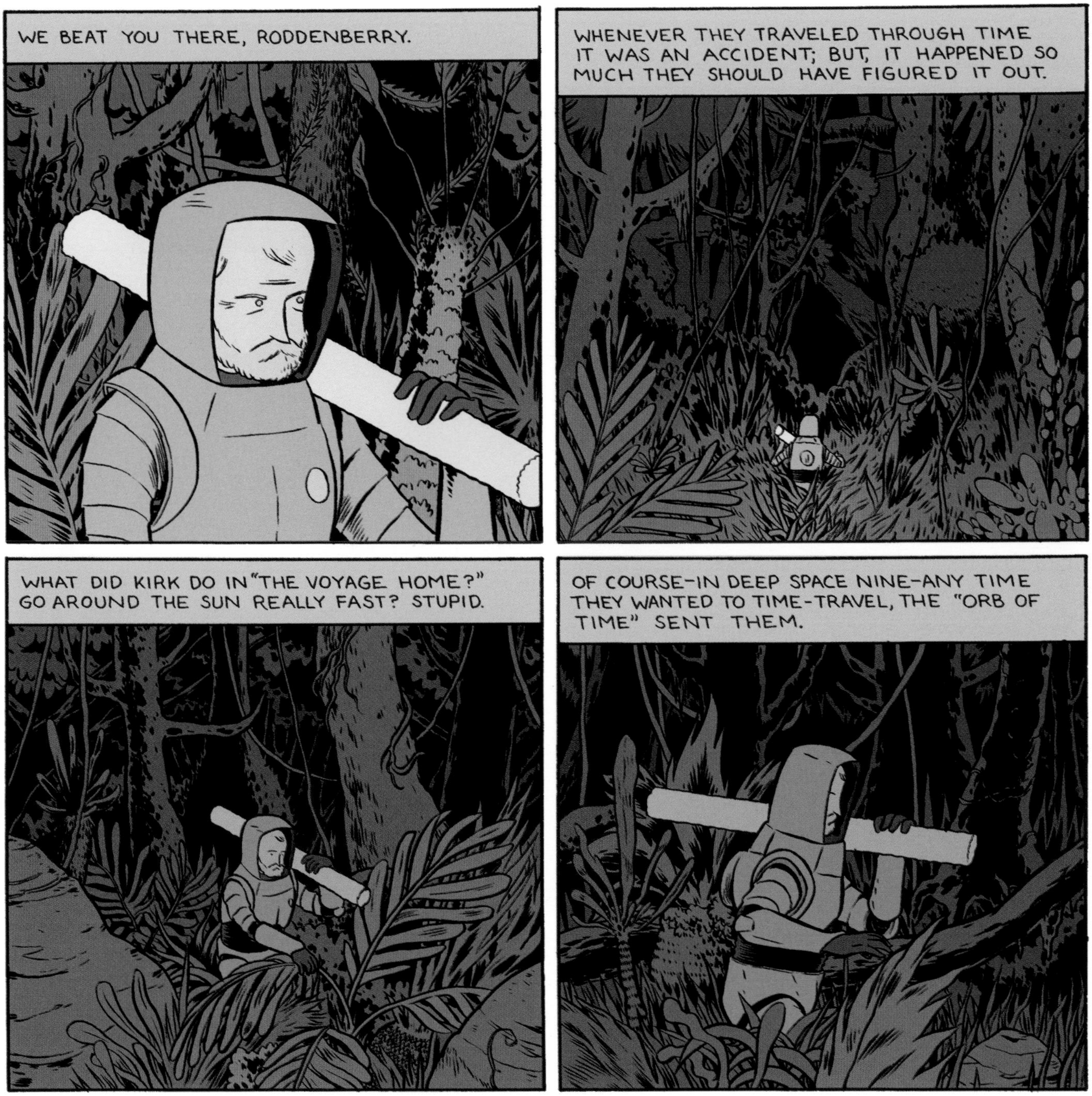
WE BEAT YOU THERE, RODDENBERRY.
WHENEVER THEY TRAVELED THROUGH TIME IT WAS AN ACCIDENT; BUT, IT HAPPENED SO MUCH THEY SHOULD HAVE FIGURED IT OUT.
WHAT DID KIRK DO IN "THE VOYAGE HOME?" GO AROUND THE SUN REALLY FAST? STUPID.
OF COURSE-IN DEEP SPACE NINE-ANY TIME THEY WANTED TO TIME-TRAVEL, THE "ORB OF TIME" SENT THEM.

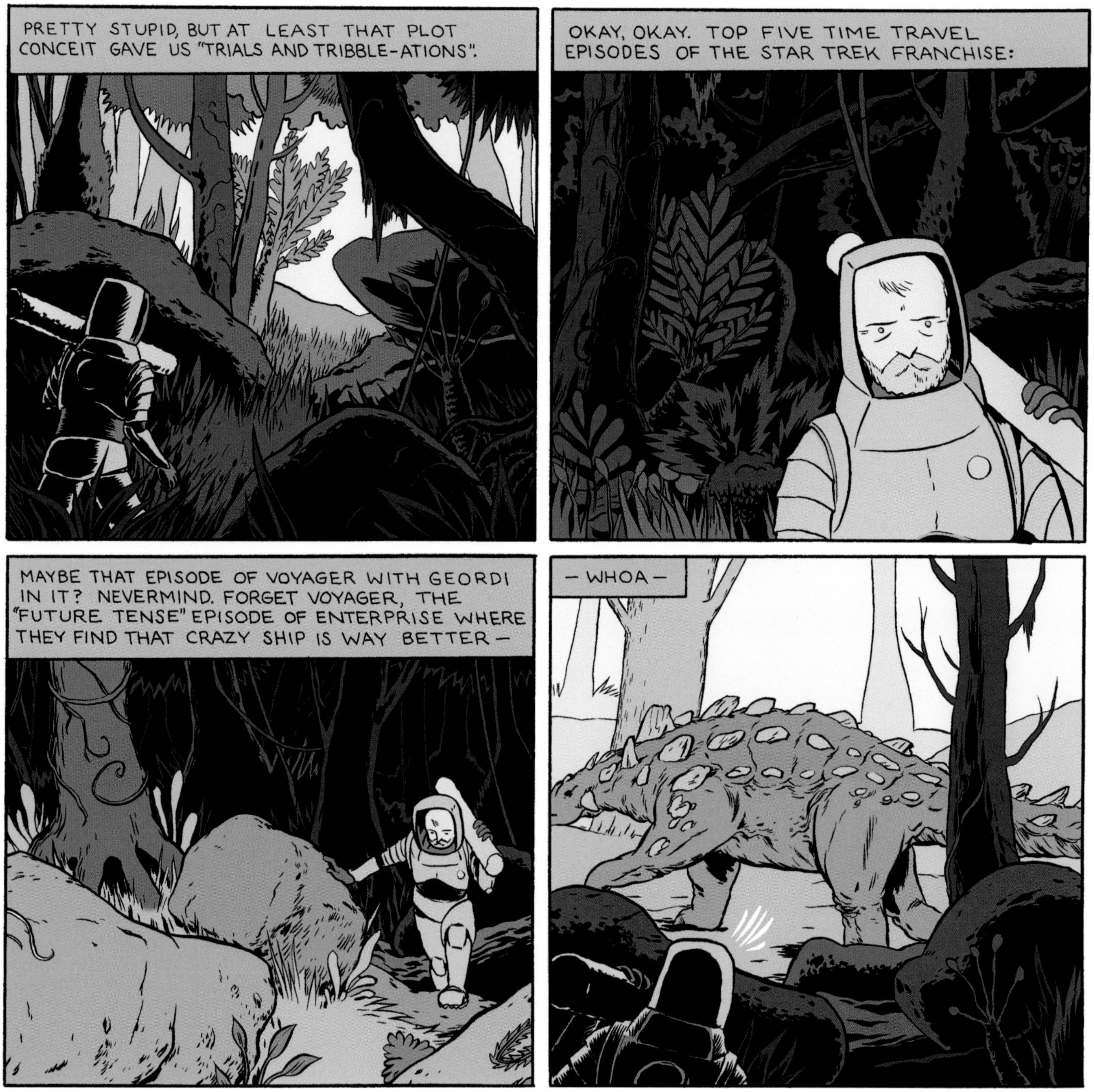
PRETTY STUPID, BUT AT LEAST THAT PLOT CONCEIT GAVE US "TRIALS AND TRIBBLE-ATIONS".
OKAY, OKAY. TOP FIVE TIME TRAVEL EPISODES OF THE STAR TREK FRANCHISE:
MAYBE THAT EPISODE OF VOYAGER WITH GEORDI IN IT? NEVERMIND. FORGET VOYAGER, THE "FUTURE TENSE" EPISODE OF ENTERPRISE WHERE THEY FIND THAT CRAZY SHIP IS WAY BETTER —
— WHOA —

VOYAGER WAS SUCH A CRAPPY SHOW.

ANYWAY, THAT EPISODE OF NEXT GENERATION WITH MARK TWAIN AND DATA'S HEAD IS PROBABLY NUMBER FOUR.

NEXT GENERATION'S "ALL GOOD THINGS," I'D PUT THAT AT NUMBER THREE.

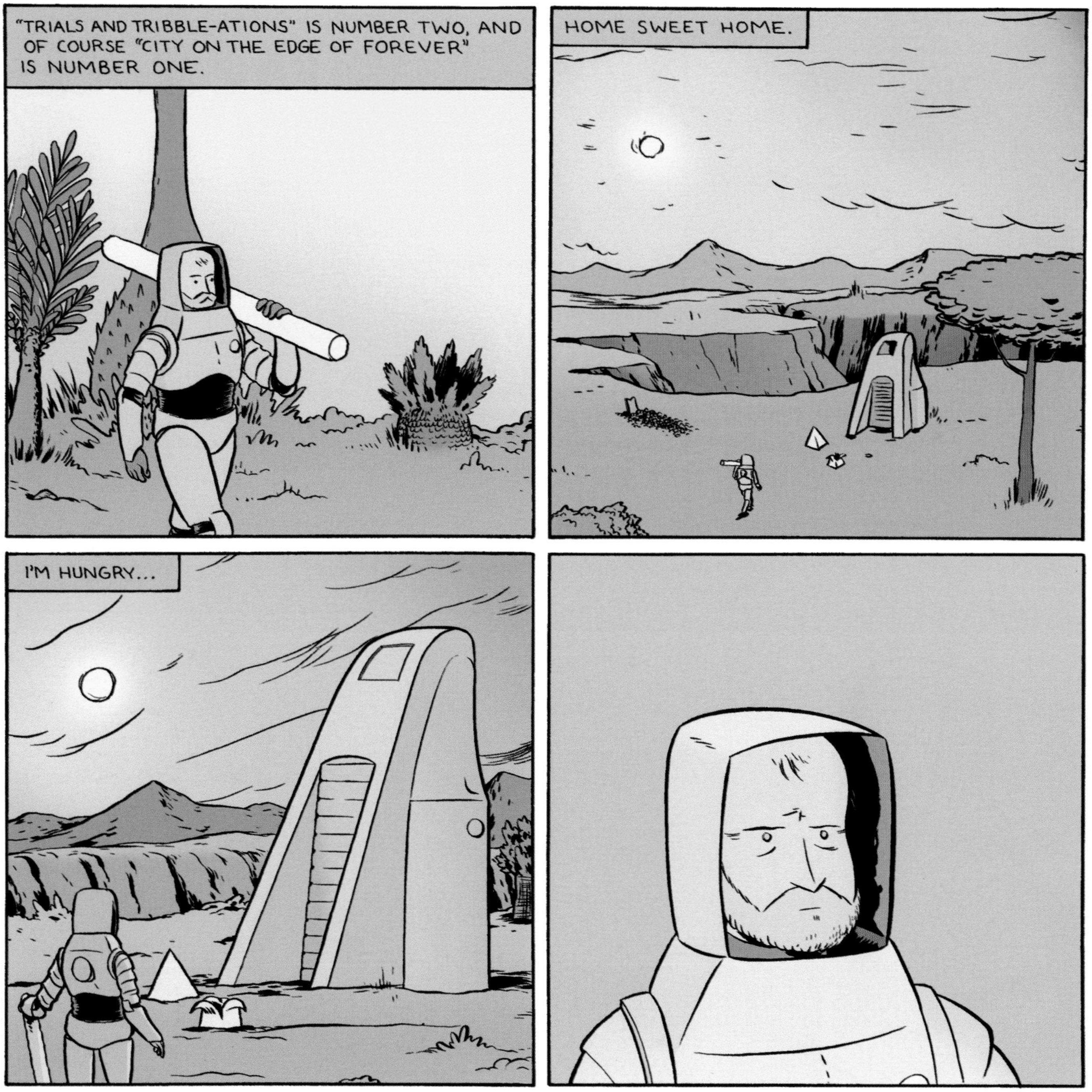
"TRIALS AND TRIBBLE-ATIONS" IS NUMBER TWO, AND OF COURSE "CITY ON THE EDGE OF FOREVER" IS NUMBER ONE.
HOME SWEET HOME.
I'M HUNGRY...

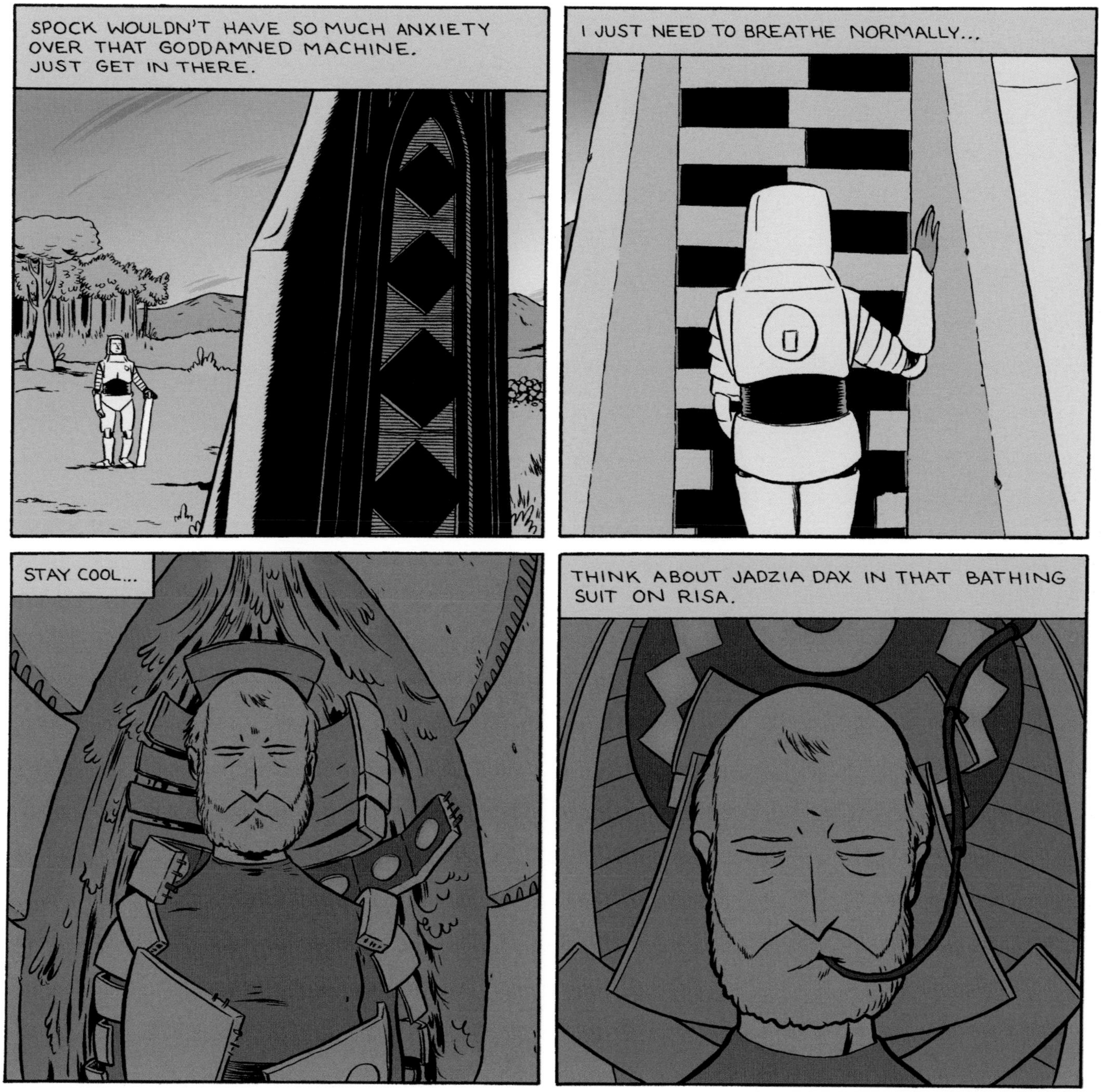
SPOCK WOULDN'T HAVE SO MUCH ANXIETY OVER THAT GODDAMNED MACHINE. JUST GET IN THERE.
I JUST NEED TO BREATHE NORMALLY...
STAY COOL...
THINK ABOUT JADZIA DAX IN THAT BATHING SUIT ON RISA.

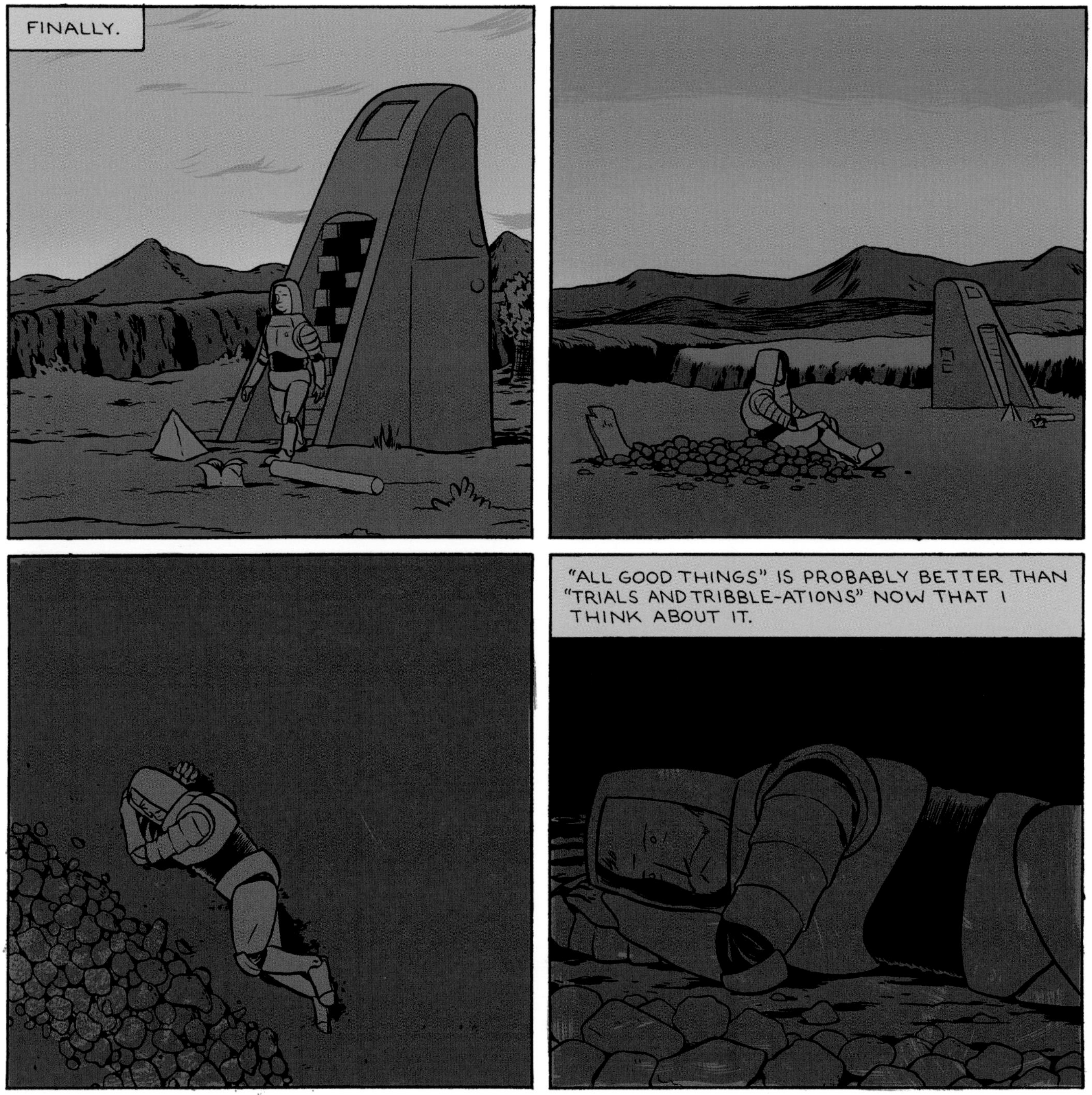
FINALLY.
"ALL GOOD THINGS" IS PROBABLY BETTER THAN "TRIALS AND TRIBBLE-ATIONS" NOW THAT I THINK ABOUT IT.

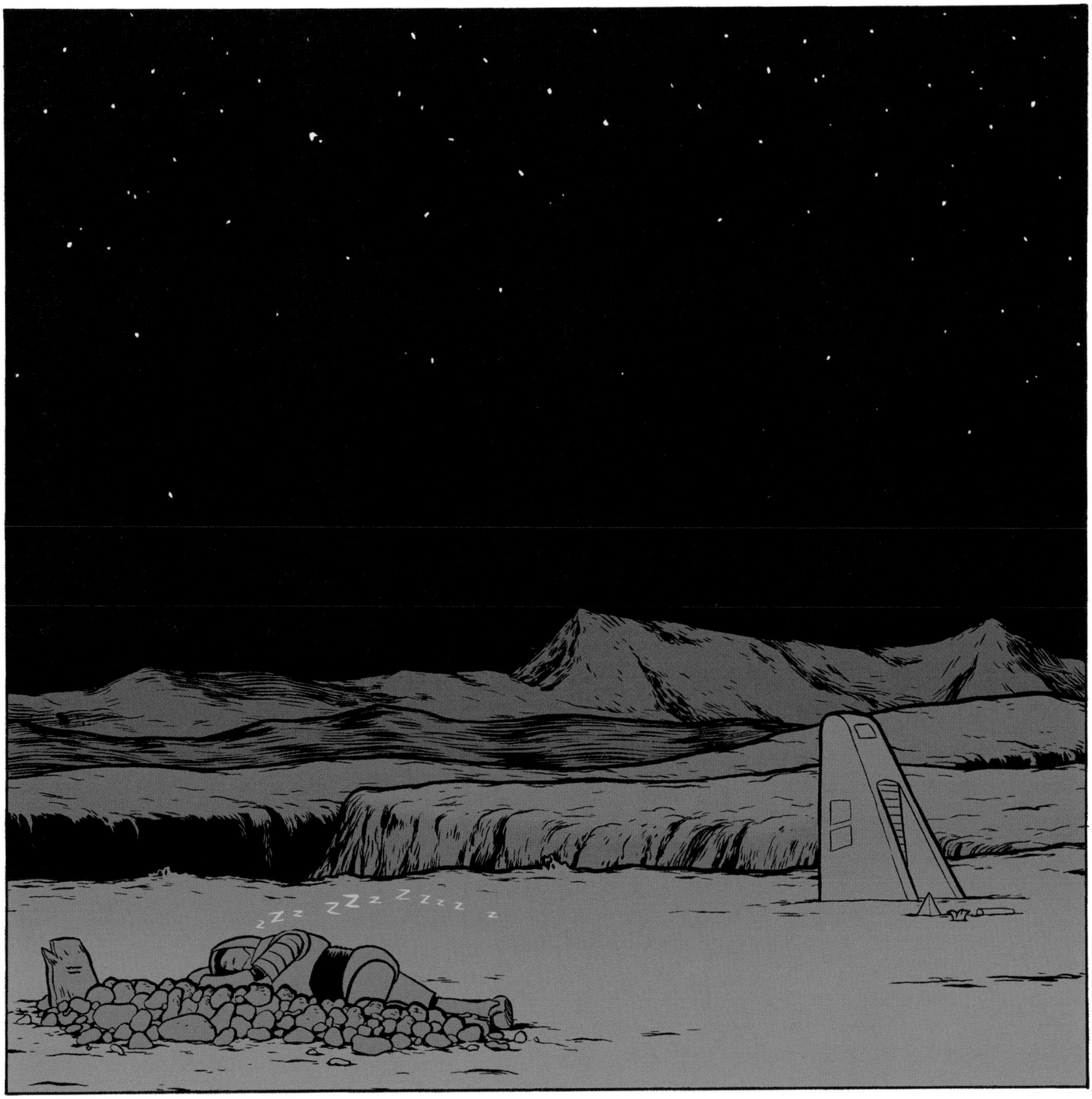
zZz ZZzZzzz z

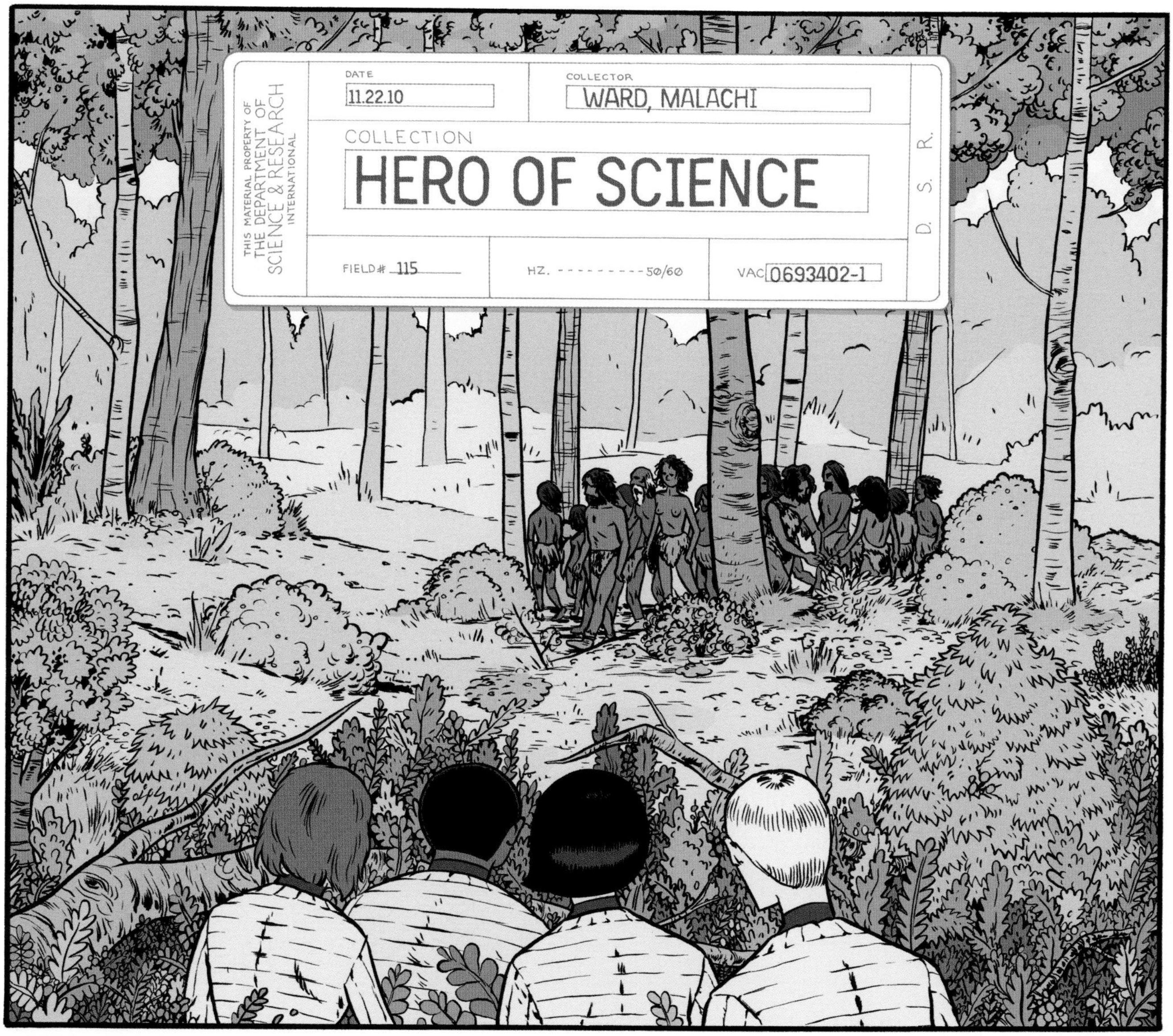
THIS MATERIAL PROPERTY OF THE DEPARTMENT OF SCIENCE & RESEARCH INTERNATIONAL
DATE
11.22.10
COLLECTOR
WARD, MALACHI
COLLECTION
HERO OF SCIENCE
FIELD# 115
HZ. ----------50/60
VAC 0693402-1
D. S. R.

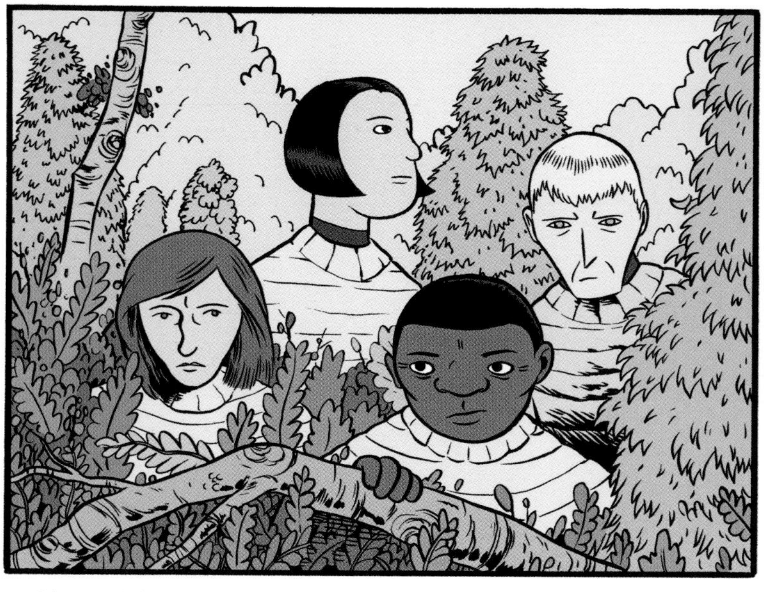

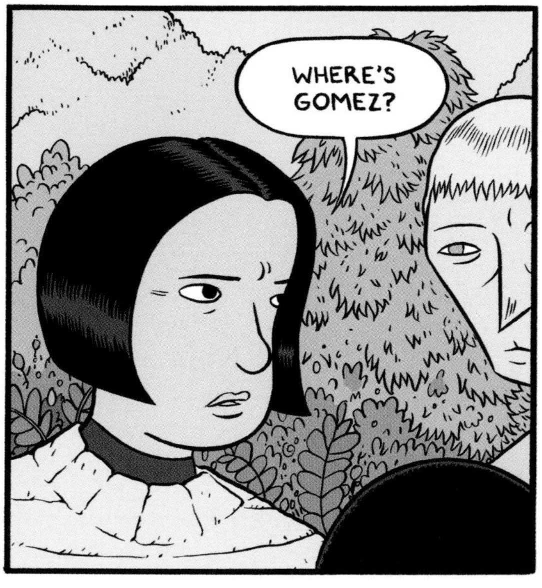
WHERE'S GOMEZ?

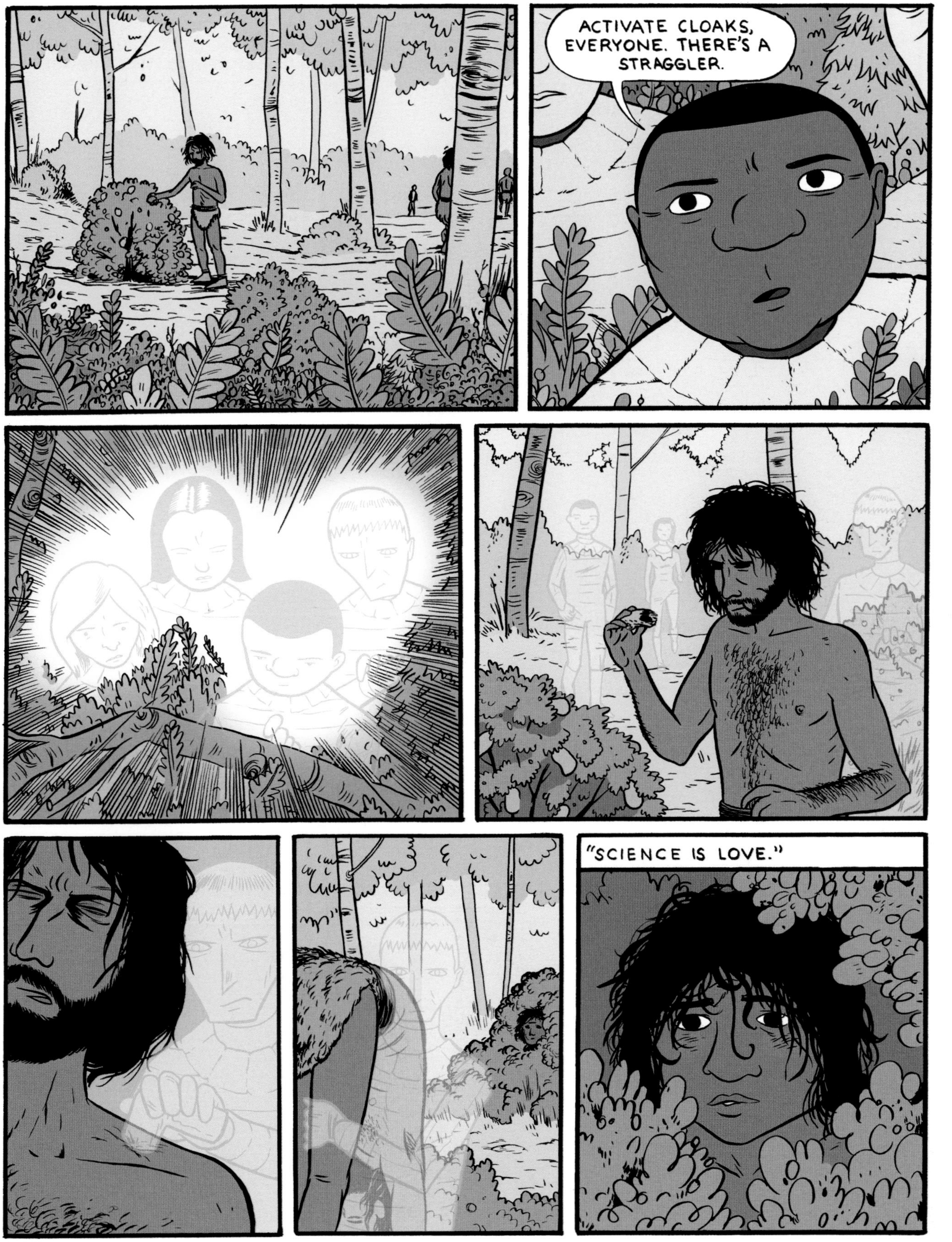

ACTIVATE CLOAKS, EVERYONE. THERE'S A STRAGGLER.
"SCIENCE IS LOVE."

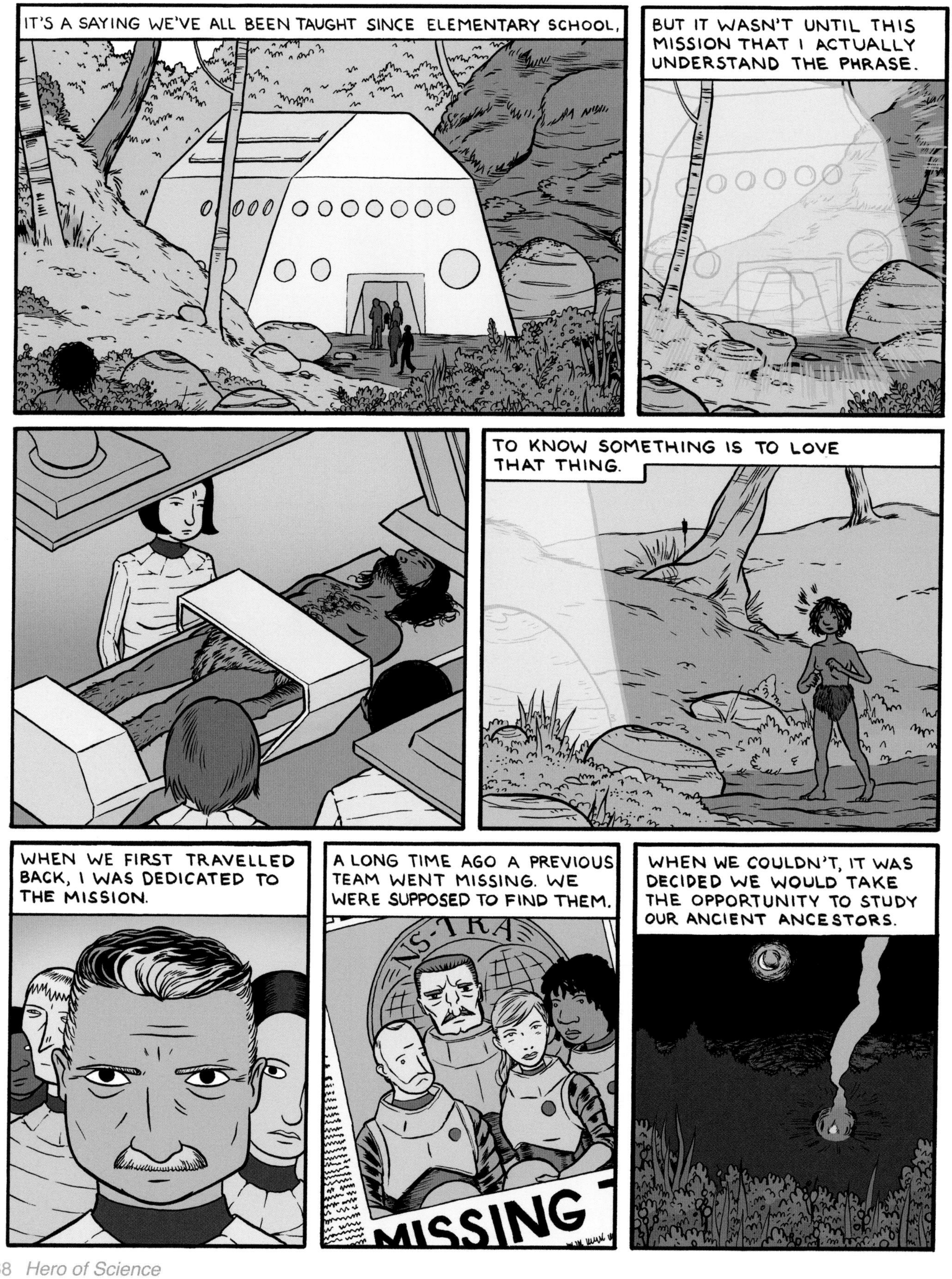
IT'S A SAYING WE'VE ALL BEEN TAUGHT SINCE ELEMENTARY SCHOOL,
BUT IT WASN'T UNTIL THIS MISSION THAT I ACTUALLY UNDERSTAND THE PHRASE.
TO KNOW SOMETHING IS TO LOVE THAT THING.
WHEN WE FIRST TRAVELLED BACK, I WAS DEDICATED TO THE MISSION.
A LONG TIME AGO A PREVIOUS TEAM WENT MISSING. WE WERE SUPPOSED TO FIND THEM.
NS-TRA
MISSING
WHEN WE COULDN'T, IT WAS DECIDED WE WOULD TAKE THE OPPORTUNITY TO STUDY OUR ANCIENT ANCESTORS.

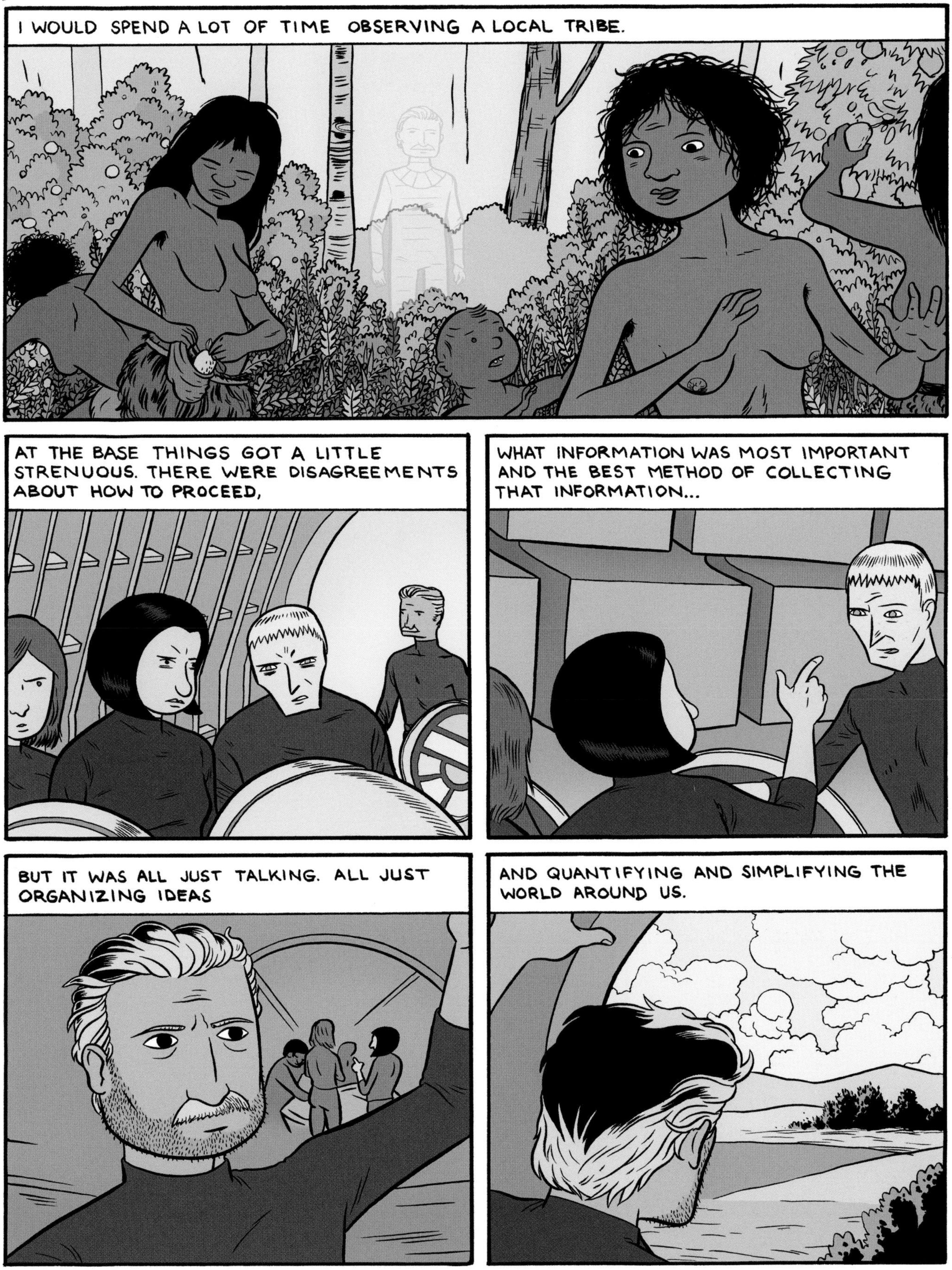
I WOULD SPEND A LOT OF TIME OBSERVING A LOCAL TRIBE.
AT THE BASE THINGS GOT A LITTLE STRENUOUS. THERE WERE DISAGREEMENTS ABOUT HOW TO PROCEED,
WHAT INFORMATION WAS MOST IMPORTANT AND THE BEST METHOD OF COLLECTING THAT INFORMATION...
BUT IT WAS ALL JUST TALKING. ALL JUST ORGANIZING IDEAS
AND QUANTIFYING AND SIMPLIFYING THE WORLD AROUND US.

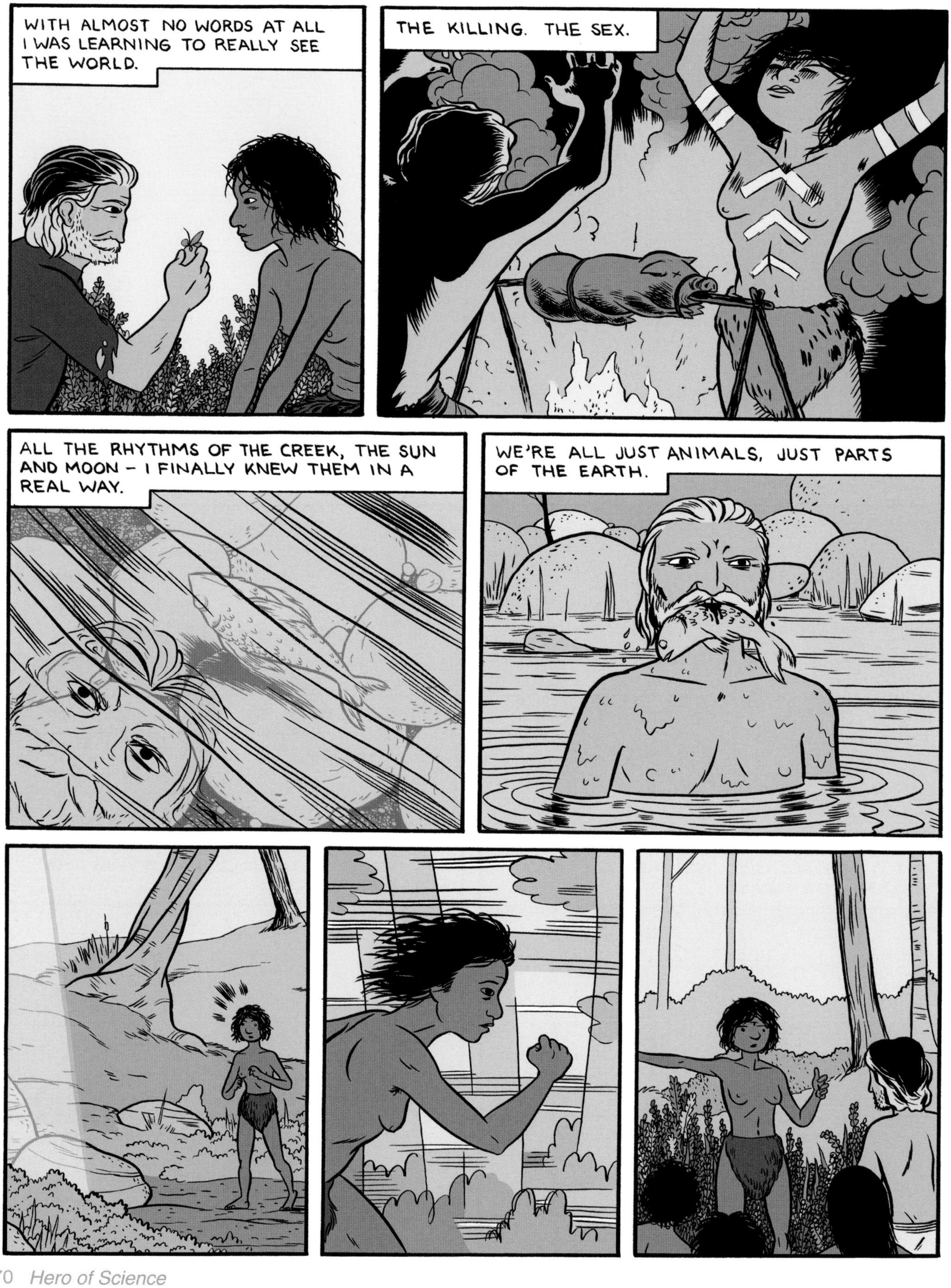
WITH ALMOST NO WORDS AT ALL I WAS LEARNING TO REALLY SEE THE WORLD.
THE KILLING. THE SEX.
ALL THE RHYTHMS OF THE CREEK, THE SUN AND MOON – I FINALLY KNEW THEM IN A REAL WAY.
WE'RE ALL JUST ANIMALS, JUST PARTS OF THE EARTH.

THEY DON'T KNOW THE WORLD, SO THEY DON'T KNOW ME.

THEY DON'T KNOW MY TRIBE.

FOR US, PROBLEMS HAVE SIMPLE, ELEGANT SOLUTIONS.

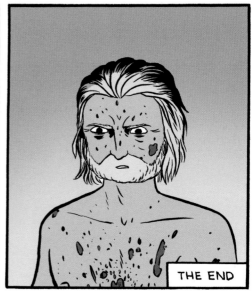

THE END

71

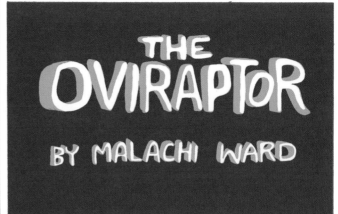

THE OVIRAPTOR

BY MALACHI WARD

ANY SIGNS OF PAIGE?

NOTHING YET.

ASHUR IS RE-CALIBRATING THE SENSORS.

I THOUGHT I KNEW WHAT I WAS GETTING INTO WHEN I SIGNED UP FOR THIS MISSION.

I KNEW... I KNEW THERE'D BE ISOLATION... THAT I WAS GOING TO DIE IN A FOREIGN TIME...

BUT I **FOUGHT** FOR A POSITION ON THIS TEAM.

HASANEGA SAYS THAT ALL THINGS DONE IN PURSUIT OF SCIENCE ARE GUIDED BY NATURE.

THERE ARE NO MISTAKES.

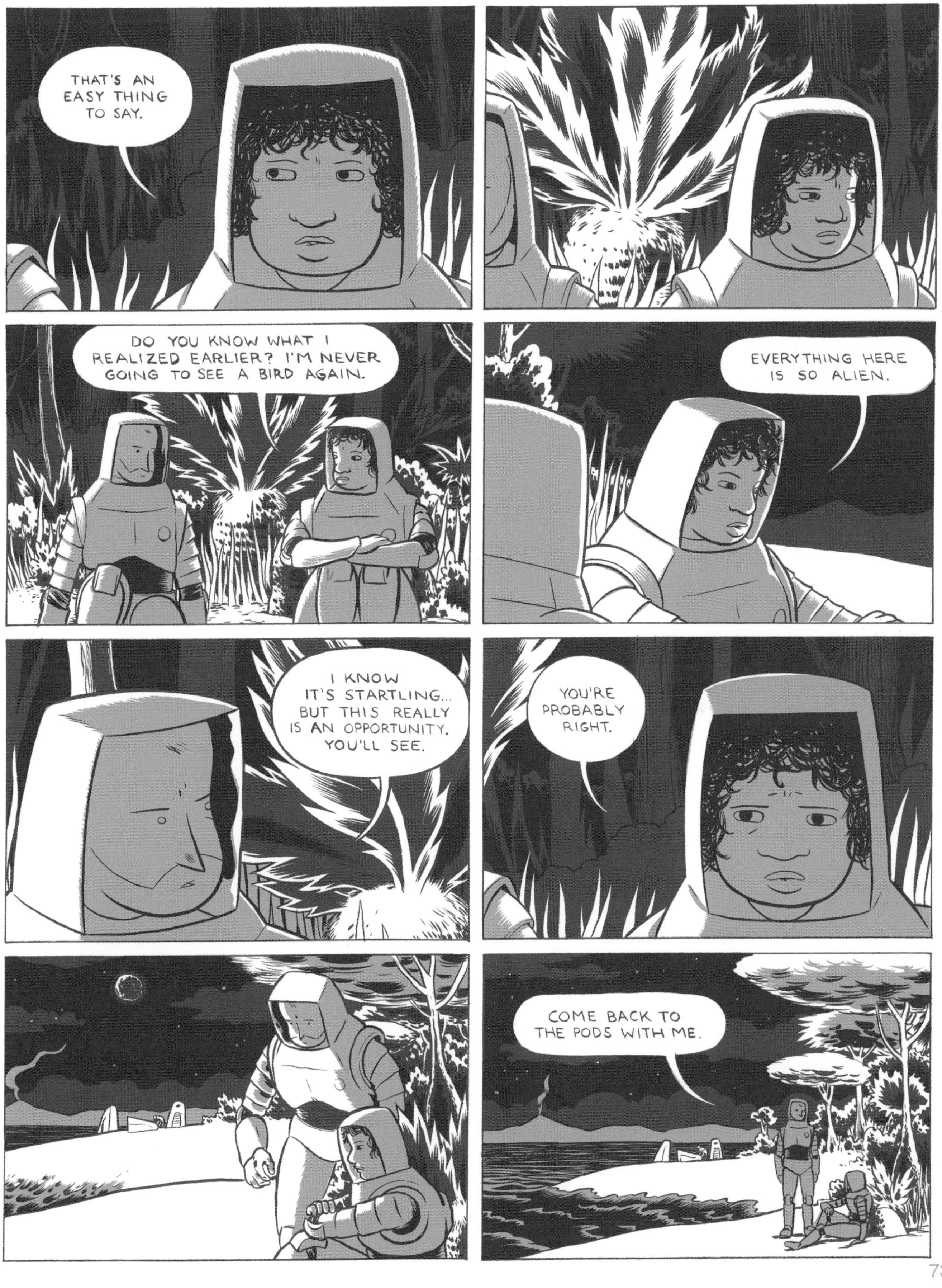
THAT'S AN EASY THING TO SAY.
DO YOU KNOW WHAT I REALIZED EARLIER? I'M NEVER GOING TO SEE A BIRD AGAIN.
EVERYTHING HERE IS SO ALIEN.
I KNOW IT'S STARTLING... BUT THIS REALLY IS AN OPPORTUNITY. YOU'LL SEE.
YOU'RE PROBABLY RIGHT.
COME BACK TO THE PODS WITH ME.

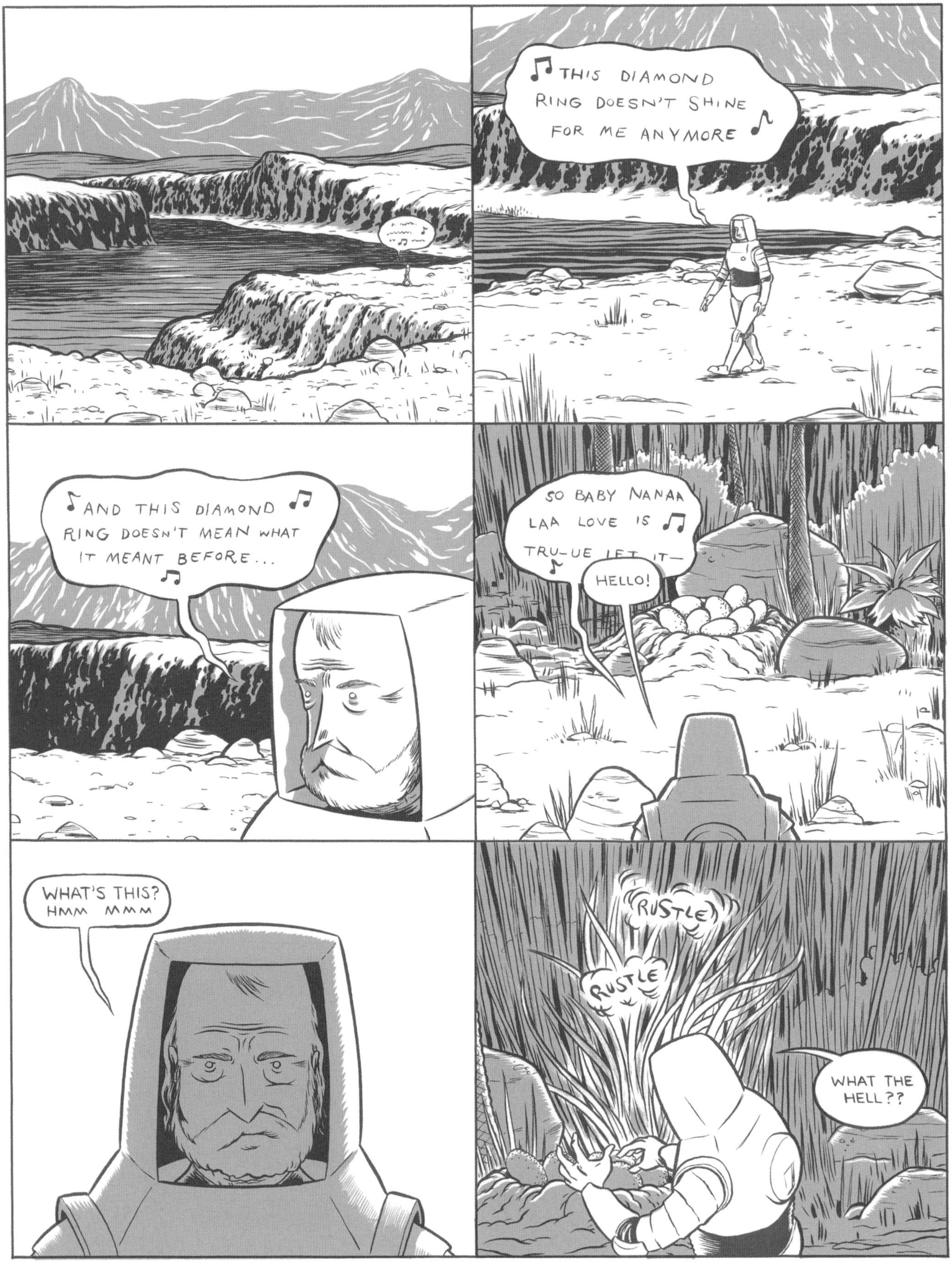

THIS DIAMOND RING DOESN'T SHINE FOR ME ANYMORE
AND THIS DIAMOND RING DOESN'T MEAN WHAT IT MEANT BEFORE...
SO BABY NANAA LAA LOVE IS TRU-UE LET IT—
HELLO!
WHAT'S THIS? HMM MMM
RUSTLE
RUSTLE
WHAT THE HELL??

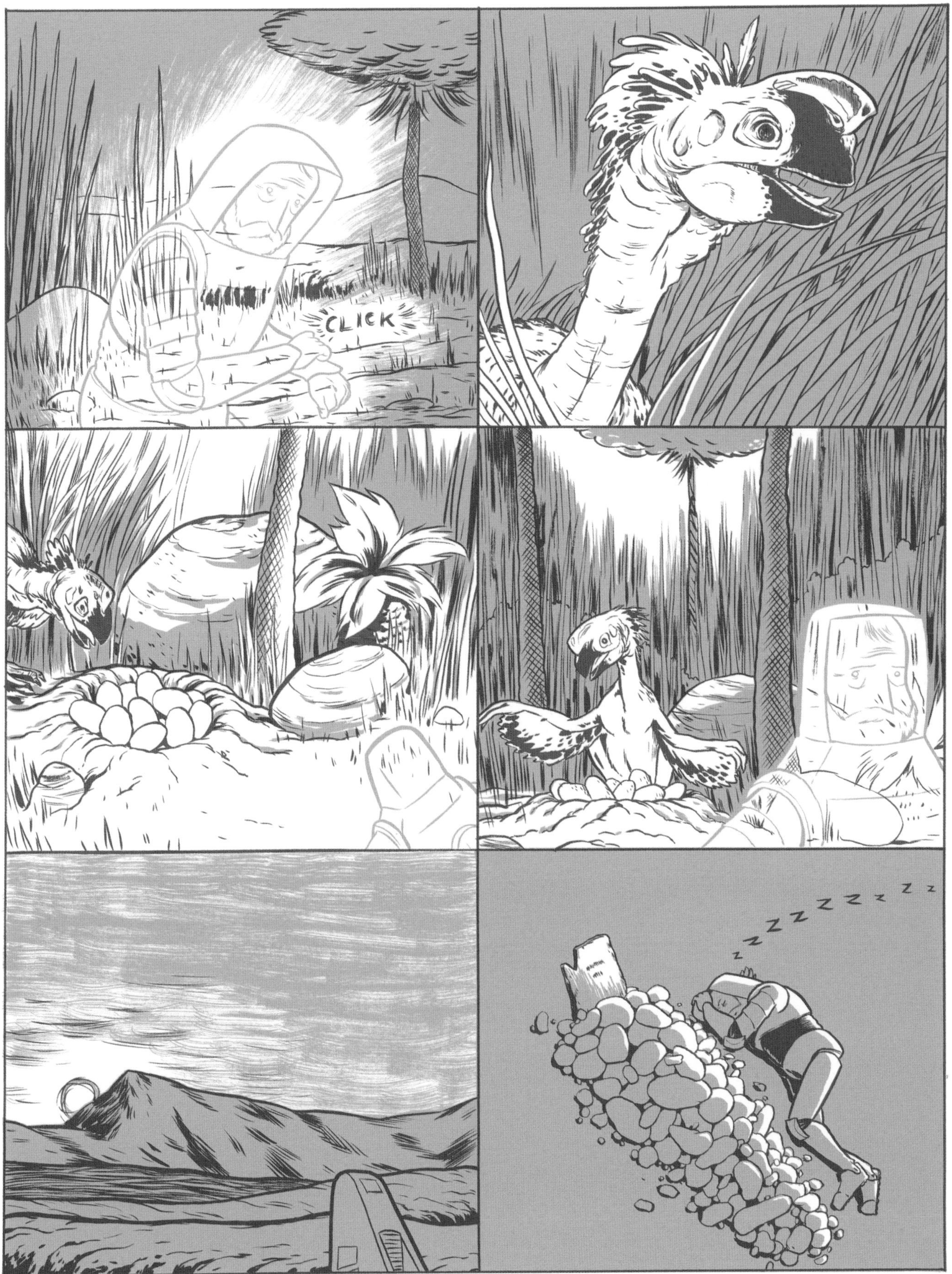
CLICK
Z Z Z Z Z Z Z z Z z

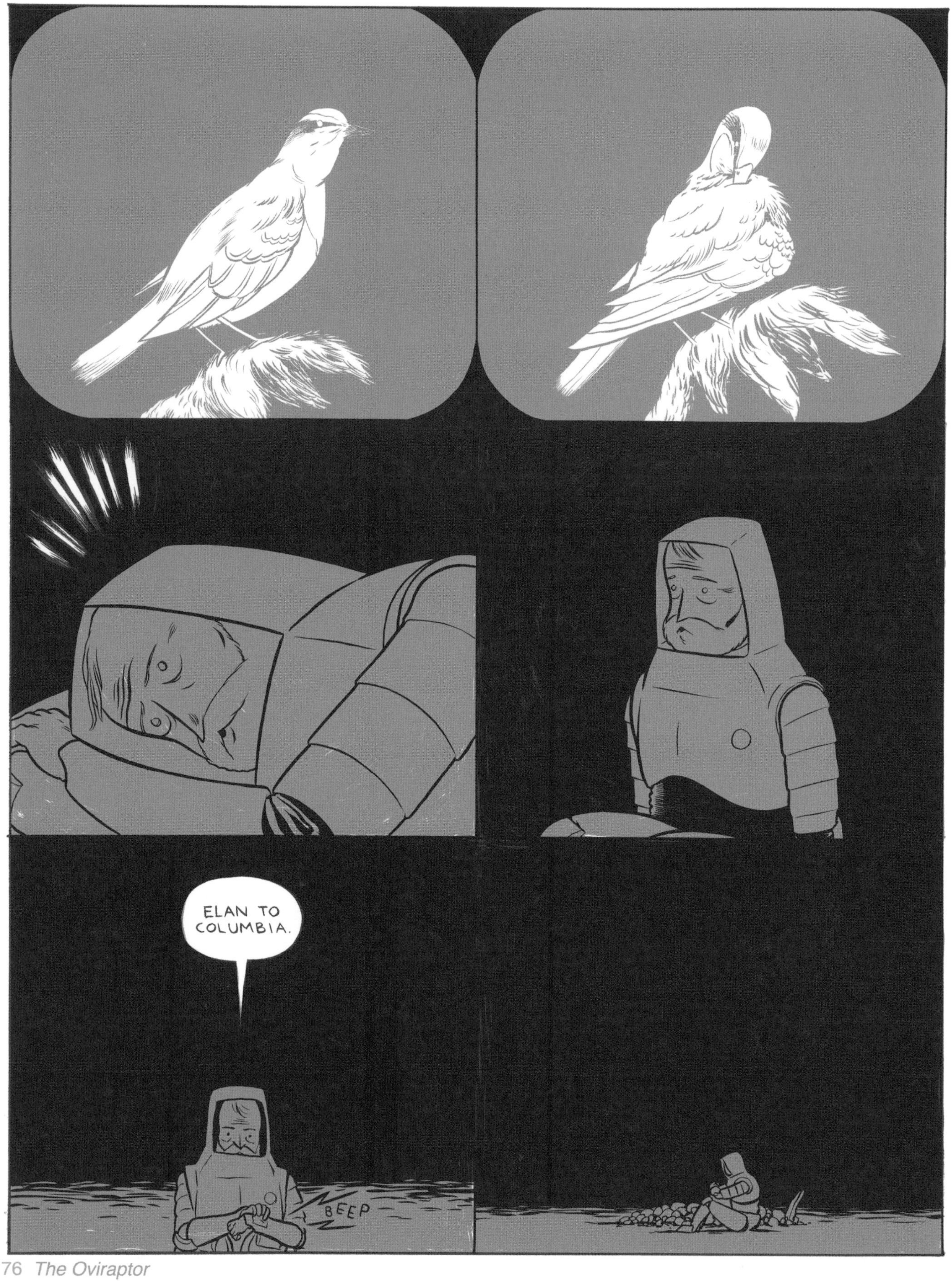
ELAN TO COLUMBIA.
BEEP

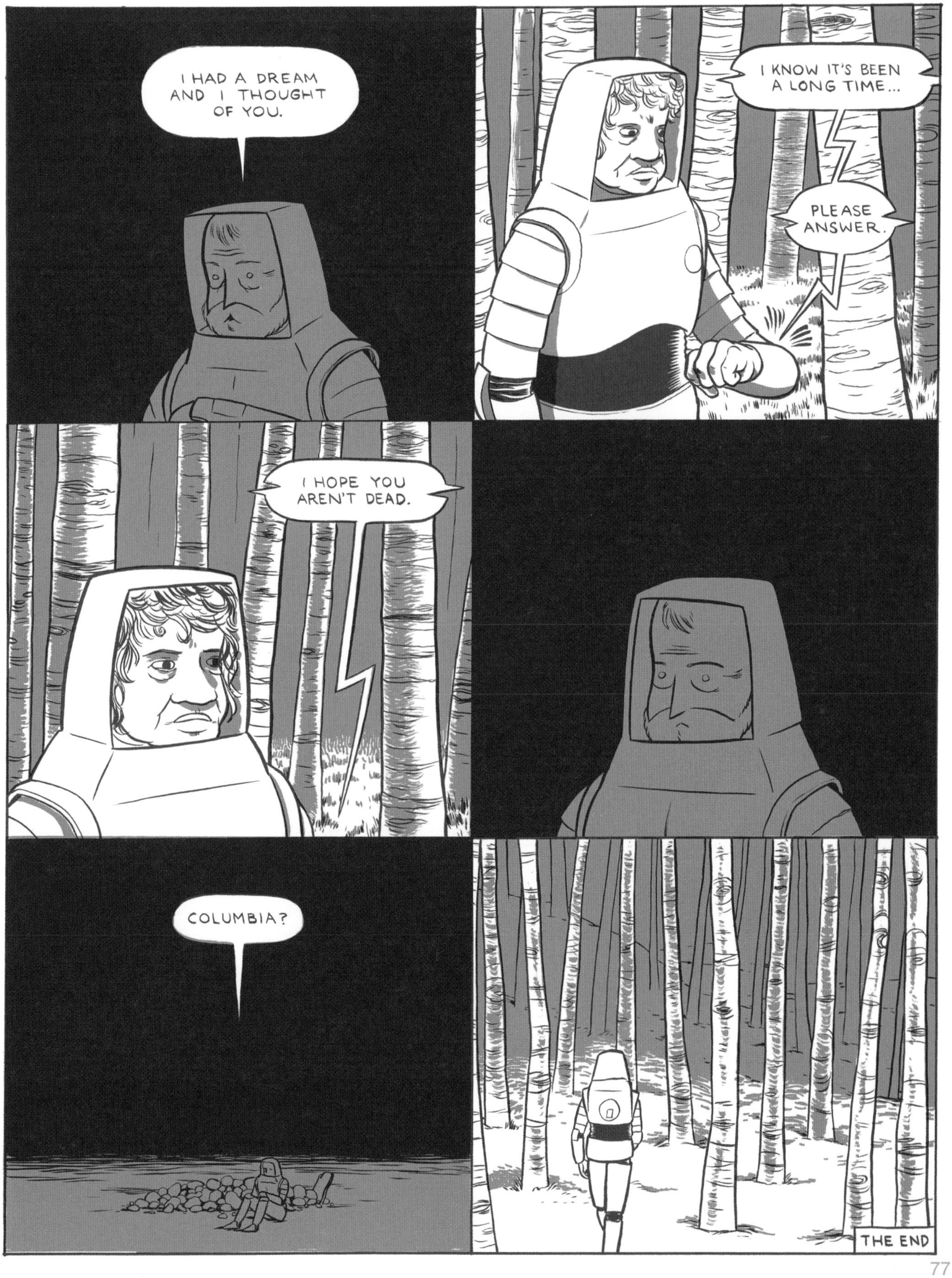
I HAD A DREAM AND I THOUGHT OF YOU.
I KNOW IT'S BEEN A LONG TIME...
PLEASE ANSWER.
I HOPE YOU AREN'T DEAD.
COLUMBIA?
THE END

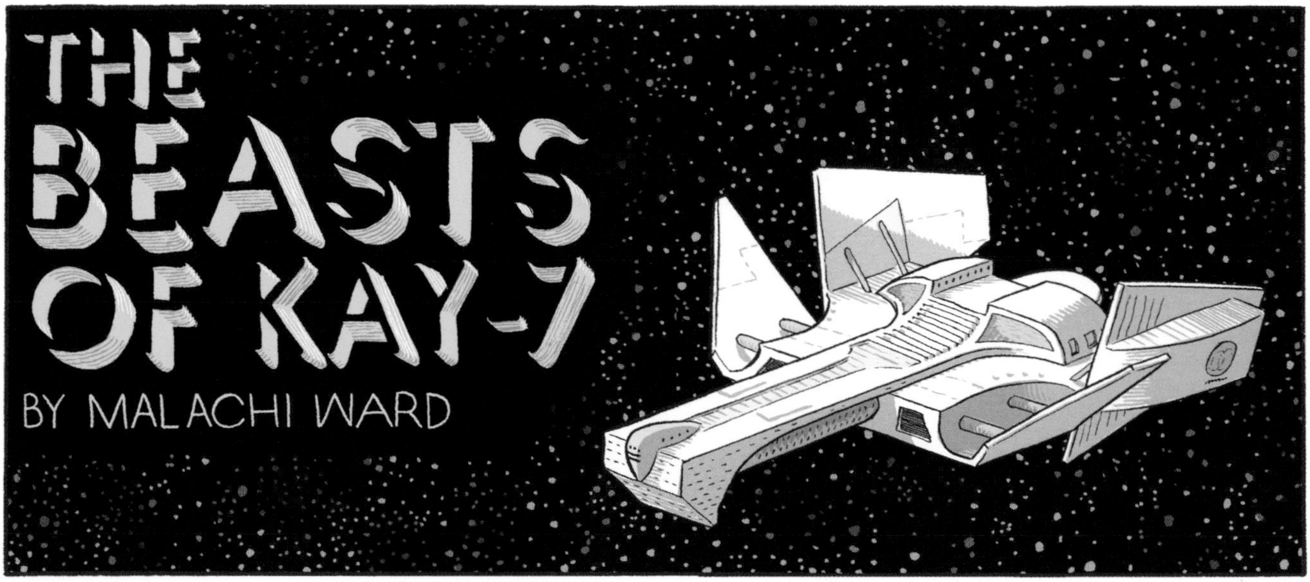
THE BEASTS OF KAY-7
BY MALACHI WARD

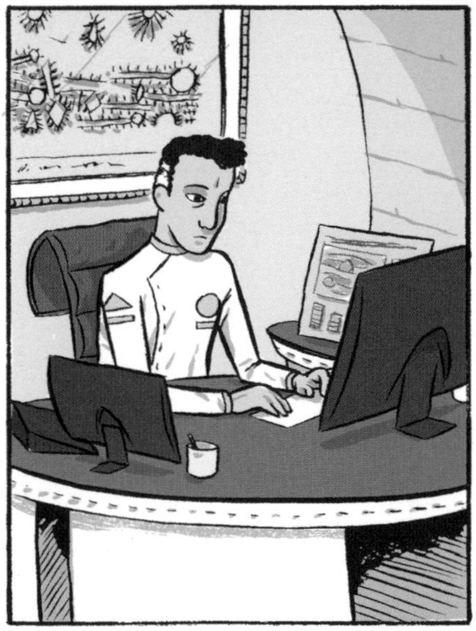

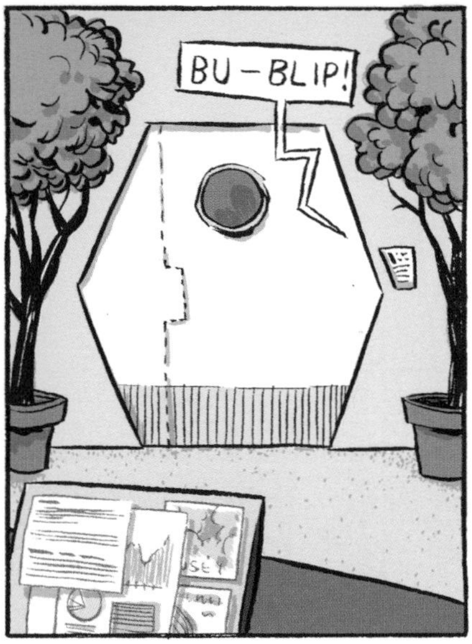
BU-BLIP!

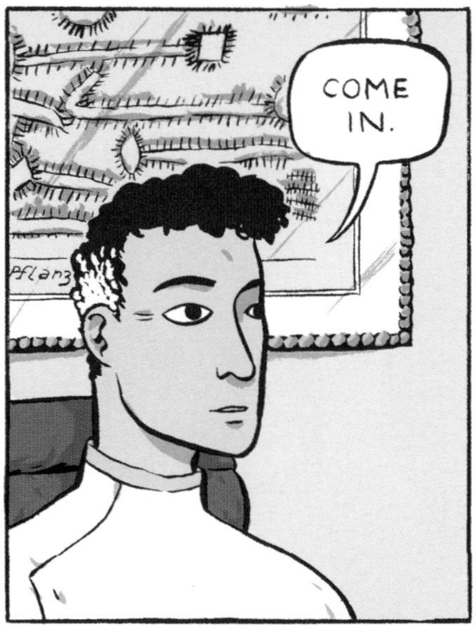
COME IN.

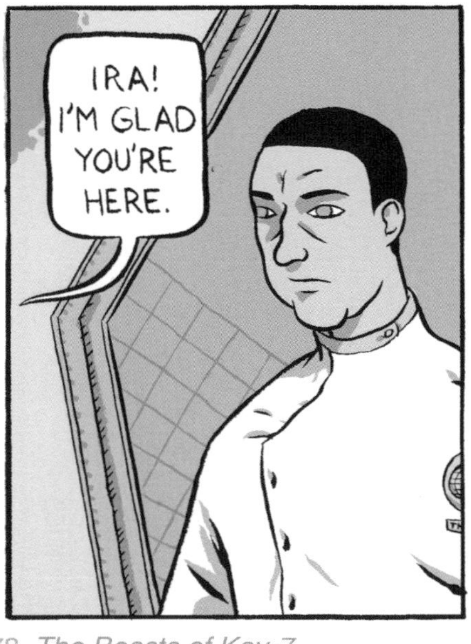
IRA! I'M GLAD YOU'RE HERE.

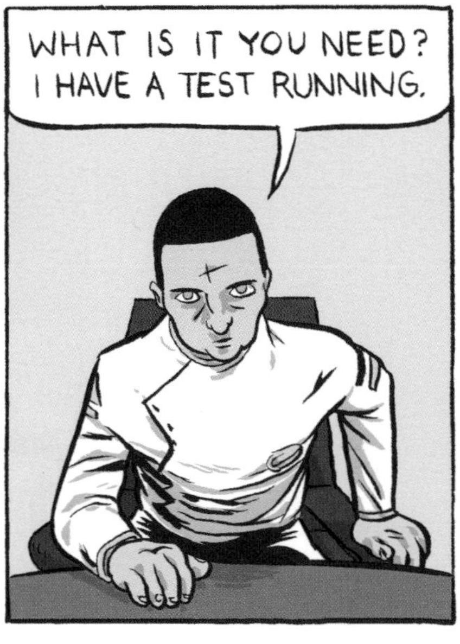
WHAT IS IT YOU NEED? I HAVE A TEST RUNNING.

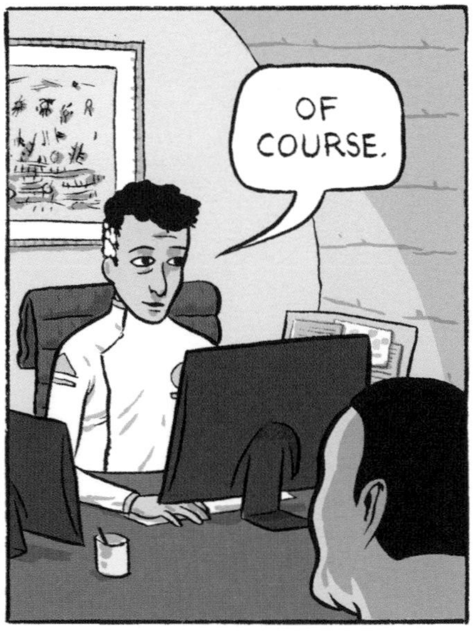
OF COURSE.

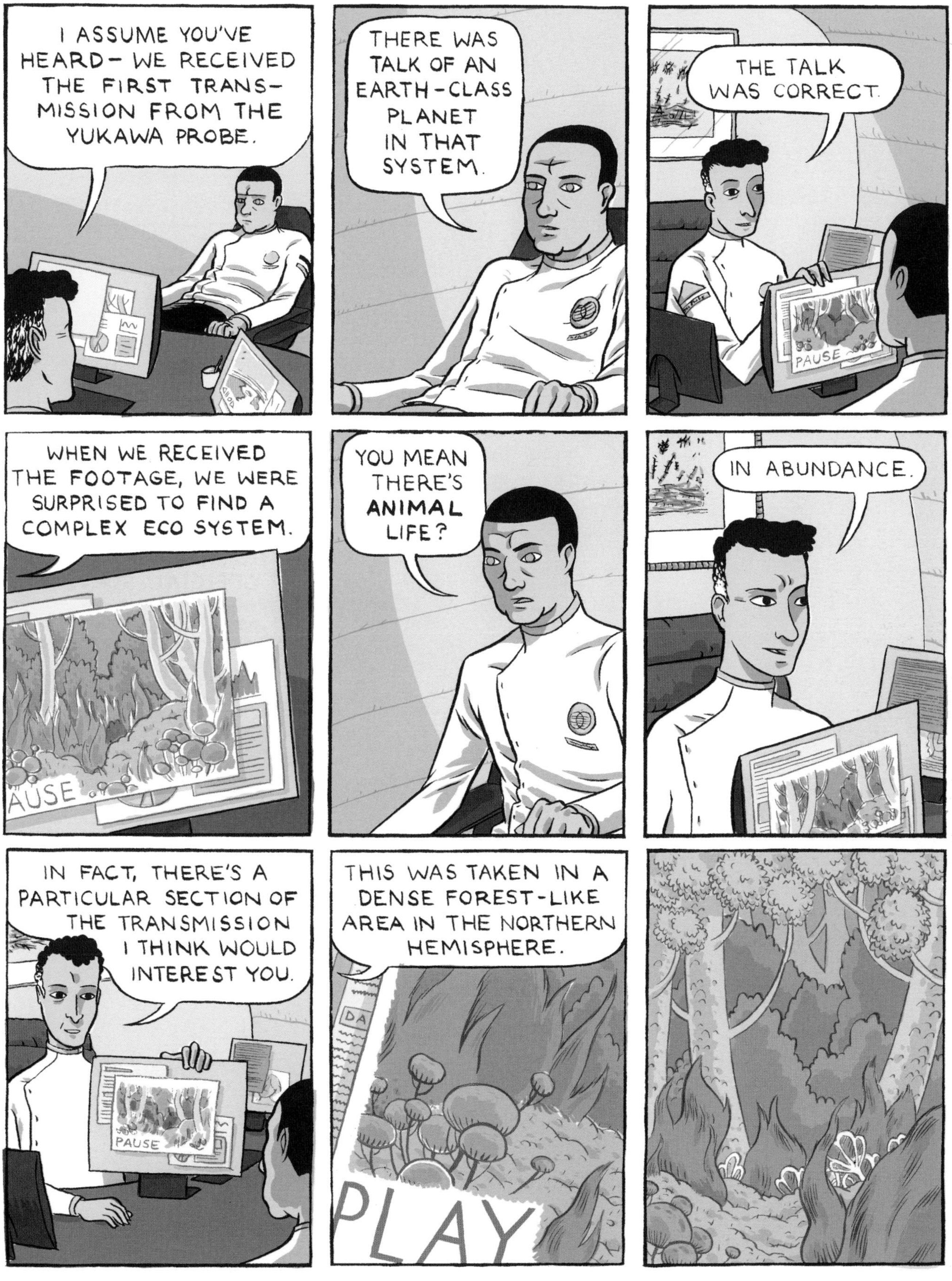
I ASSUME YOU'VE HEARD- WE RECEIVED THE FIRST TRANS-MISSION FROM THE YUKAWA PROBE.
THERE WAS TALK OF AN EARTH-CLASS PLANET IN THAT SYSTEM.
THE TALK WAS CORRECT.
PAUSE
WHEN WE RECEIVED THE FOOTAGE, WE WERE SURPRISED TO FIND A COMPLEX ECO SYSTEM.
AUSE
YOU MEAN THERE'S **ANIMAL** LIFE?
IN ABUNDANCE.
IN FACT, THERE'S A PARTICULAR SECTION OF THE TRANSMISSION I THINK WOULD INTEREST YOU.
PAUSE
THIS WAS TAKEN IN A DENSE FOREST-LIKE AREA IN THE NORTHERN HEMISPHERE.
PLAY

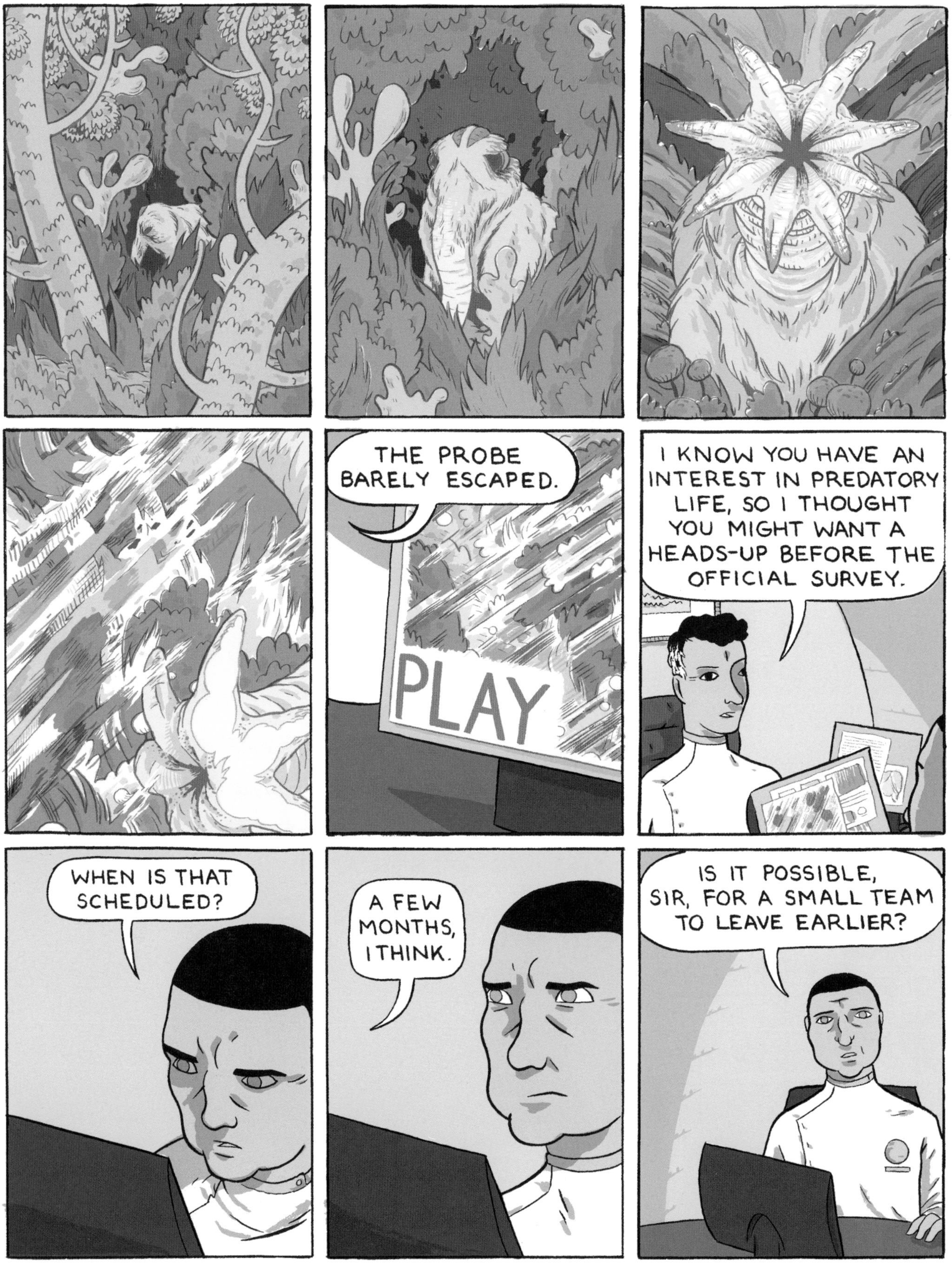
THE PROBE BARELY ESCAPED.
PLAY
I KNOW YOU HAVE AN INTEREST IN PREDATORY LIFE, SO I THOUGHT YOU MIGHT WANT A HEADS-UP BEFORE THE OFFICIAL SURVEY.
WHEN IS THAT SCHEDULED?
A FEW MONTHS, I THINK.
IS IT POSSIBLE, SIR, FOR A SMALL TEAM TO LEAVE EARLIER?

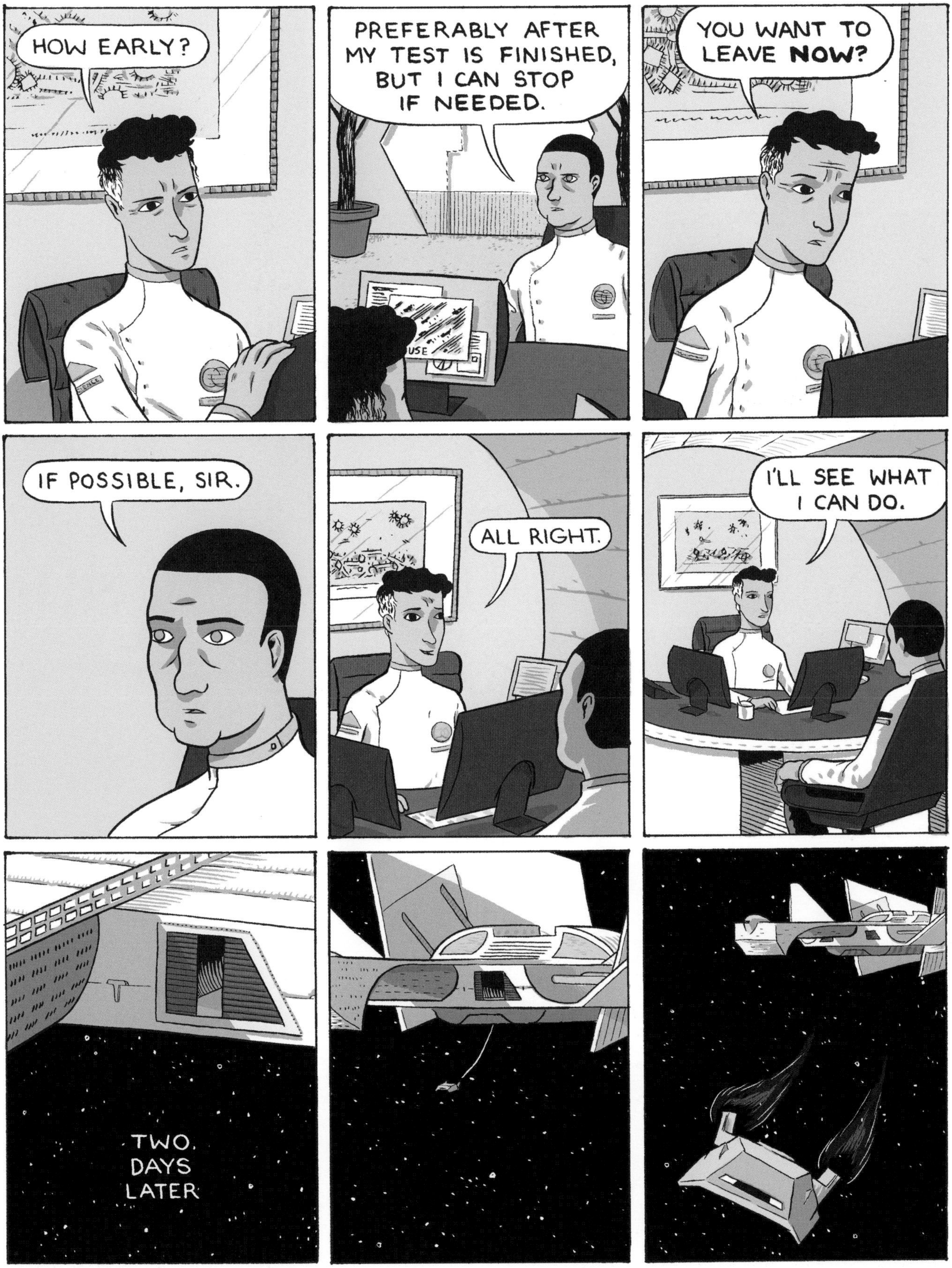
HOW EARLY?
PREFERABLY AFTER MY TEST IS FINISHED, BUT I CAN STOP IF NEEDED.
YOU WANT TO LEAVE **NOW?**
IF POSSIBLE, SIR.
ALL RIGHT.
I'LL SEE WHAT I CAN DO.
TWO DAYS LATER

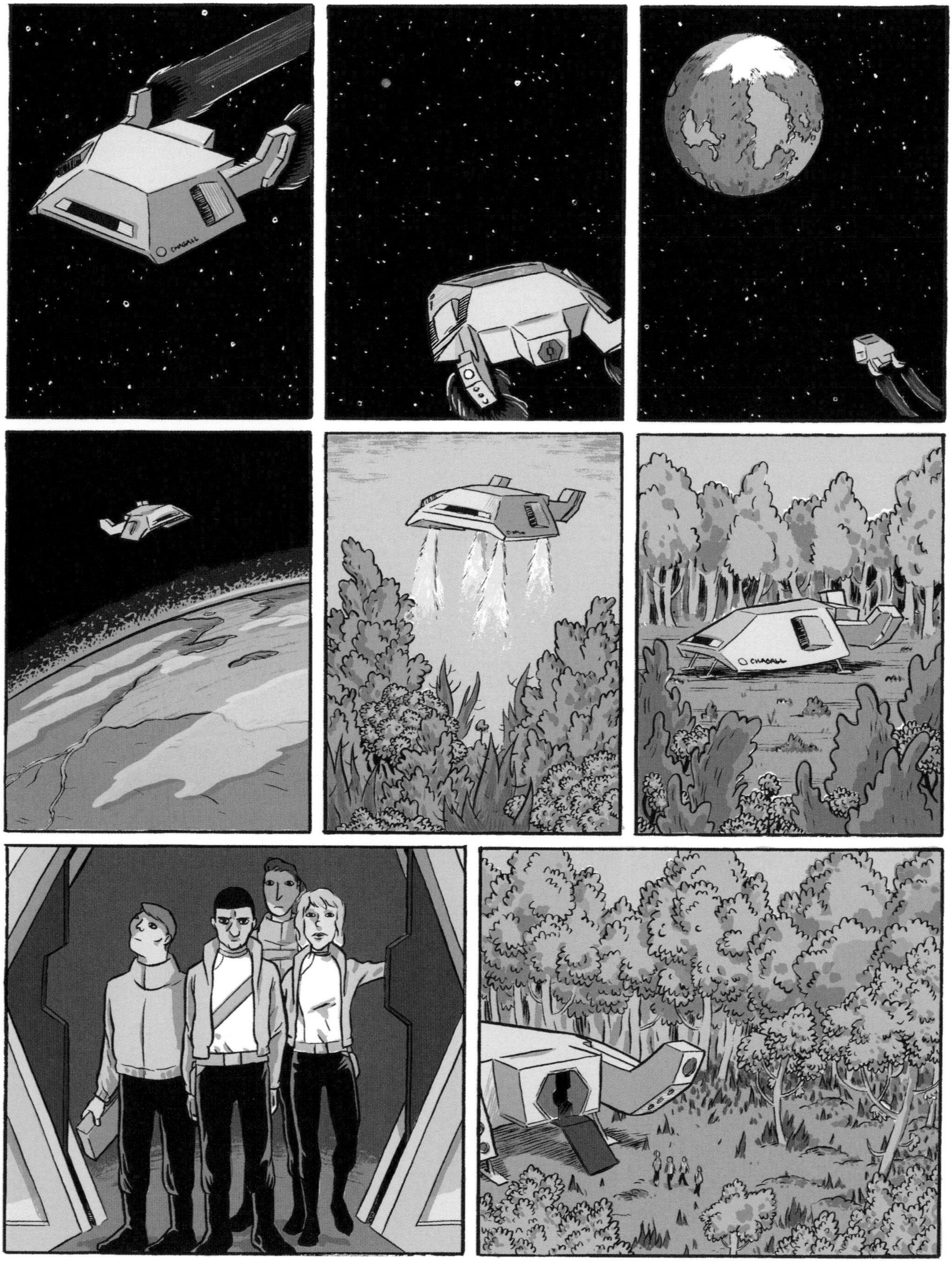
CHAGALL
CHAGALL

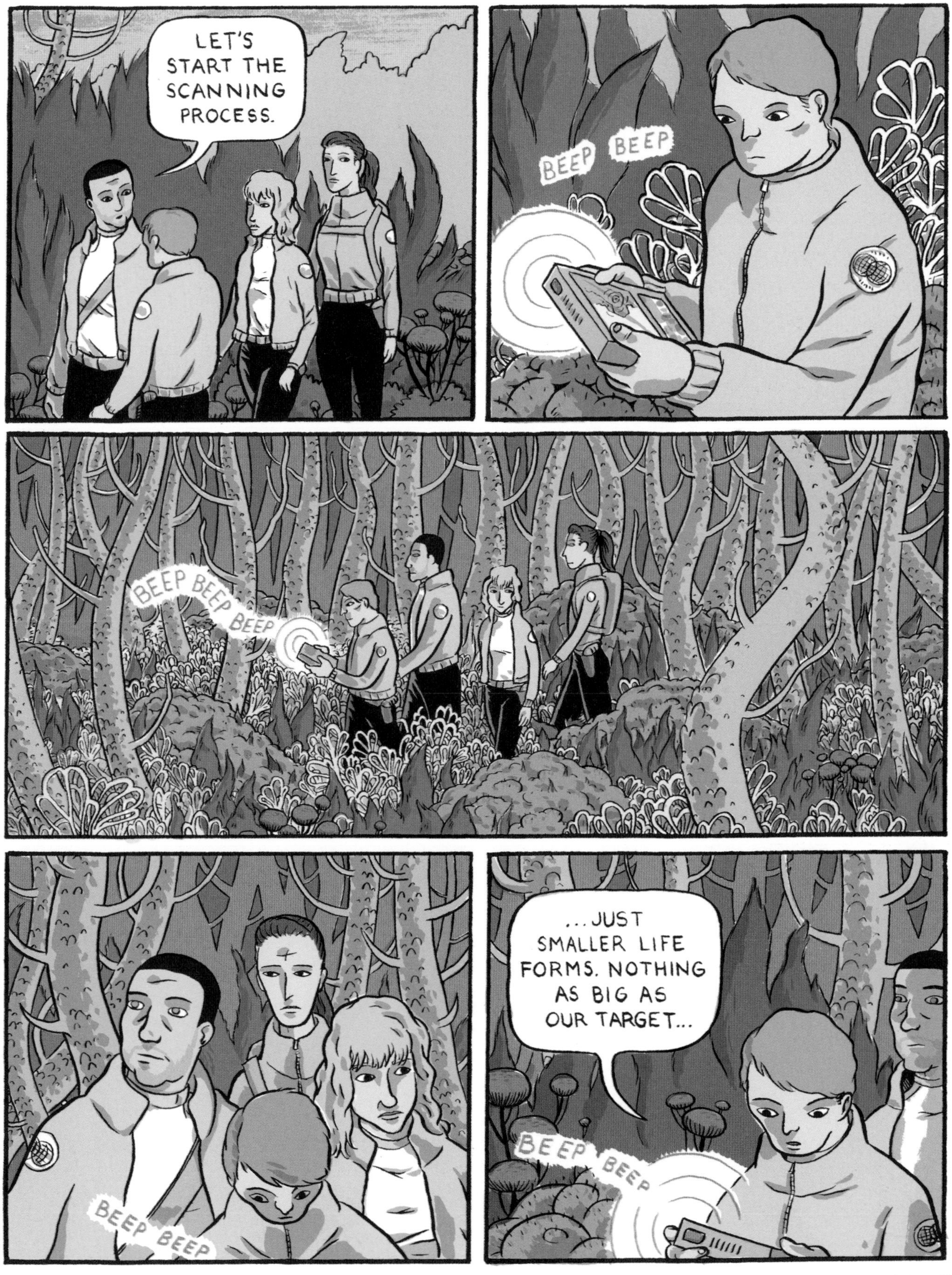
LET'S START THE SCANNING PROCESS.
BEEP BEEP
BEEP BEEP BEEP
BEEP BEEP
...JUST SMALLER LIFE FORMS. NOTHING AS BIG AS OUR TARGET...
BEEP BEEP

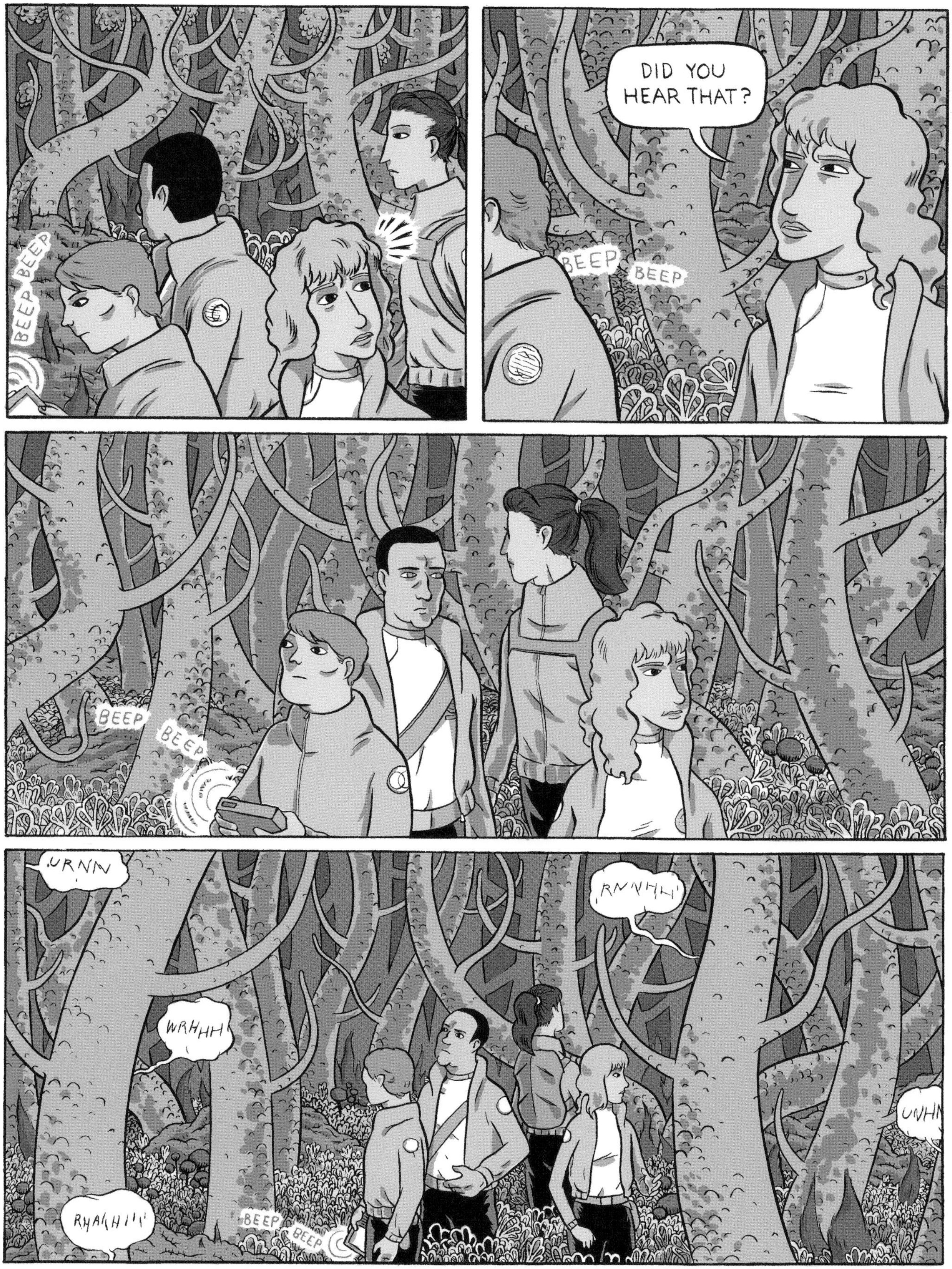
BEEP BEEP
BEEP
DID YOU HEAR THAT?
BEEP BEEP
BEEP
BEEP
URNN
RNNHH
WRHHH
UNHN
RHAHH
BEEP
BEEP

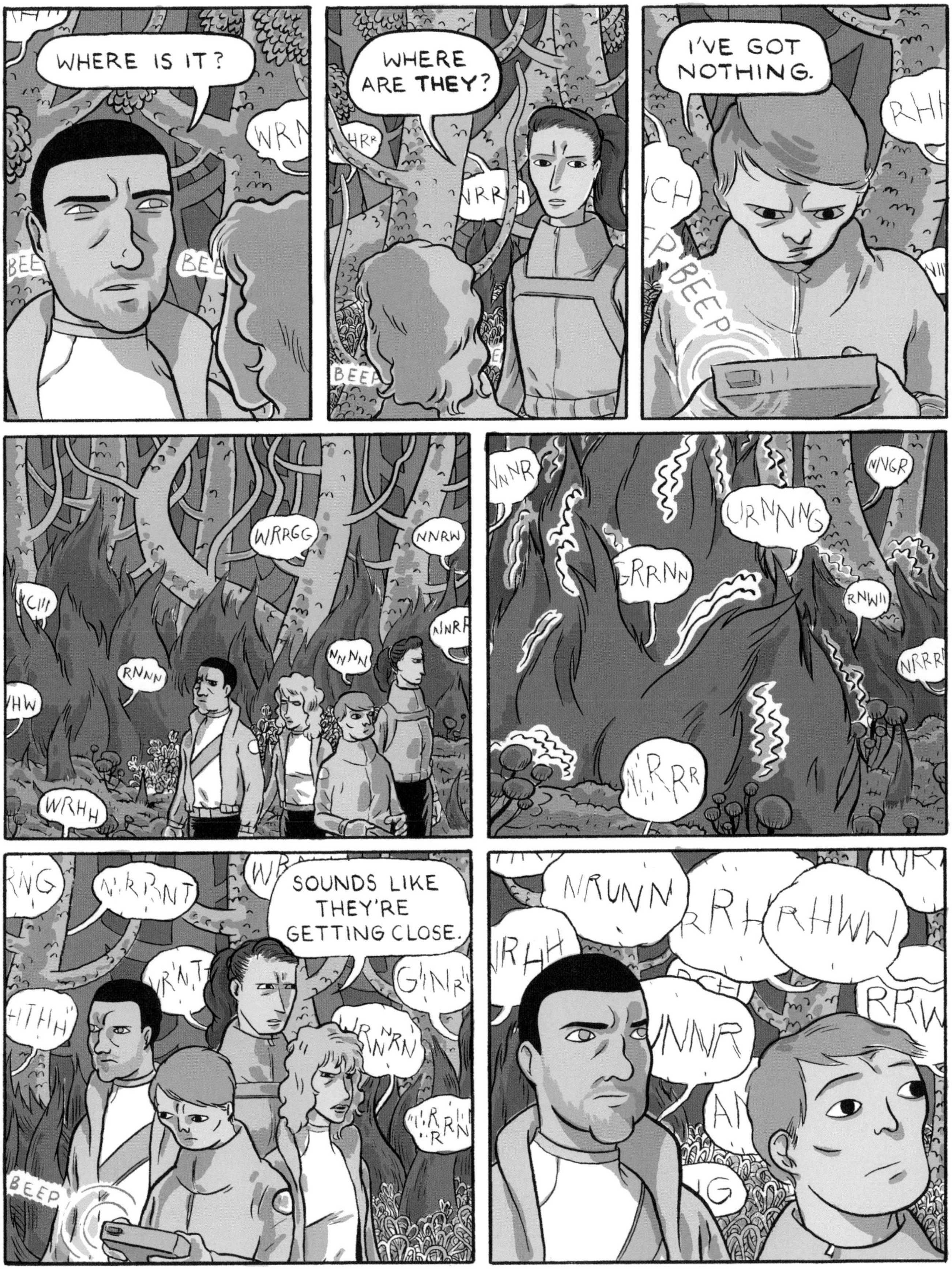

WHERE IS IT?
WRN
BEE
BEE
WHERE ARE THEY?
HRR
NRR
BEEP
I'VE GOT NOTHING.
RHH
CH
BEEP
WRRGG
NNRW
RNNN
NNNN
WRHH
URNNNG
GRRNN
NNGR
RNW
NRRR
NIRRR
SOUNDS LIKE THEY'RE GETTING CLOSE.
NRRNT
RNG
BEEP
NRUNN
RRH
RHWW
RRW
NNR

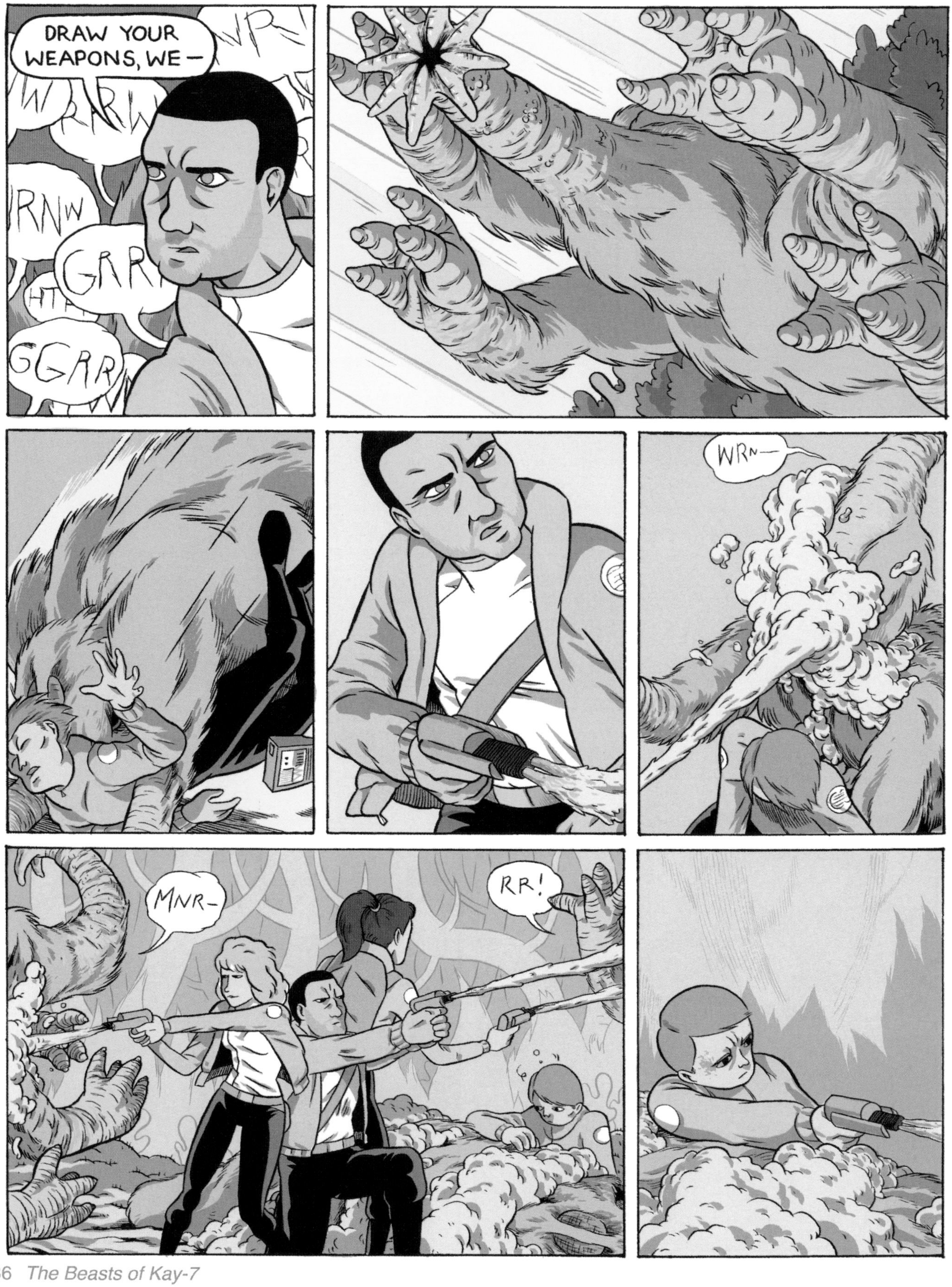
DRAW YOUR WEAPONS, WE—
WRNW
GRR
GGRR
WRN—
MNR—
RR!

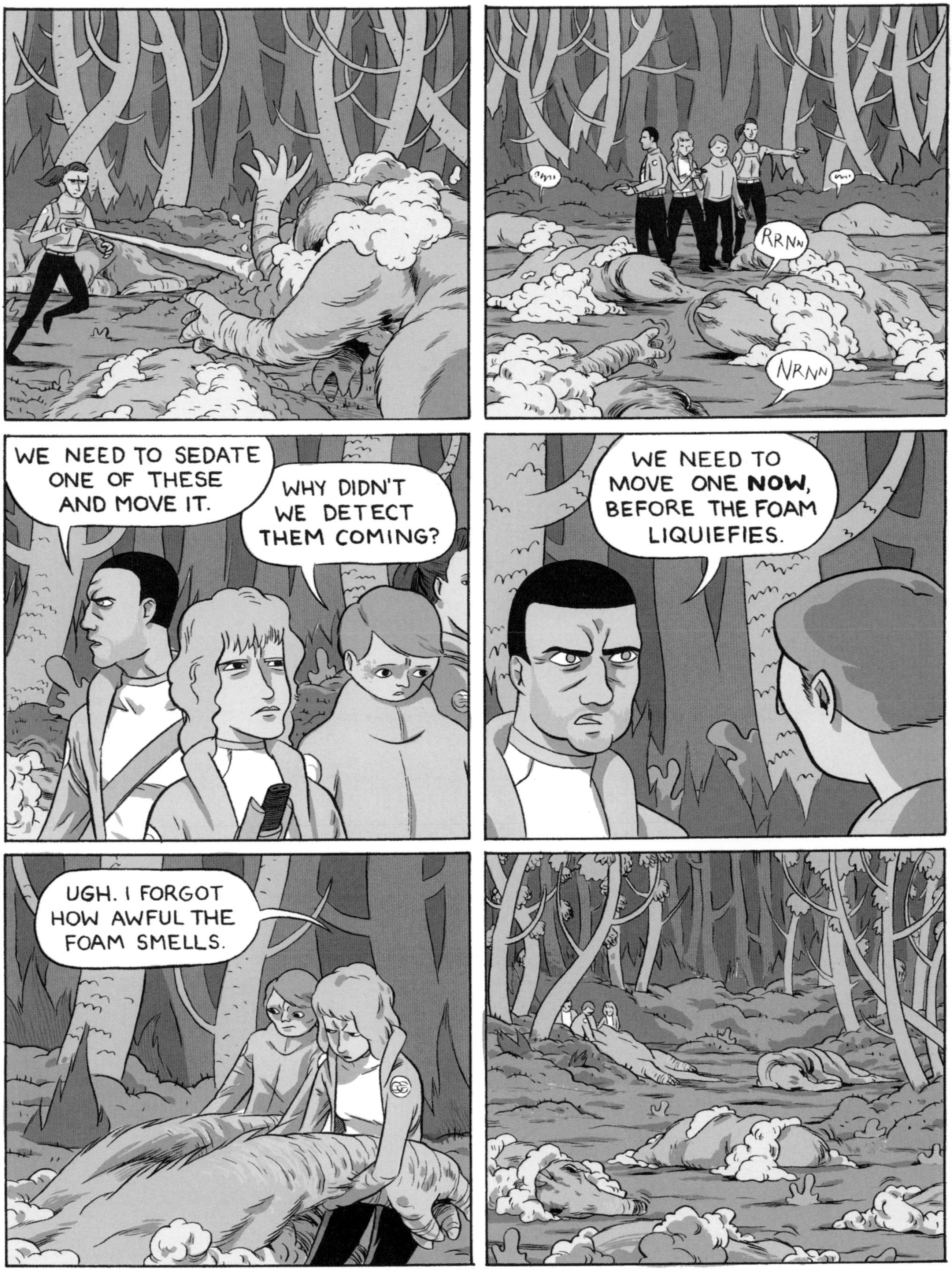
RRNN
NRNN
WE NEED TO SEDATE ONE OF THESE AND MOVE IT.
WHY DIDN'T WE DETECT THEM COMING?
WE NEED TO MOVE ONE **NOW**, BEFORE THE FOAM LIQUIEFIES.
UGH. I FORGOT HOW AWFUL THE FOAM SMELLS.

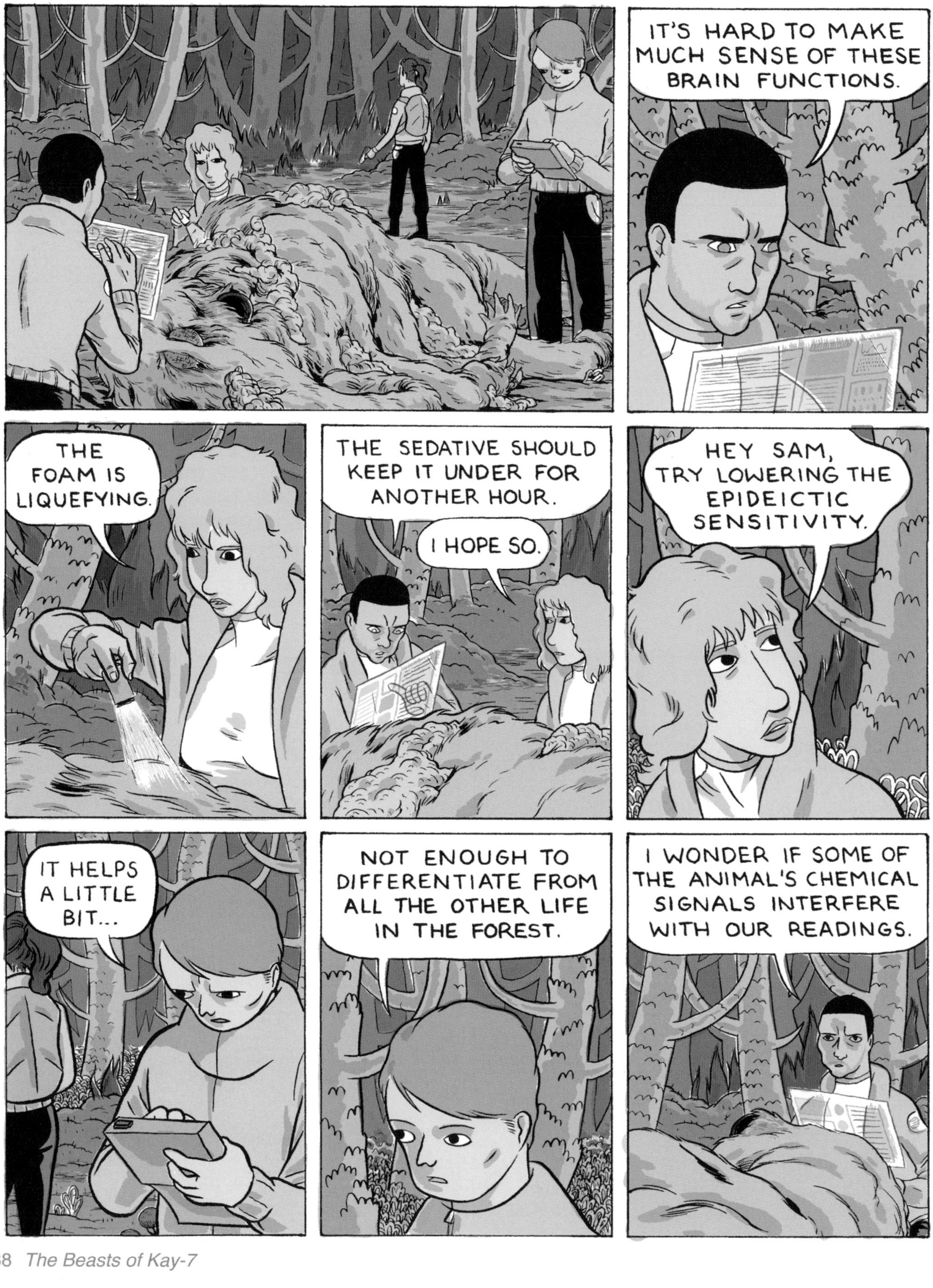
IT'S HARD TO MAKE MUCH SENSE OF THESE BRAIN FUNCTIONS.
THE FOAM IS LIQUEFYING.
THE SEDATIVE SHOULD KEEP IT UNDER FOR ANOTHER HOUR.
I HOPE SO.
HEY SAM, TRY LOWERING THE EPIDEICTIC SENSITIVITY.
IT HELPS A LITTLE BIT...
NOT ENOUGH TO DIFFERENTIATE FROM ALL THE OTHER LIFE IN THE FOREST.
I WONDER IF SOME OF THE ANIMAL'S CHEMICAL SIGNALS INTERFERE WITH OUR READINGS.

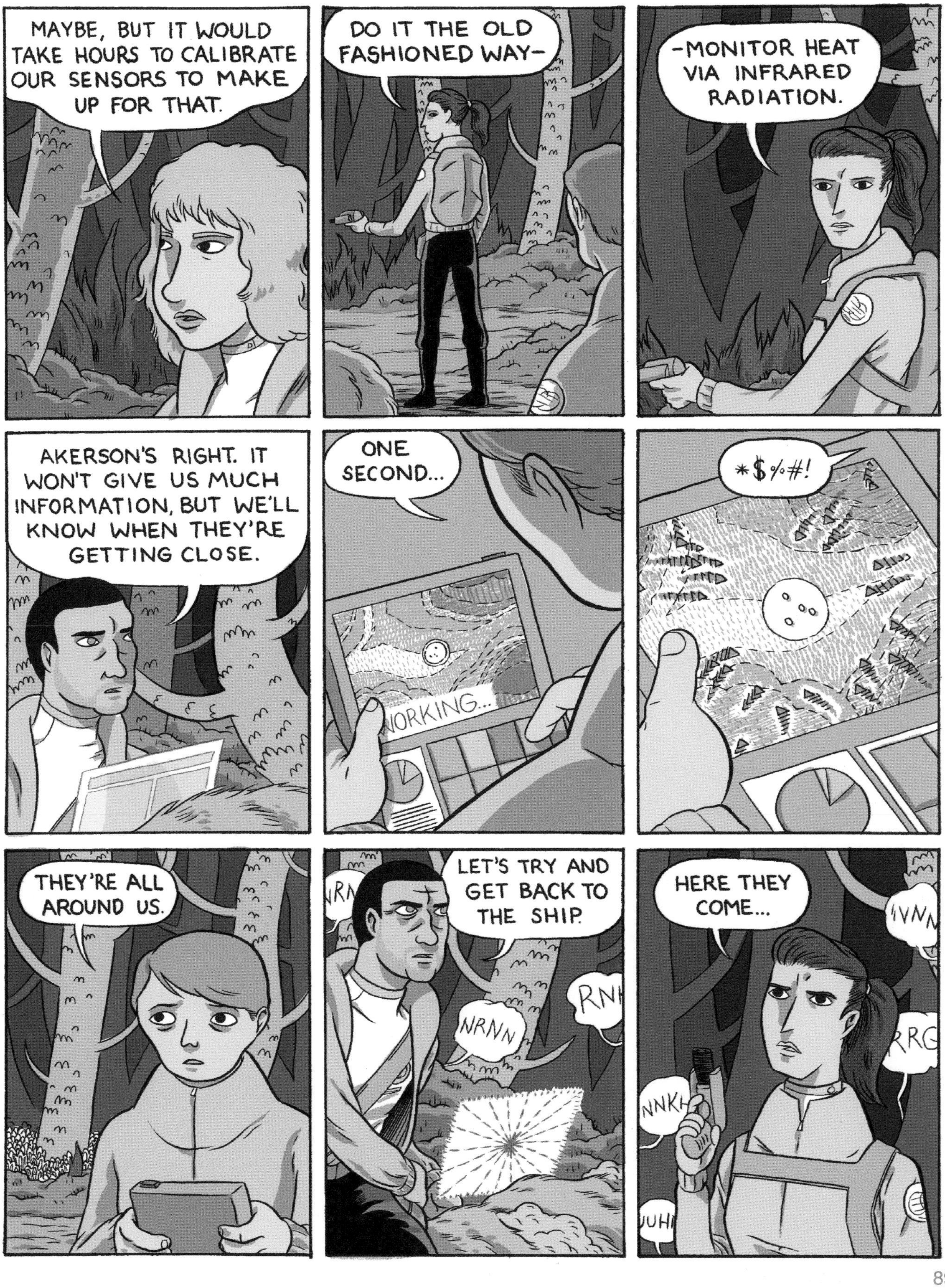
MAYBE, BUT IT WOULD TAKE HOURS TO CALIBRATE OUR SENSORS TO MAKE UP FOR THAT.
DO IT THE OLD FASHIONED WAY-
-MONITOR HEAT VIA INFRARED RADIATION.
AKERSON'S RIGHT. IT WON'T GIVE US MUCH INFORMATION, BUT WE'LL KNOW WHEN THEY'RE GETTING CLOSE.
ONE SECOND...
WORKING...
*$%#!
THEY'RE ALL AROUND US.
LET'S TRY AND GET BACK TO THE SHIP.
NRNN
HERE THEY COME...
NNKH

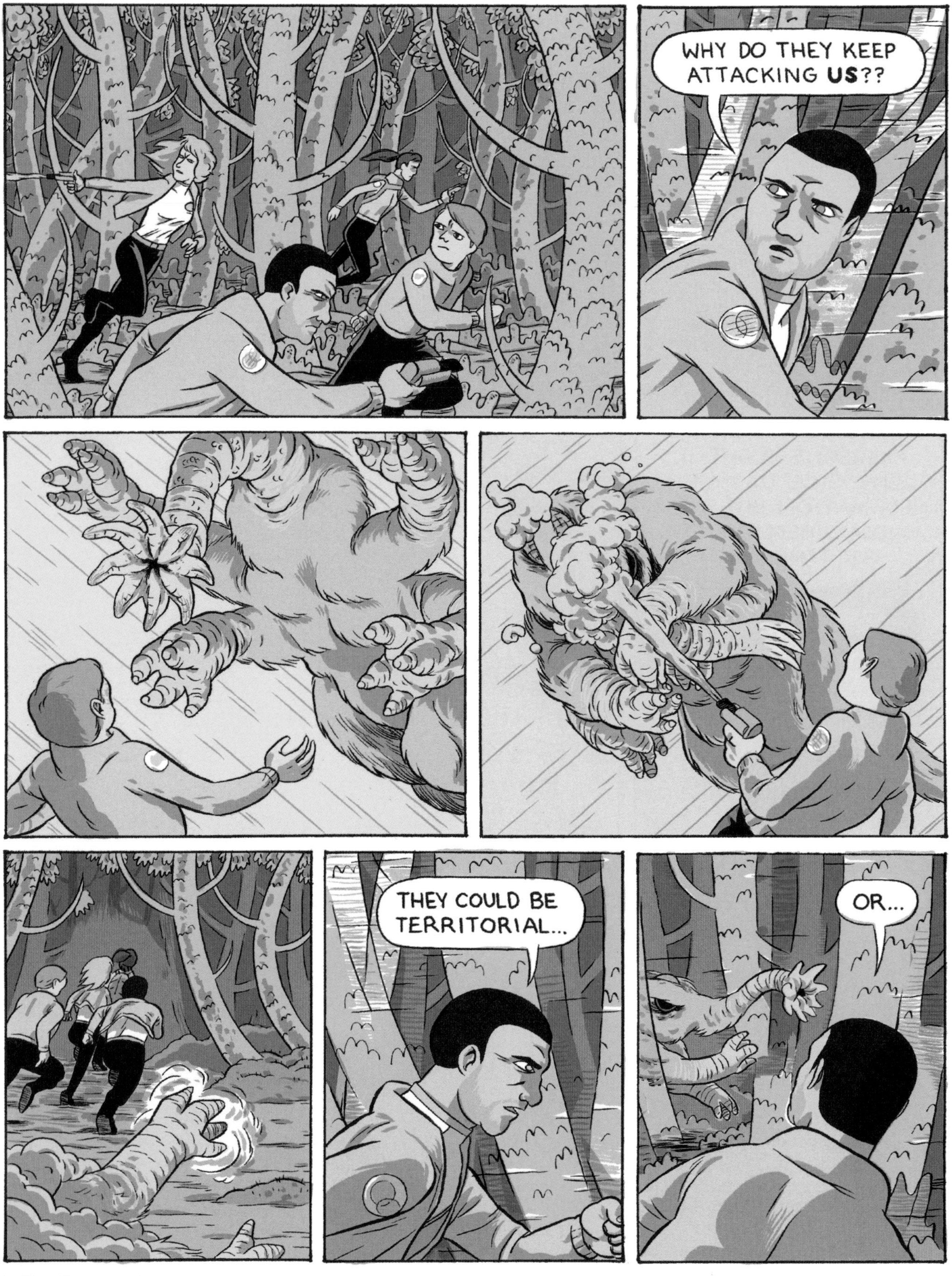
WHY DO THEY KEEP ATTACKING **US**??
THEY COULD BE TERRITORIAL...
OR...

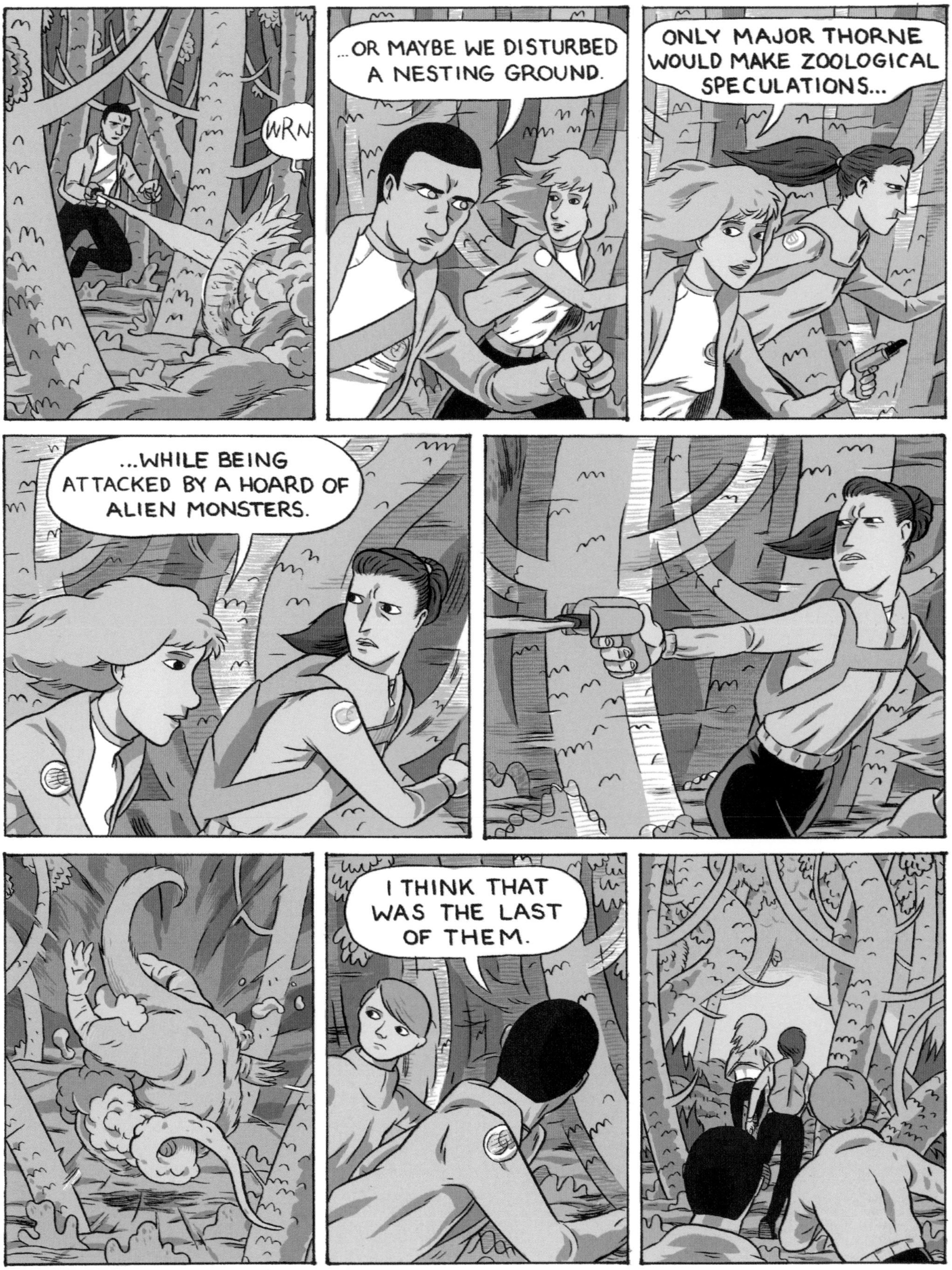
WRN
...OR MAYBE WE DISTURBED A NESTING GROUND.
ONLY MAJOR THORNE WOULD MAKE ZOOLOGICAL SPECULATIONS...
...WHILE BEING ATTACKED BY A HOARD OF ALIEN MONSTERS.
I THINK THAT WAS THE LAST OF THEM.

MORGAN, LOOK AT THIS.

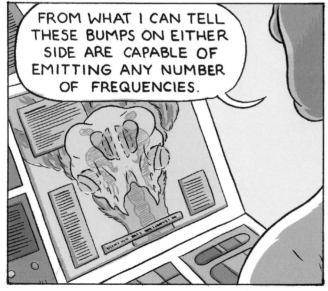

FROM WHAT I CAN TELL THESE BUMPS ON EITHER SIDE ARE CAPABLE OF EMITTING ANY NUMBER OF FREQUENCIES.

...SO IT COULD DEFLECT LEVEL THREE SCANS.

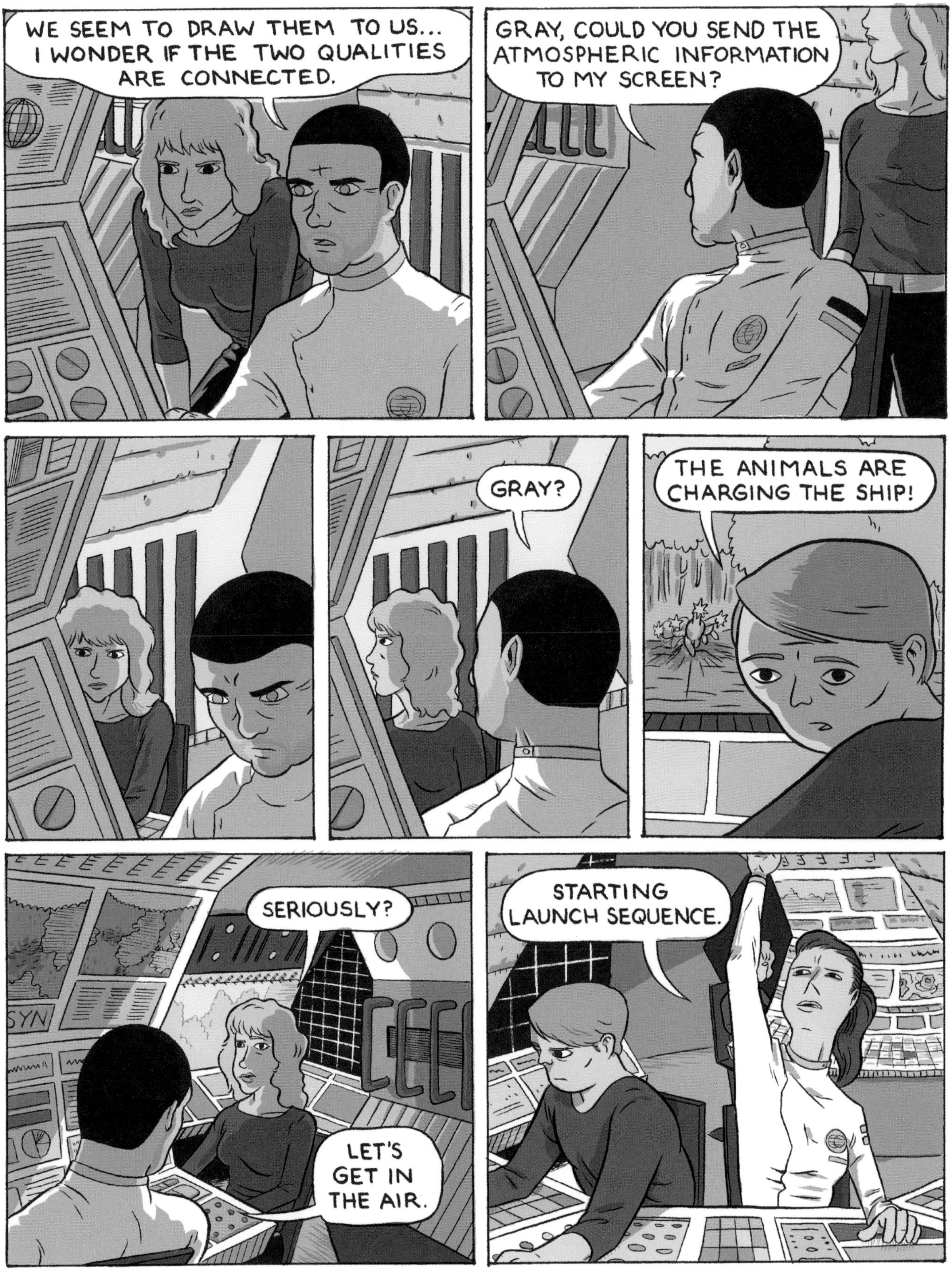
WE SEEM TO DRAW THEM TO US... I WONDER IF THE TWO QUALITIES ARE CONNECTED.
GRAY, COULD YOU SEND THE ATMOSPHERIC INFORMATION TO MY SCREEN?
GRAY?
THE ANIMALS ARE CHARGING THE SHIP!
SERIOUSLY?
LET'S GET IN THE AIR.
STARTING LAUNCH SEQUENCE.

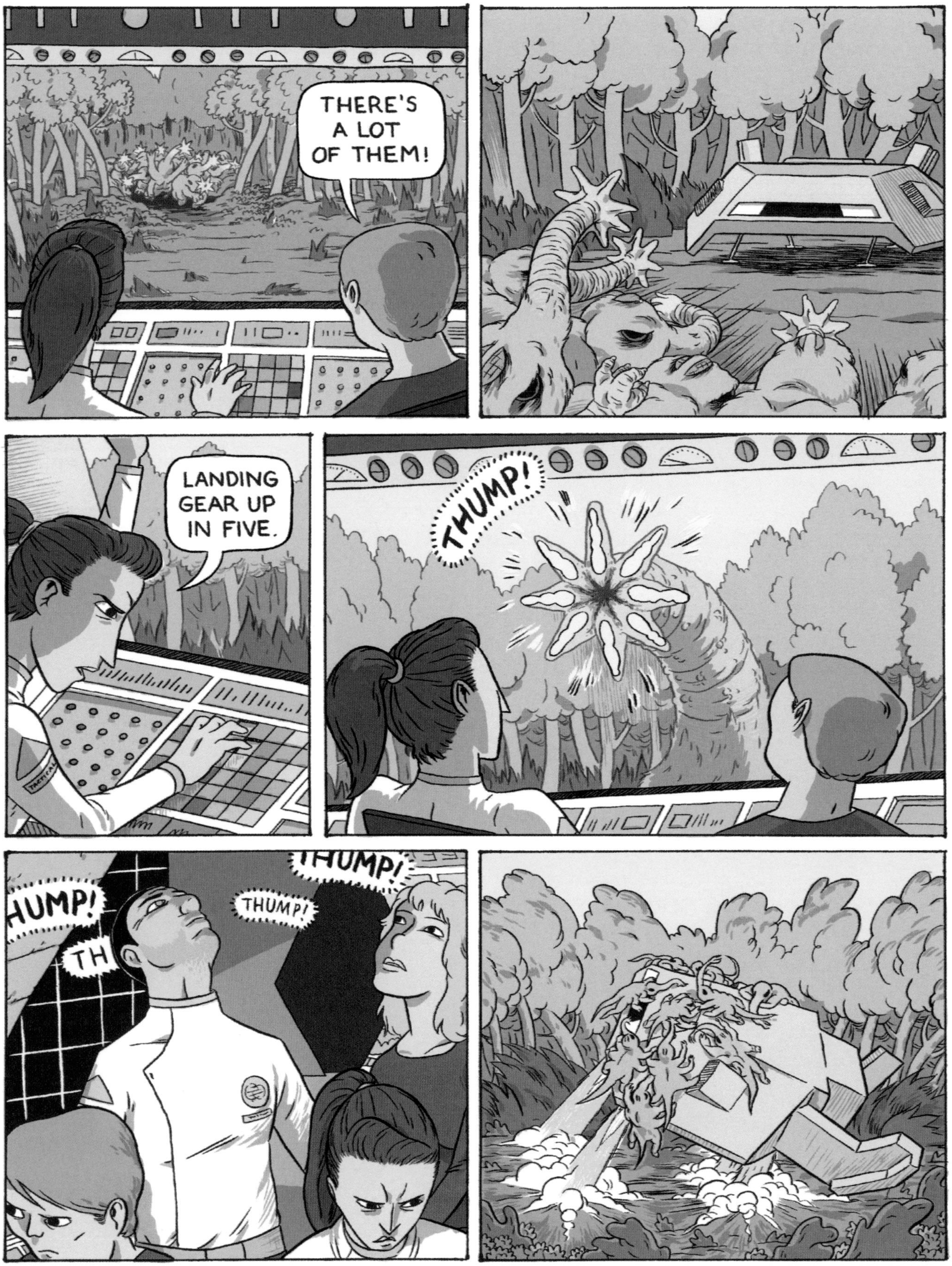
THERE'S A LOT OF THEM!
LANDING GEAR UP IN FIVE.
THUMP!
THUMP!
HUMP!
THUMP!
TH

SIT DOWN, MAJOR!

THE SHIFTING WEIGHT IS THROWING OFF THRUSTER ALIGNMENT.

URNT! URNT! URNT! URNT!

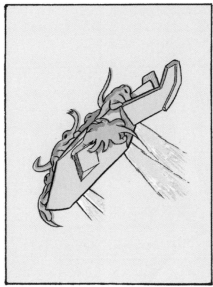

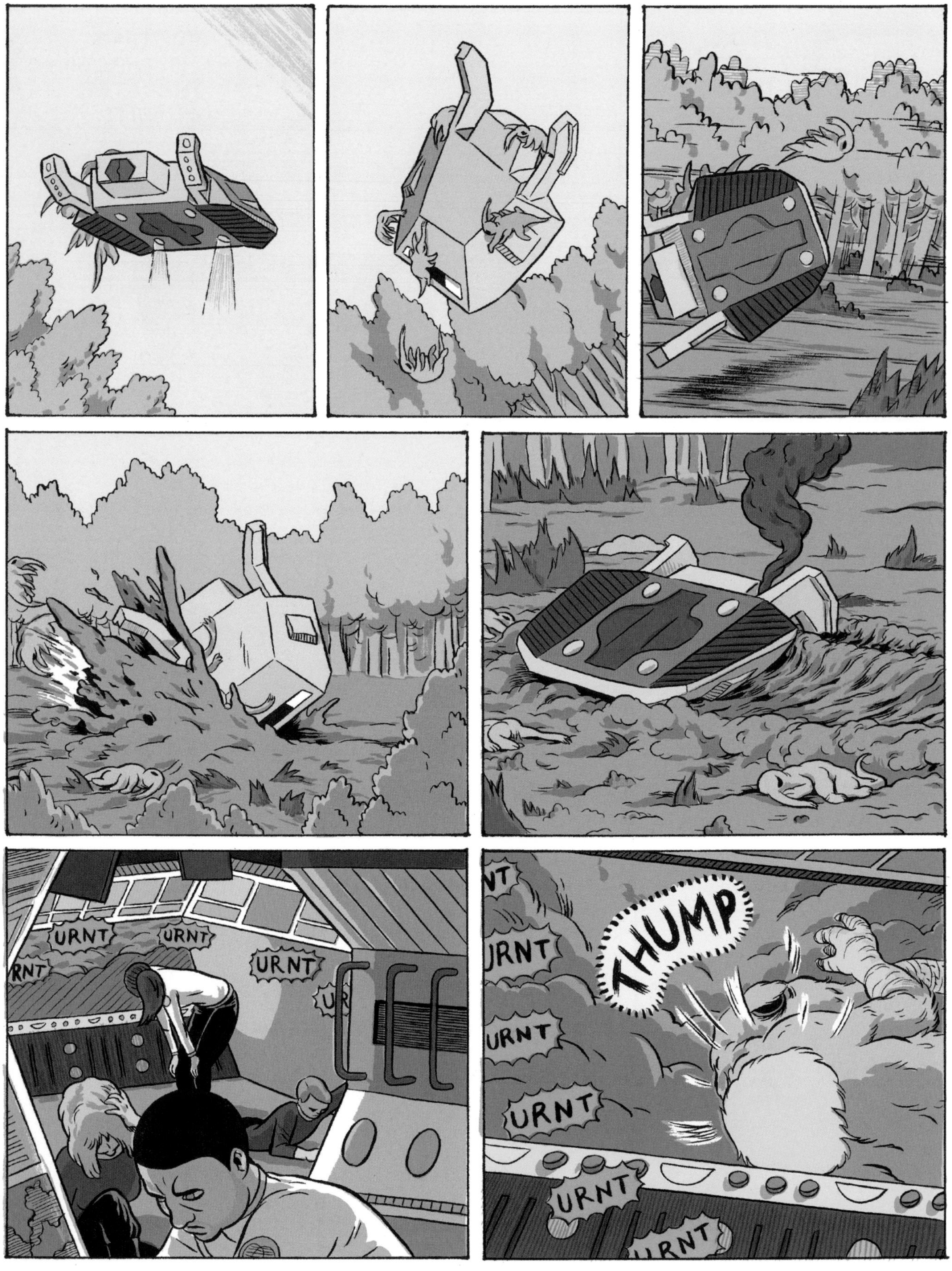
URNT
URNT
RNT
URNT
UR
NT
URNT
THUMP
URNT
URNT
URNT
RNT
URNT
URNT

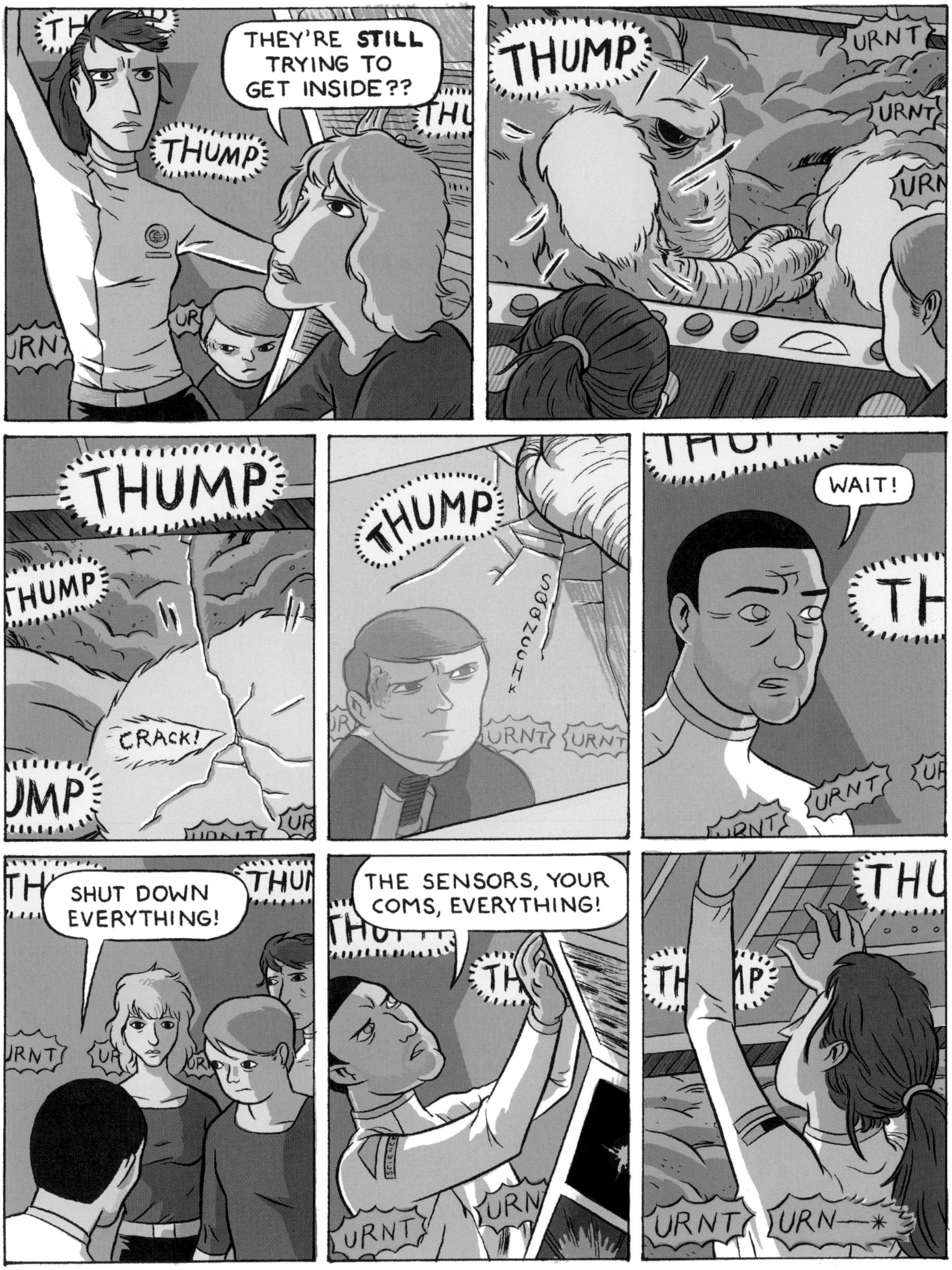
THEY'RE **STILL** TRYING TO GET INSIDE??
THUMP
URNT
THUMP
URNT
URNT
THUMP
THUMP
CRACK!
THUMP
URNT
URNT
WAIT!
URNT
SHUT DOWN EVERYTHING!
URNT
THE SENSORS, YOUR COMS, EVERYTHING!
URNT
URNT
URN—

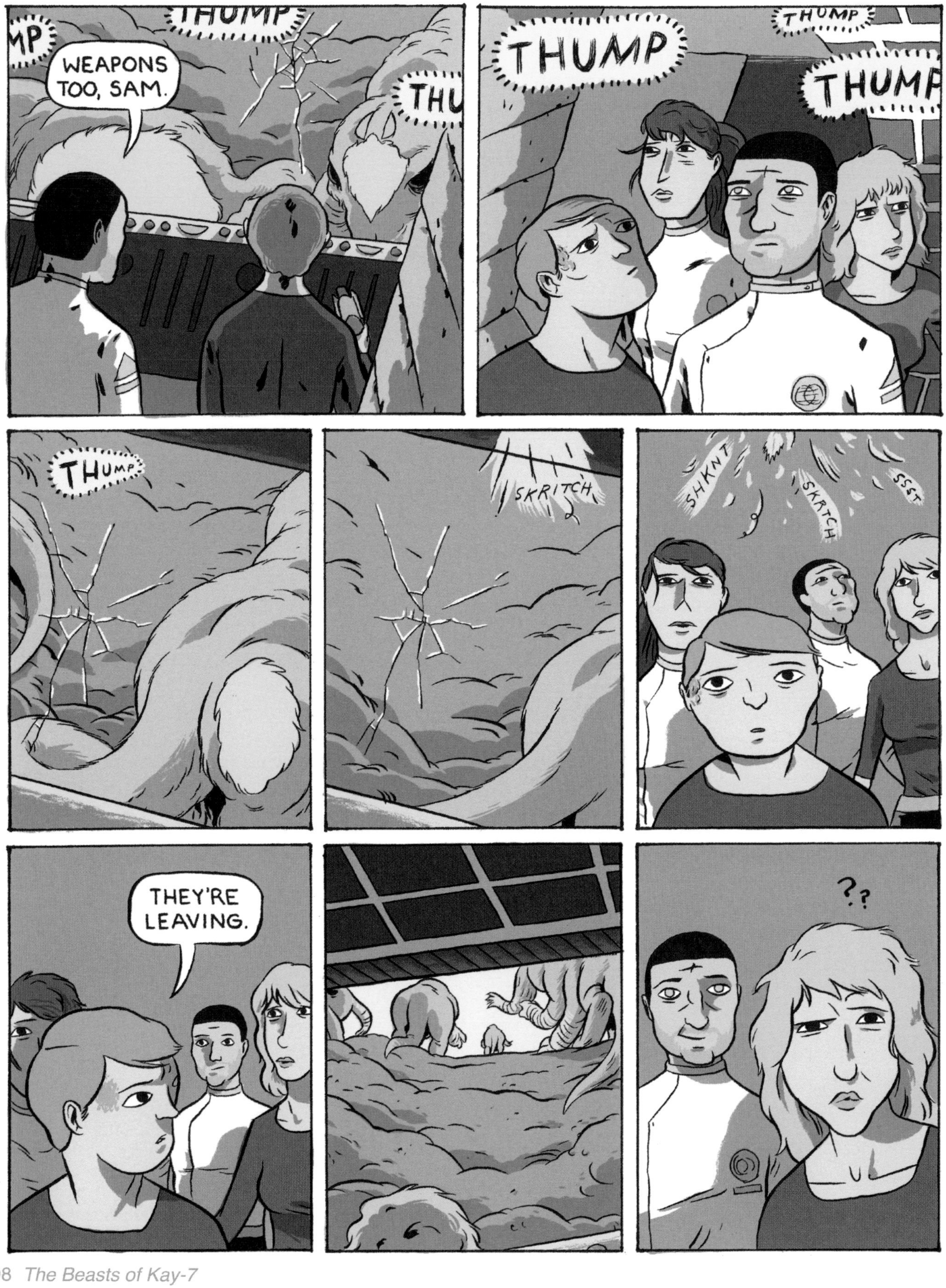
MP
THUMP
WEAPONS TOO, SAM.
THU
THUMP
THUMP
THUMP
THump
SKRITCH
SHKNT
SKRTCH
SSST
THEY'RE LEAVING.
??

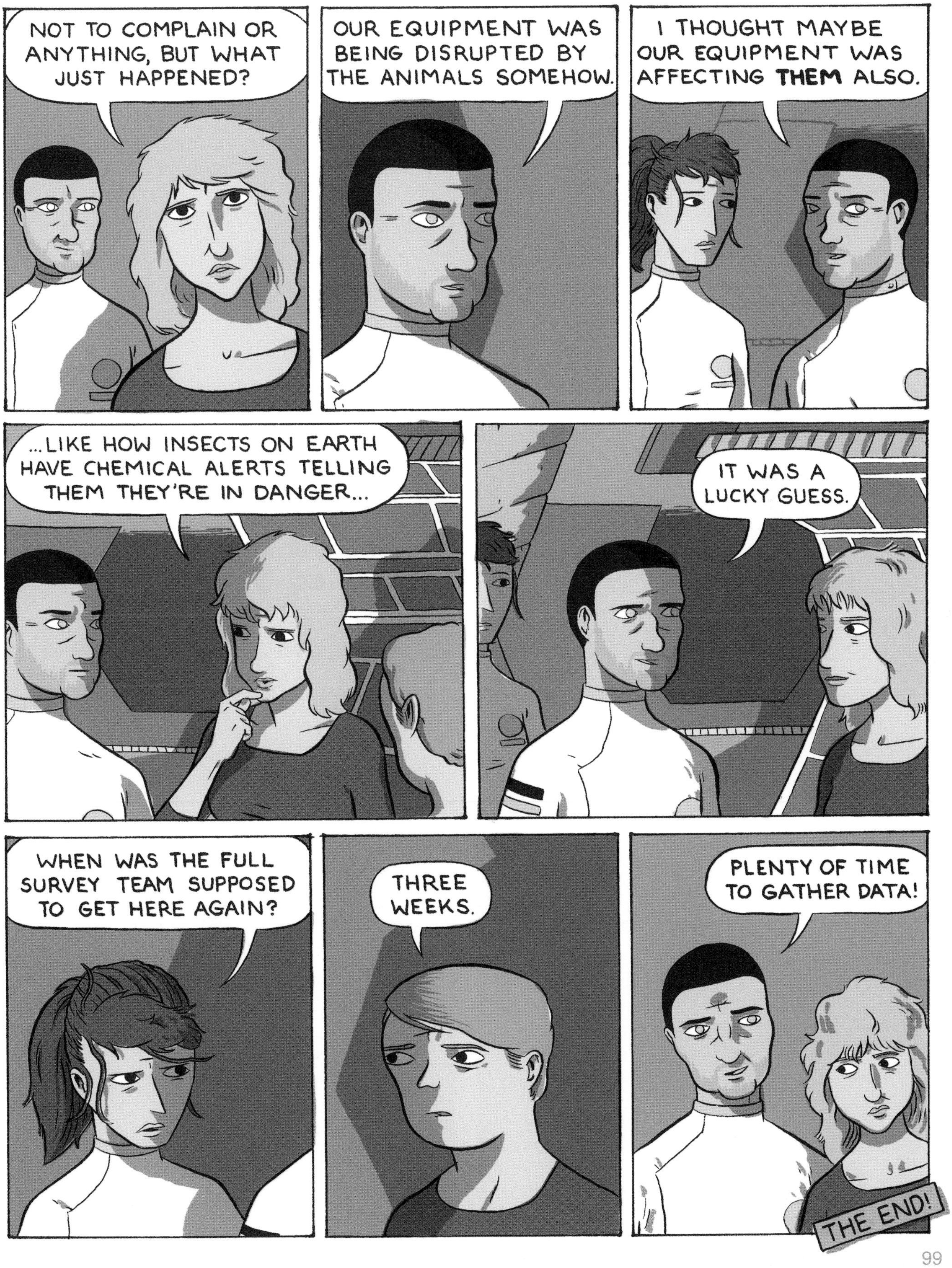
NOT TO COMPLAIN OR ANYTHING, BUT WHAT JUST HAPPENED?
OUR EQUIPMENT WAS BEING DISRUPTED BY THE ANIMALS SOMEHOW.
I THOUGHT MAYBE OUR EQUIPMENT WAS AFFECTING **THEM** ALSO.
...LIKE HOW INSECTS ON EARTH HAVE CHEMICAL ALERTS TELLING THEM THEY'RE IN DANGER...
IT WAS A LUCKY GUESS.
WHEN WAS THE FULL SURVEY TEAM SUPPOSED TO GET HERE AGAIN?
THREE WEEKS.
PLENTY OF TIME TO GATHER DATA!
THE END!

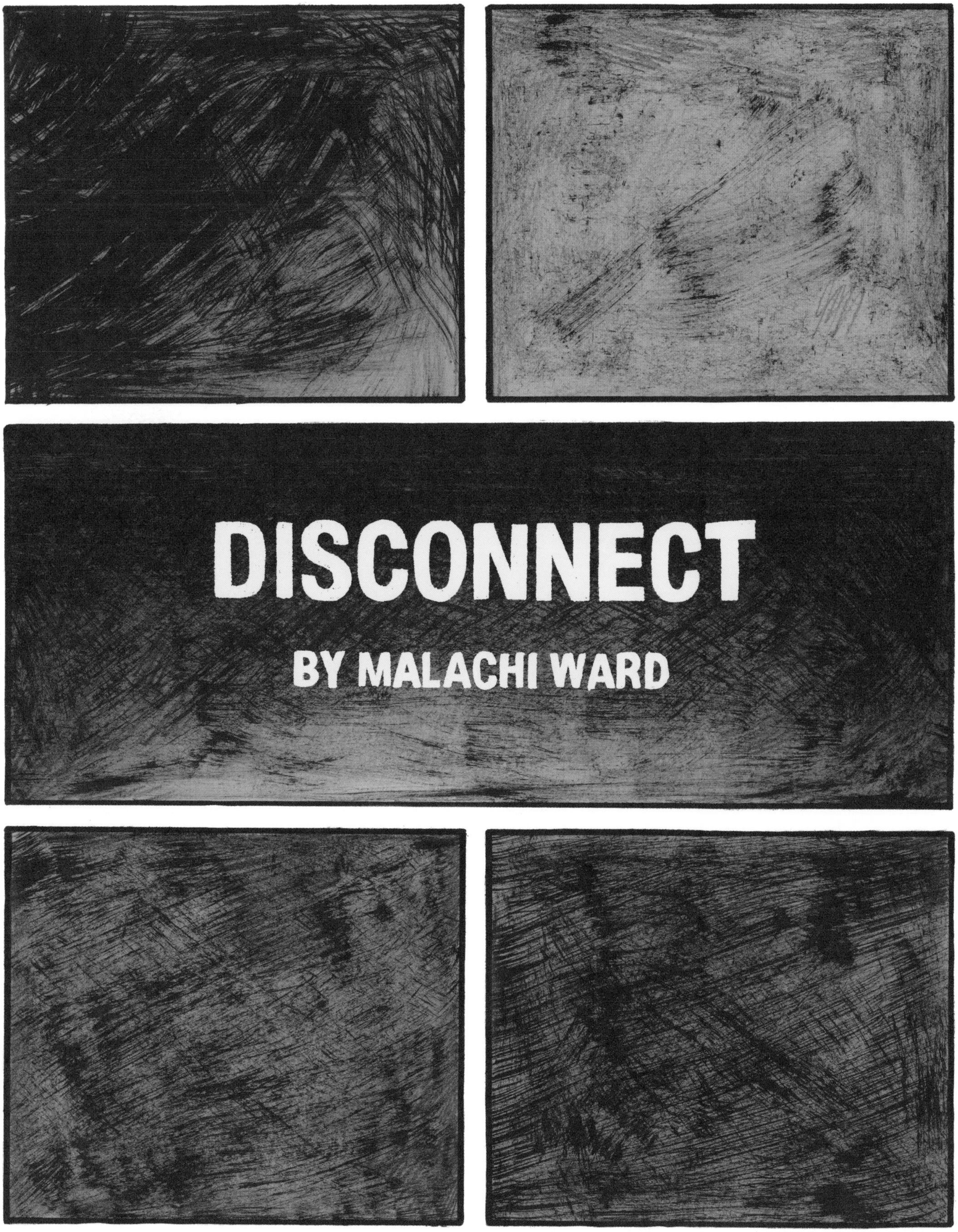
DISCONNECT
BY MALACHI WARD

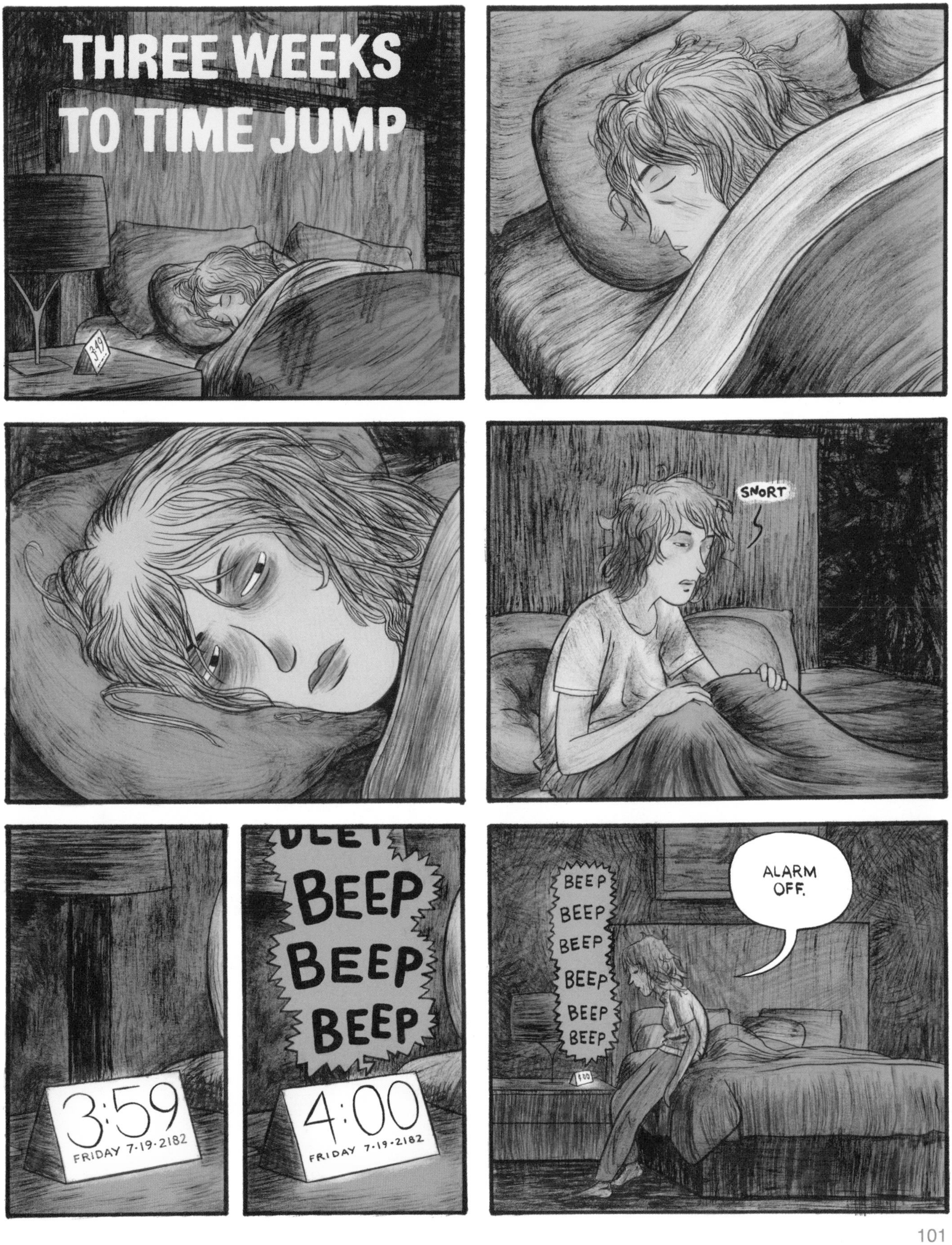
THREE WEEKS
TO TIME JUMP
3:49
SNORT
3:59
FRIDAY 7·19·2182
BEEP
BEEP
BEEP
4:00
FRIDAY 7·19·2182
BEEP
BEEP
BEEP
BEEP
BEEP
BEEP
ALARM
OFF.

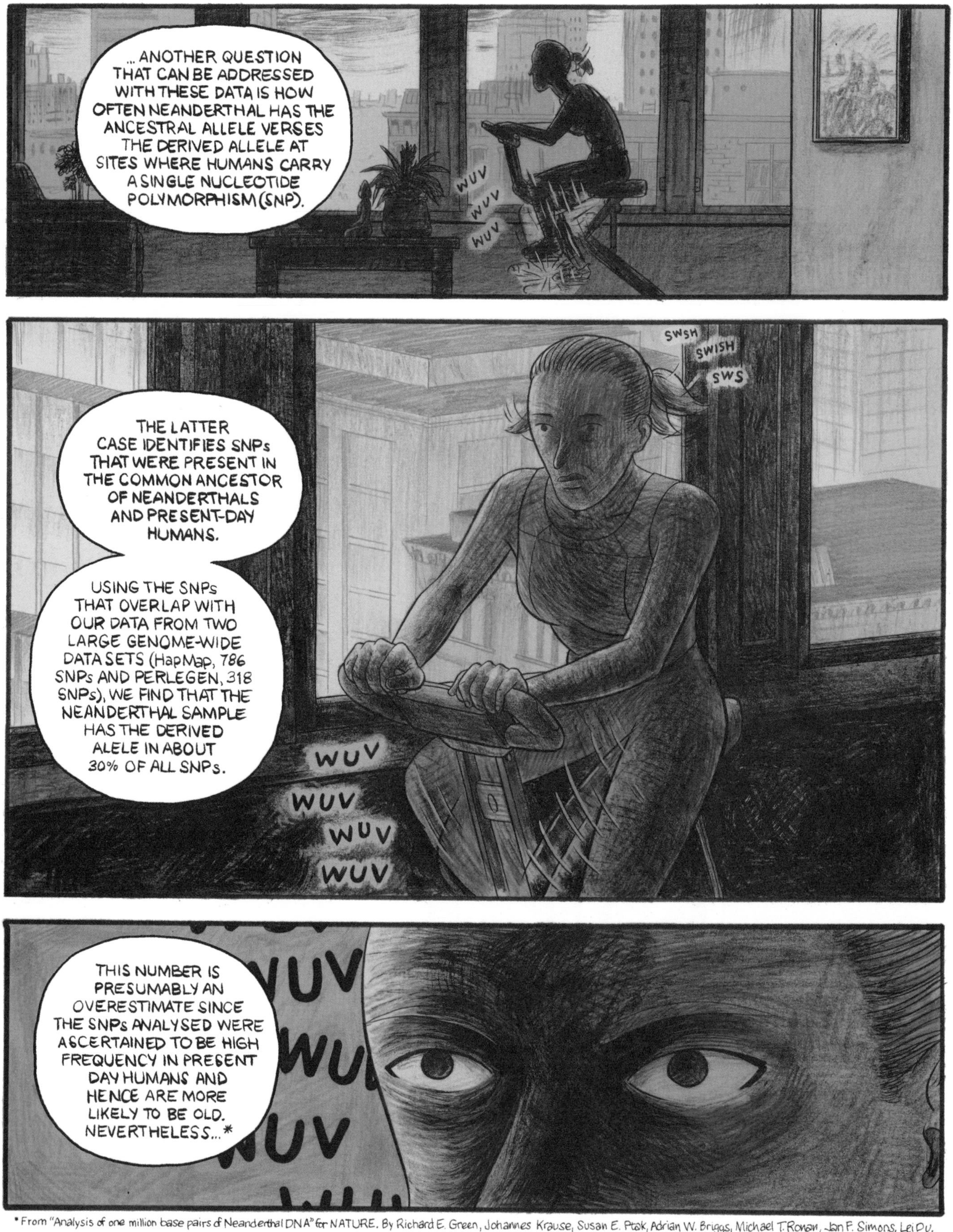
... ANOTHER QUESTION THAT CAN BE ADDRESSED WITH THESE DATA IS HOW OFTEN NEANDERTHAL HAS THE ANCESTRAL ALLELE VERSES THE DERIVED ALLELE AT SITES WHERE HUMANS CARRY A SINGLE NUCLEOTIDE POLYMORPHISM (SNP).
WUV
WUV
WUV
SWSH
SWISH
SWS
THE LATTER CASE IDENTIFIES SNPs THAT WERE PRESENT IN THE COMMON ANCESTOR OF NEANDERTHALS AND PRESENT-DAY HUMANS.
USING THE SNPs THAT OVERLAP WITH OUR DATA FROM TWO LARGE GENOME-WIDE DATA SETS (HapMap, 786 SNPs AND PERLEGEN, 318 SNPs), WE FIND THAT THE NEANDERTHAL SAMPLE HAS THE DERIVED ALELE IN ABOUT 30% OF ALL SNPs.
WUV
WUV
WUV
WUV
THIS NUMBER IS PRESUMABLY AN OVERESTIMATE SINCE THE SNPs ANALYSED WERE ASCERTAINED TO BE HIGH FREQUENCY IN PRESENT DAY HUMANS AND HENCE ARE MORE LIKELY TO BE OLD. NEVERTHELESS...*
WUV
WUV

* From "Analysis of one million base pairs of Neanderthal DNA" for NATURE. By Richard E. Green, Johannes Krause, Susan E. Ptak, Adrian W. Briggs, Michael T. Ronan, Jan F. Simons, Lei Du, Michael Egholm, Jonathan M. Rothberg, Maja Paunovic, and Svante Pääbo.

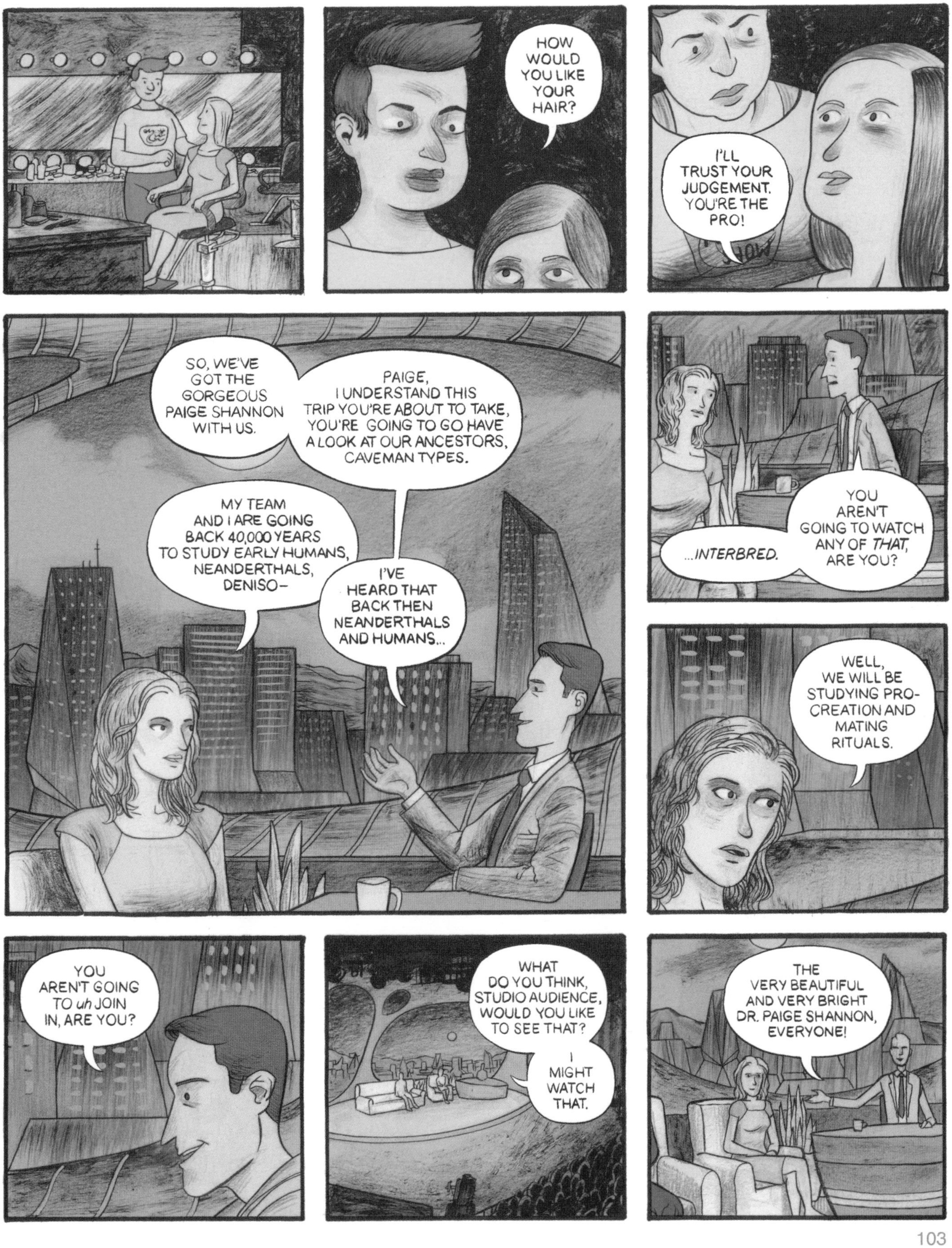
HOW WOULD YOU LIKE YOUR HAIR?
I'LL TRUST YOUR JUDGEMENT. YOU'RE THE PRO!
SO, WE'VE GOT THE GORGEOUS PAIGE SHANNON WITH US.
PAIGE, I UNDERSTAND THIS TRIP YOU'RE ABOUT TO TAKE, YOU'RE GOING TO GO HAVE A LOOK AT OUR ANCESTORS, CAVEMAN TYPES.
MY TEAM AND I ARE GOING BACK 40,000 YEARS TO STUDY EARLY HUMANS, NEANDERTHALS, DENISO–
I'VE HEARD THAT BACK THEN NEANDERTHALS AND HUMANS...
...*INTERBRED.*
YOU AREN'T GOING TO WATCH ANY OF *THAT*, ARE YOU?
WELL, WE WILL BE STUDYING PRO-CREATION AND MATING RITUALS.
YOU AREN'T GOING TO *uh* JOIN IN, ARE YOU?
WHAT DO YOU THINK, STUDIO AUDIENCE, WOULD YOU LIKE TO SEE THAT?
I MIGHT WATCH THAT.
THE VERY BEAUTIFUL AND VERY BRIGHT DR. PAIGE SHANNON, EVERYONE!

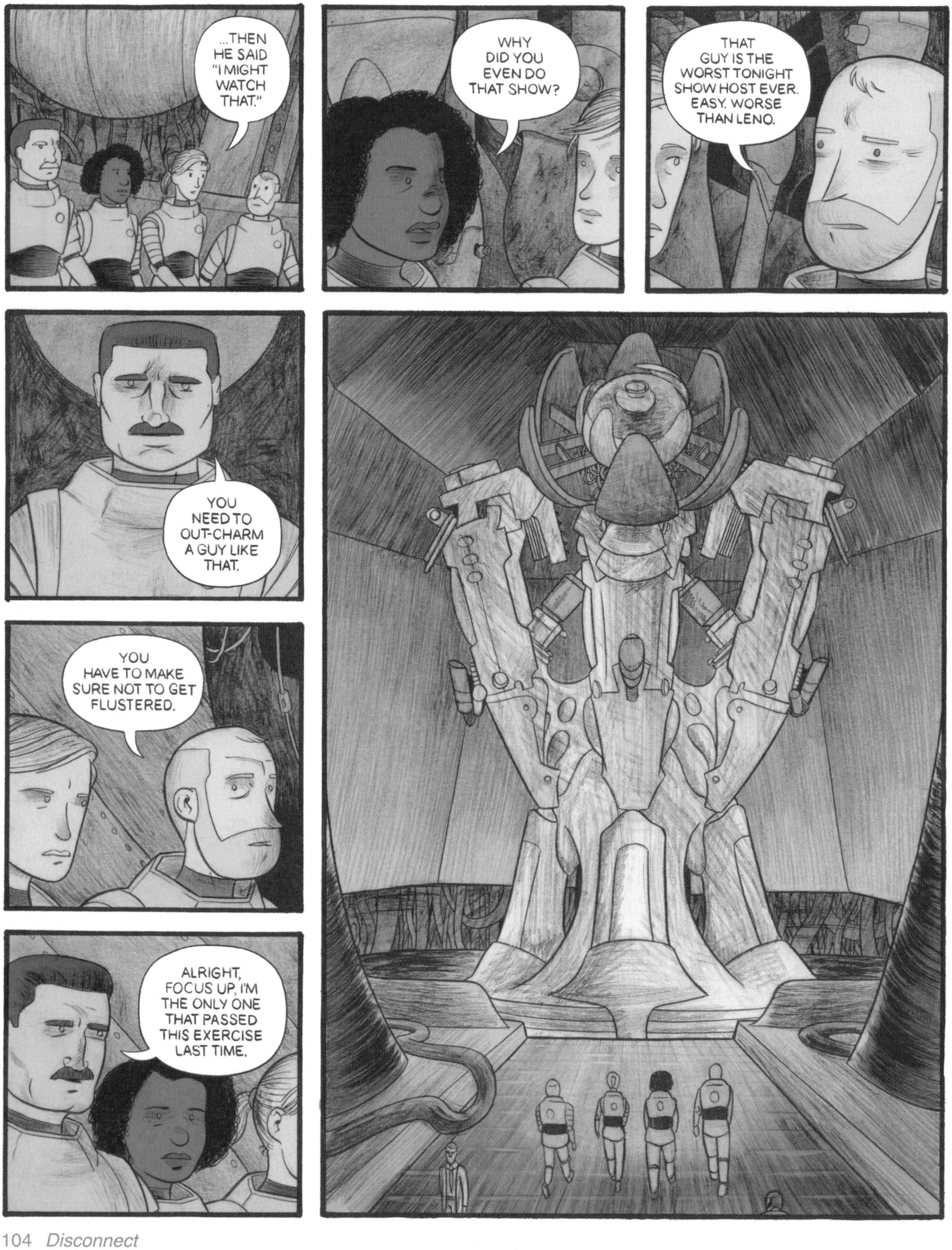
...THEN HE SAID "I MIGHT WATCH THAT."
WHY DID YOU EVEN DO THAT SHOW?
THAT GUY IS THE WORST TONIGHT SHOW HOST EVER. EASY. WORSE THAN LENO.
YOU NEED TO OUT-CHARM A GUY LIKE THAT.
YOU HAVE TO MAKE SURE NOT TO GET FLUSTERED.
ALRIGHT, FOCUS UP, I'M THE ONLY ONE THAT PASSED THIS EXERCISE LAST TIME.

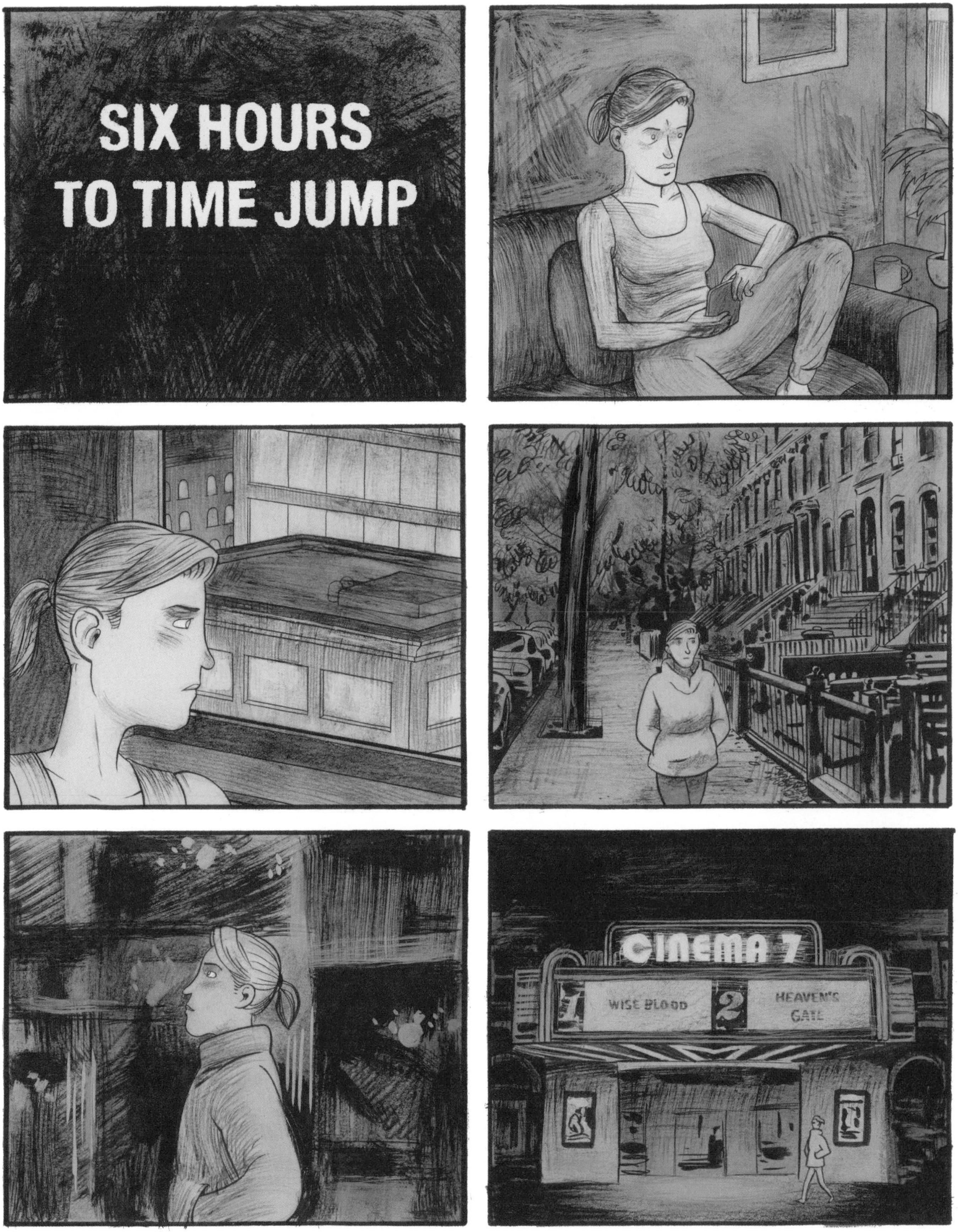
SIX HOURS TO TIME JUMP
CINEMA 7
1
WISE BLOOD
2
HEAVEN'S GATE

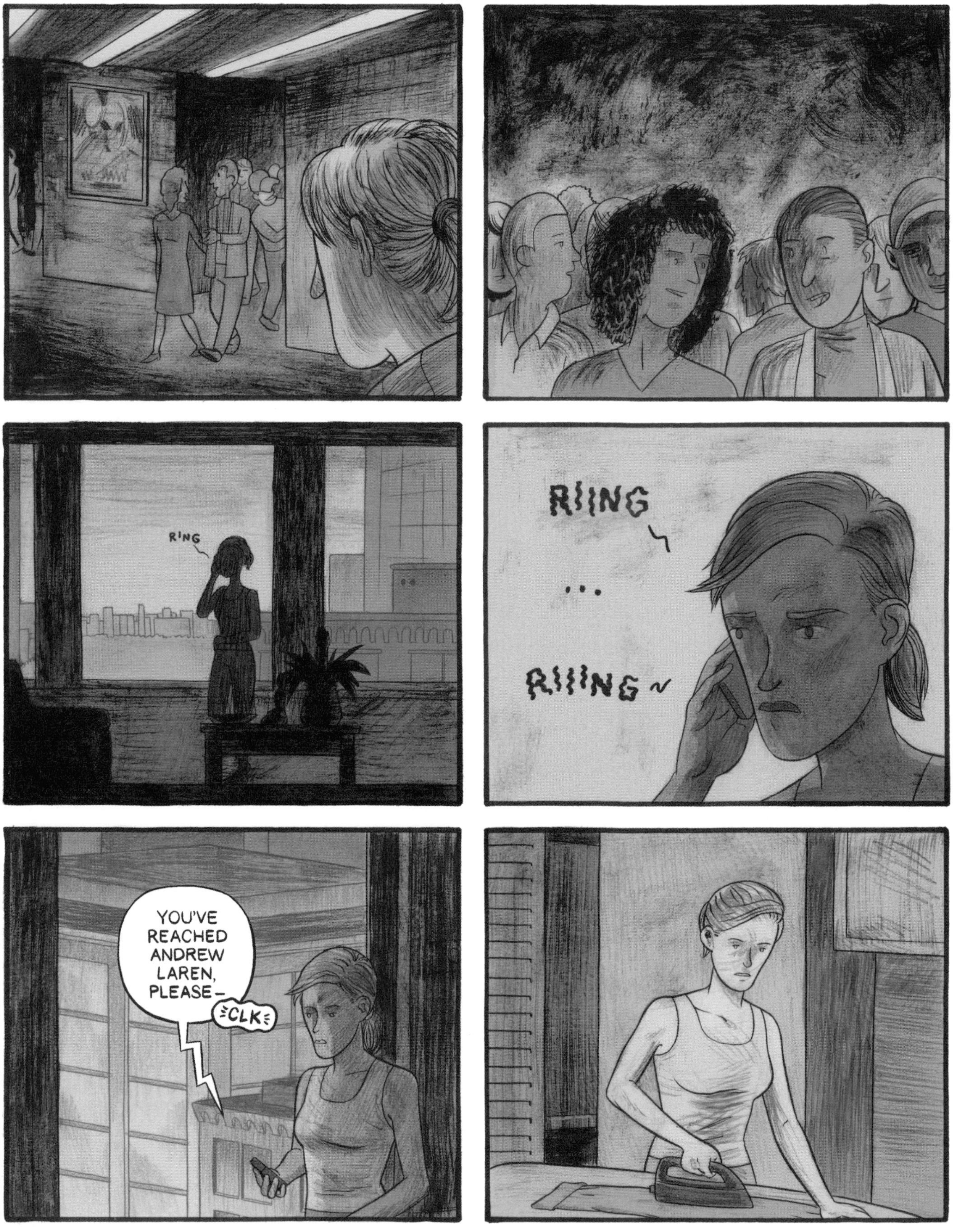
RING
RIING
...
RIIING
YOU'VE REACHED ANDREW LAREN, PLEASE—
CLK

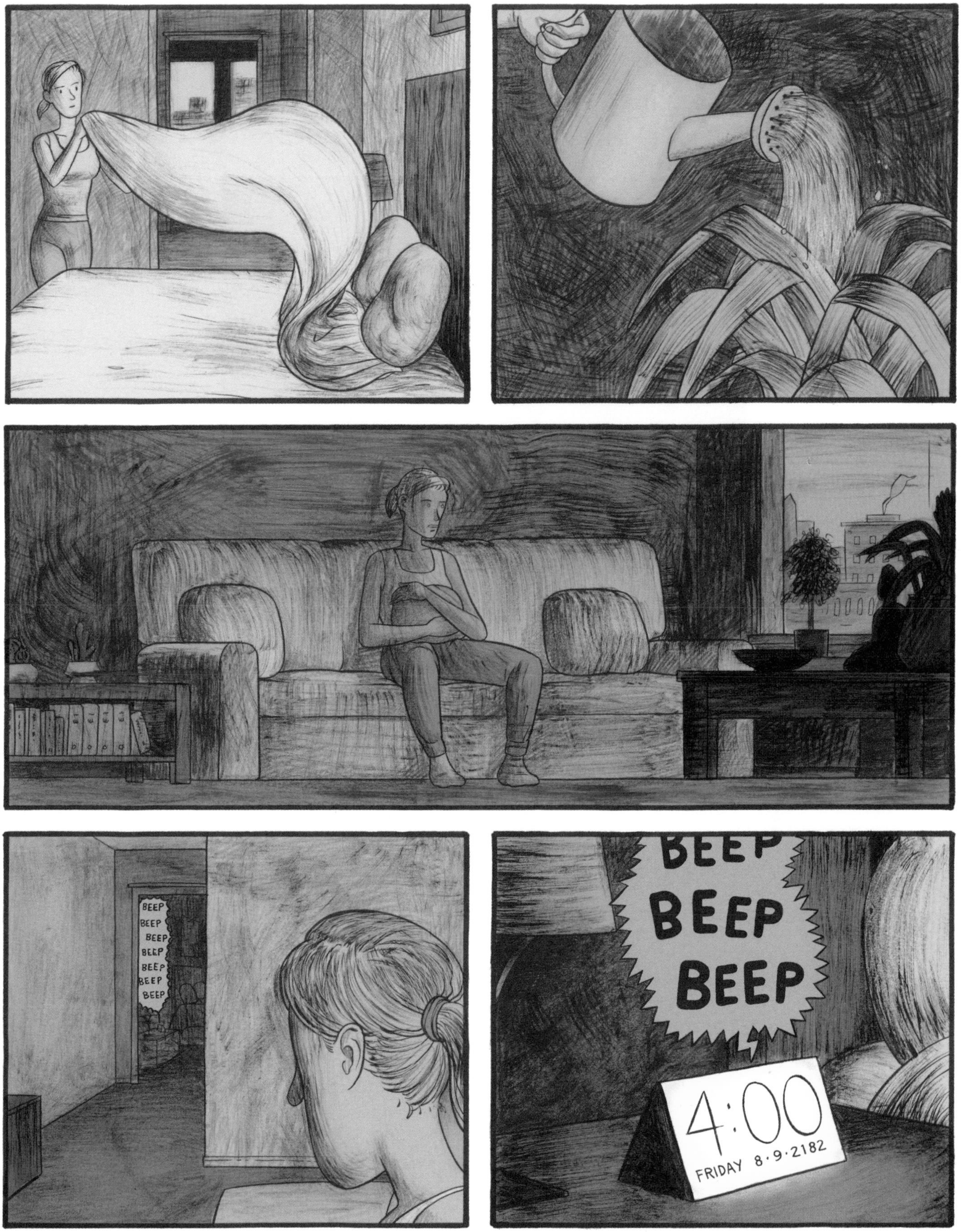
BEEP
BEEP
BEEP
BEEP
BEEP
BEEP
BEEP
BEEP
BEEP
BEEP
4:00
FRIDAY 8·9·2182

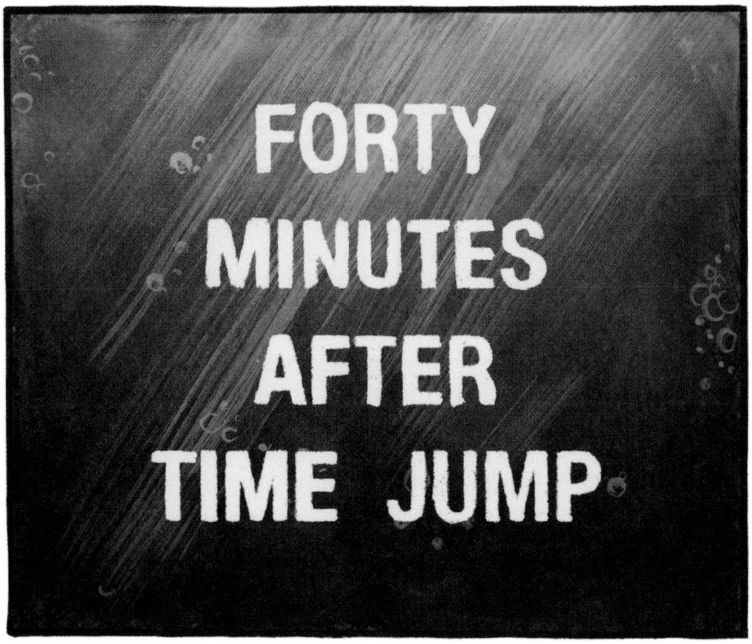
FORTY
MINUTES
AFTER
TIME JUMP

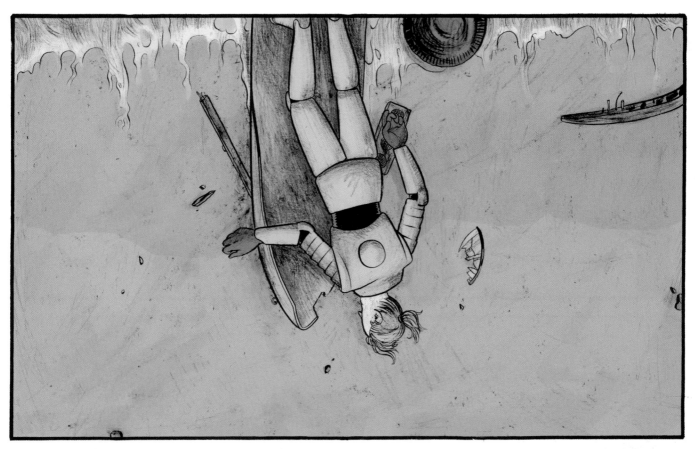

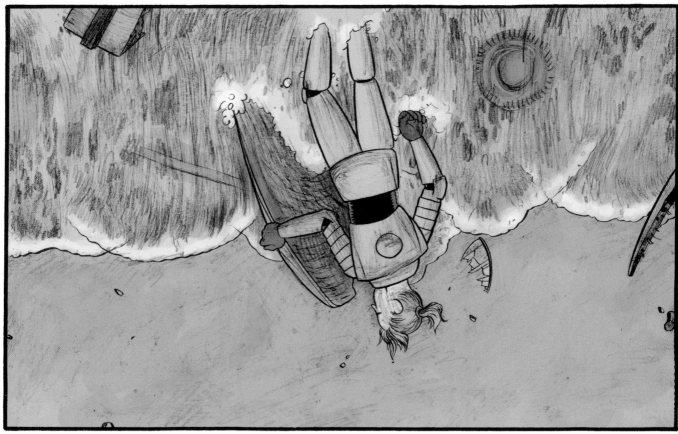

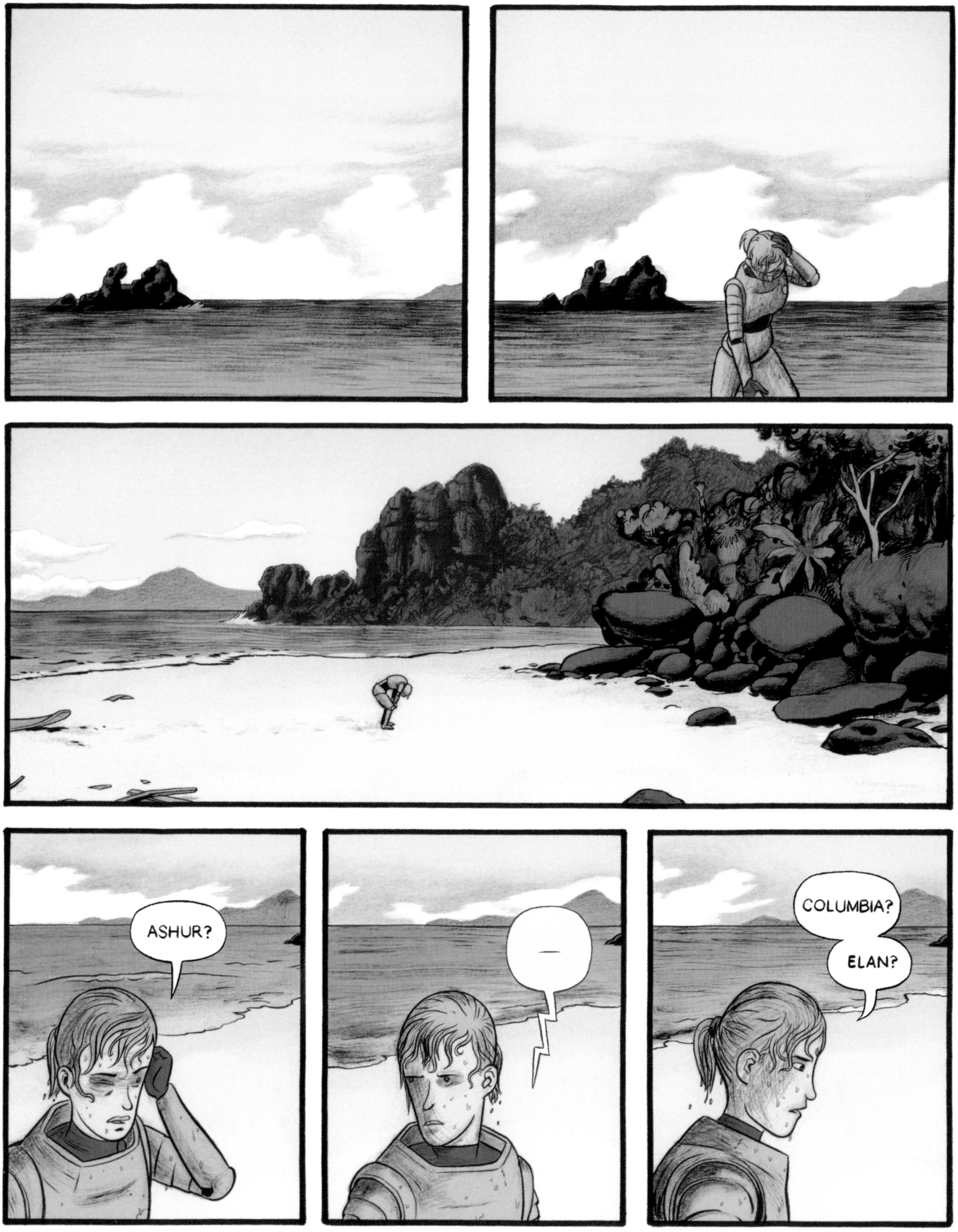
ASHUR?
—
COLUMBIA?
ELAN?

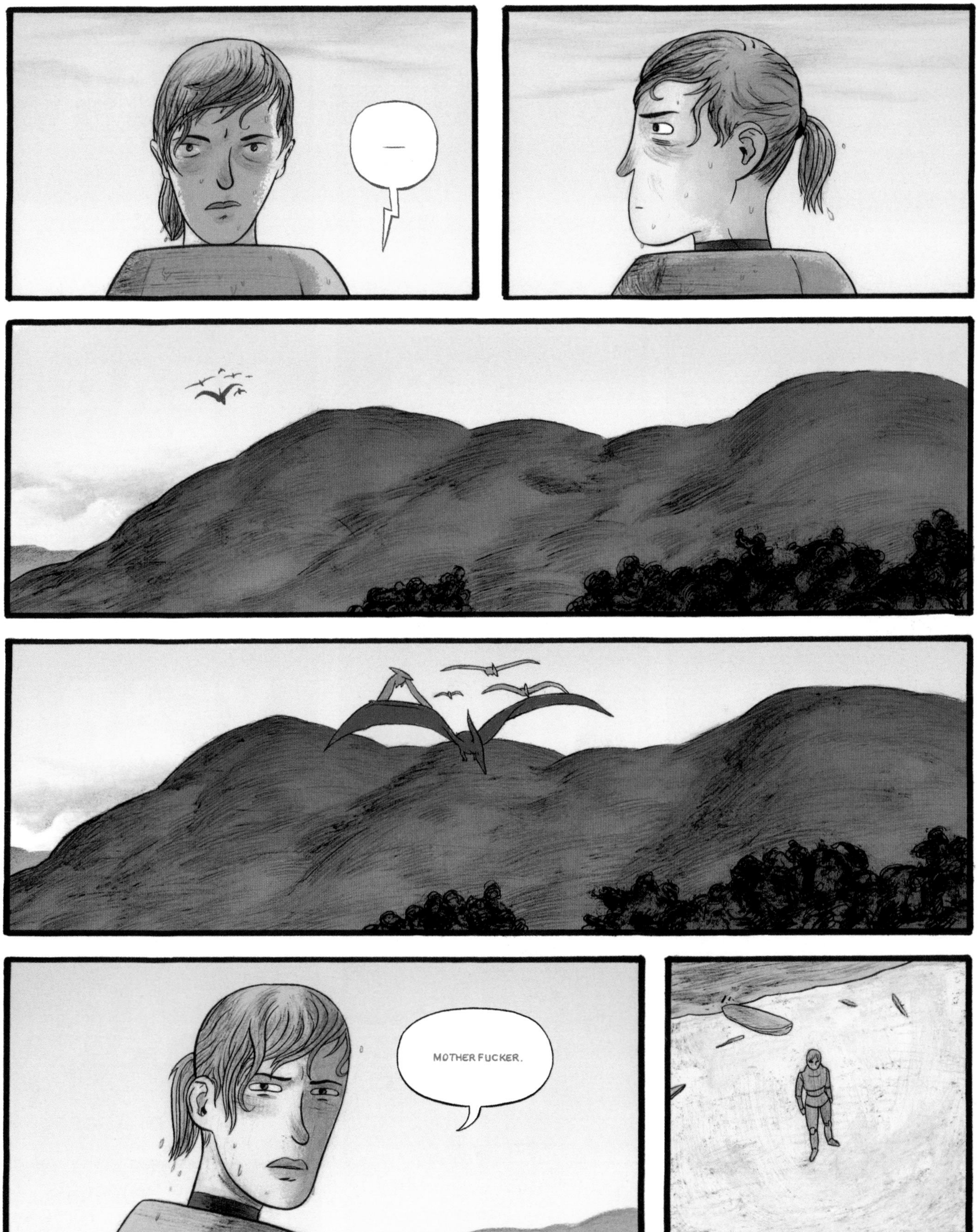
—
MOTHER FUCKER.

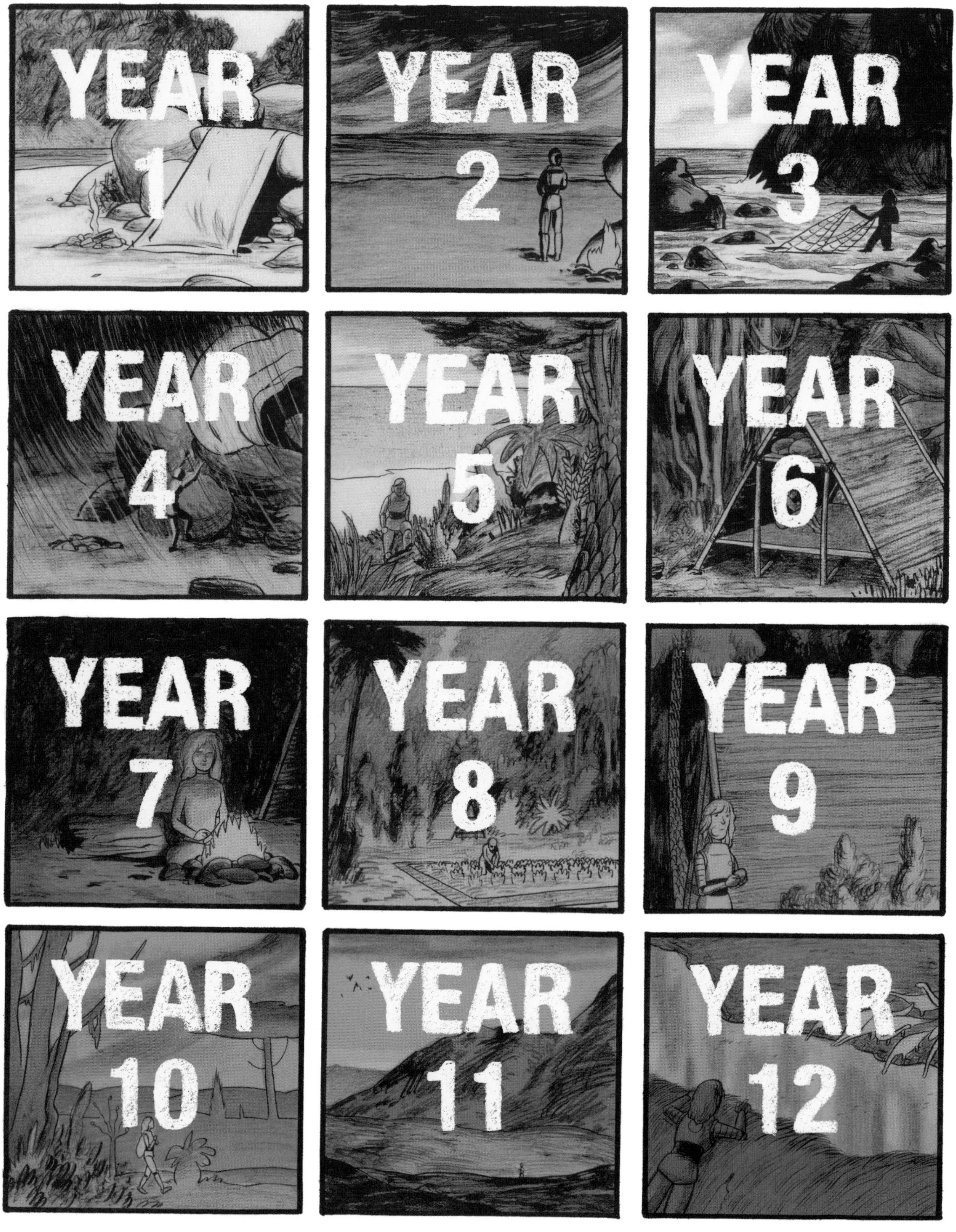
YEAR 1
YEAR 2
YEAR 3
YEAR 4
YEAR 5
YEAR 6
YEAR 7
YEAR 8
YEAR 9
YEAR 10
YEAR 11
YEAR 12

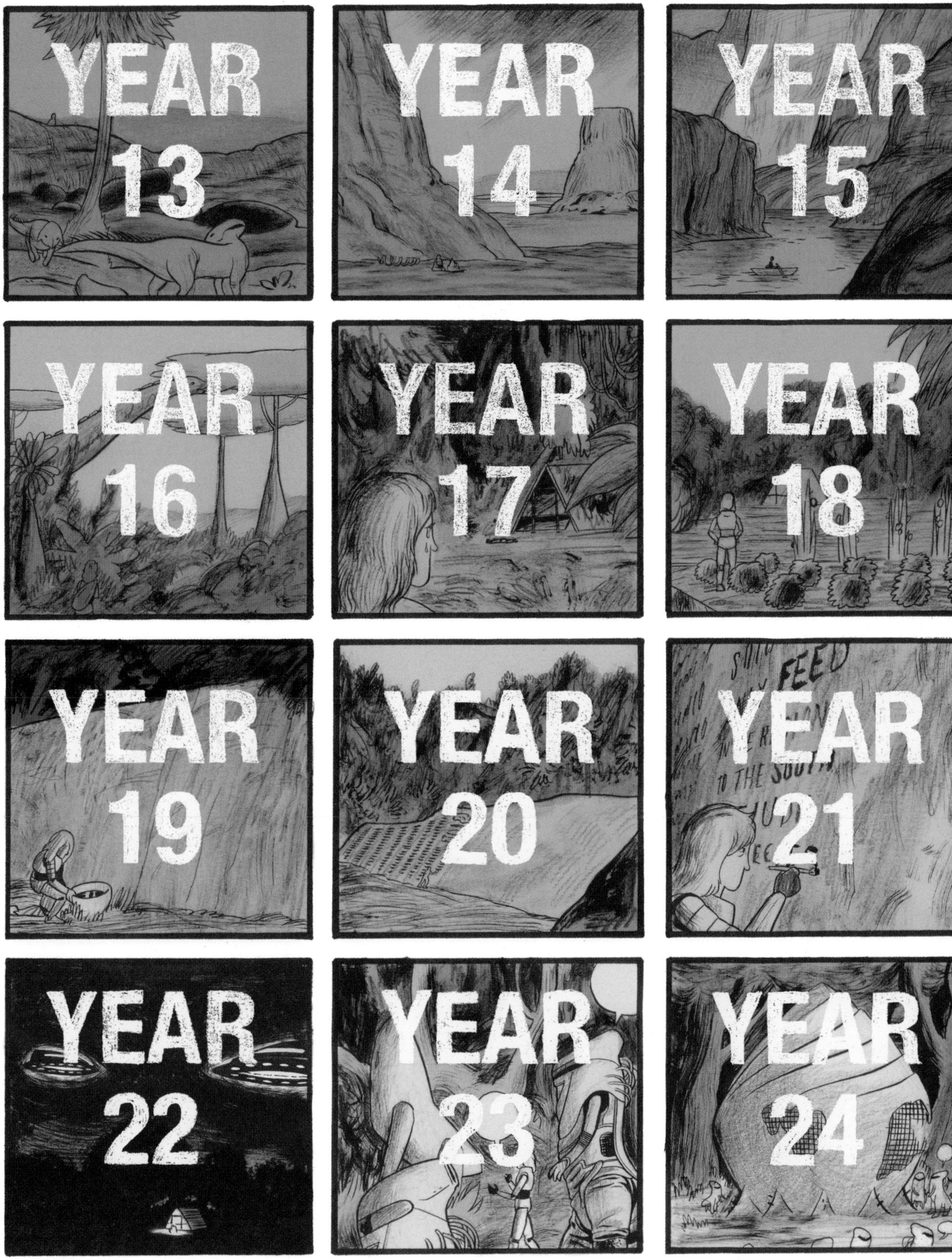
YEAR 13
YEAR 14
YEAR 15
YEAR 16
YEAR 17
YEAR 18
YEAR 19
YEAR 20
YEAR 21
YEAR 22
YEAR 23
YEAR 24

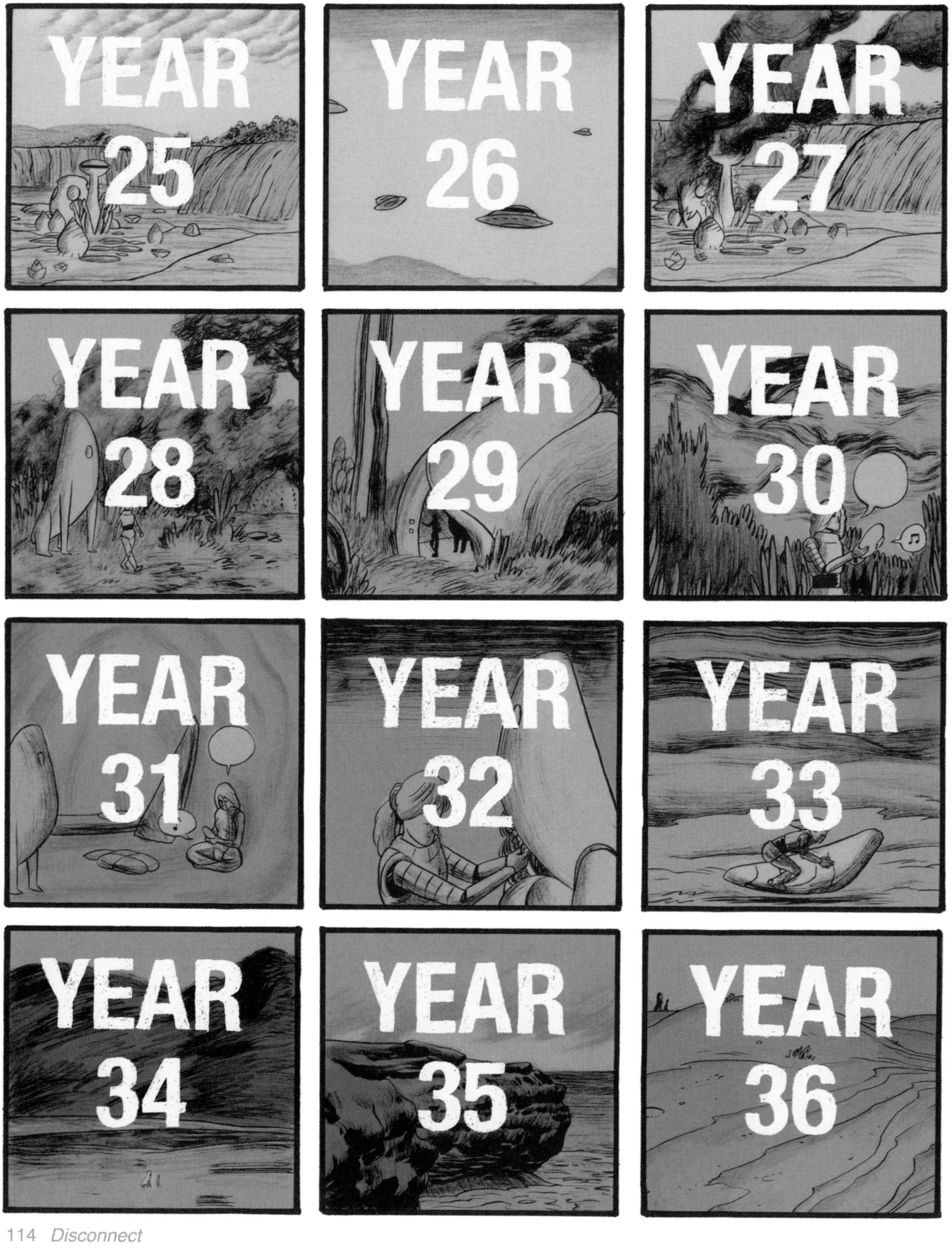
YEAR 25
YEAR 26
YEAR 27
YEAR 28
YEAR 29
YEAR 30
YEAR 31
YEAR 32
YEAR 33
YEAR 34
YEAR 35
YEAR 36

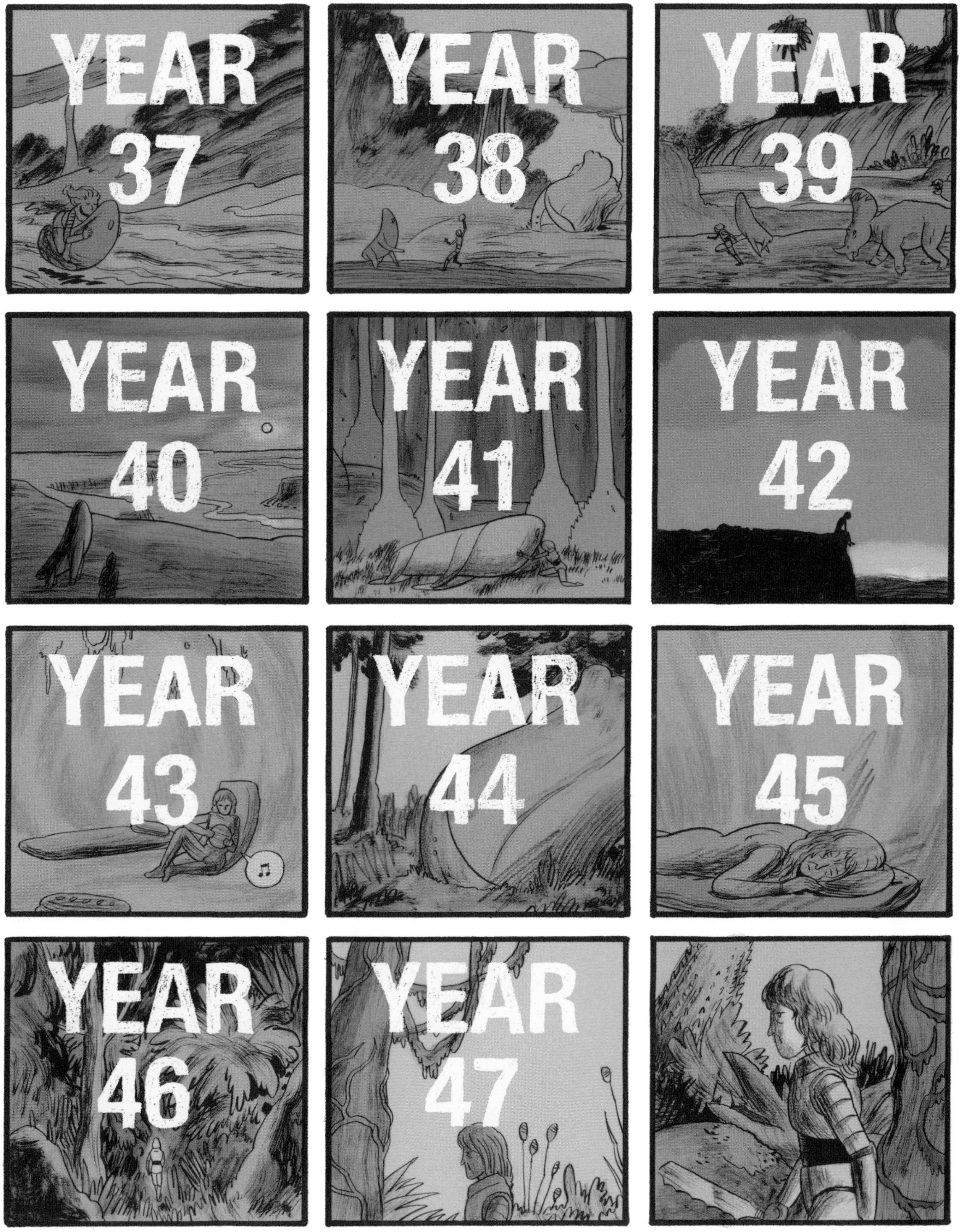
YEAR 37
YEAR 38
YEAR 39
YEAR 40
YEAR 41
YEAR 42
YEAR 43
YEAR 44
YEAR 45
YEAR 46
YEAR 47

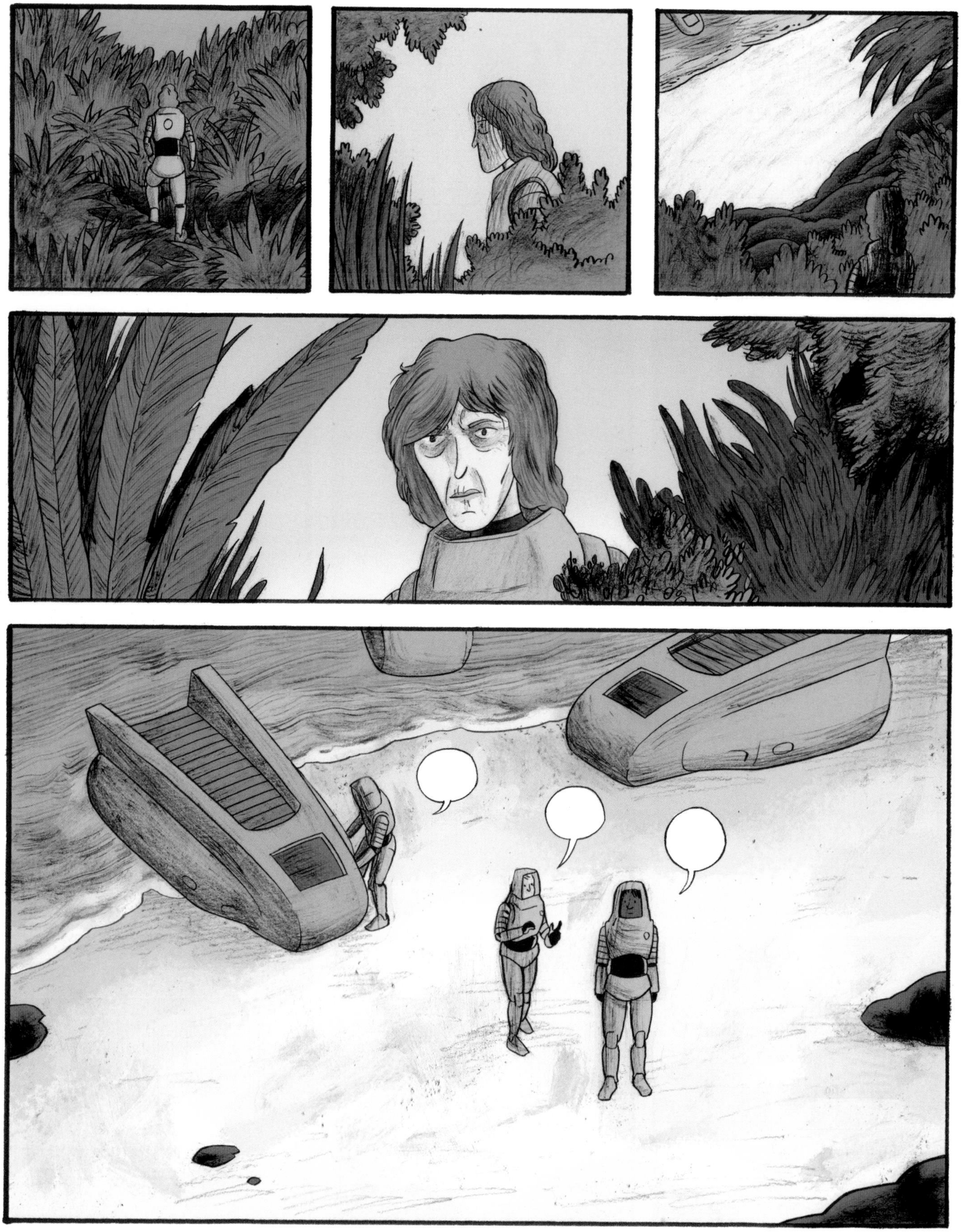

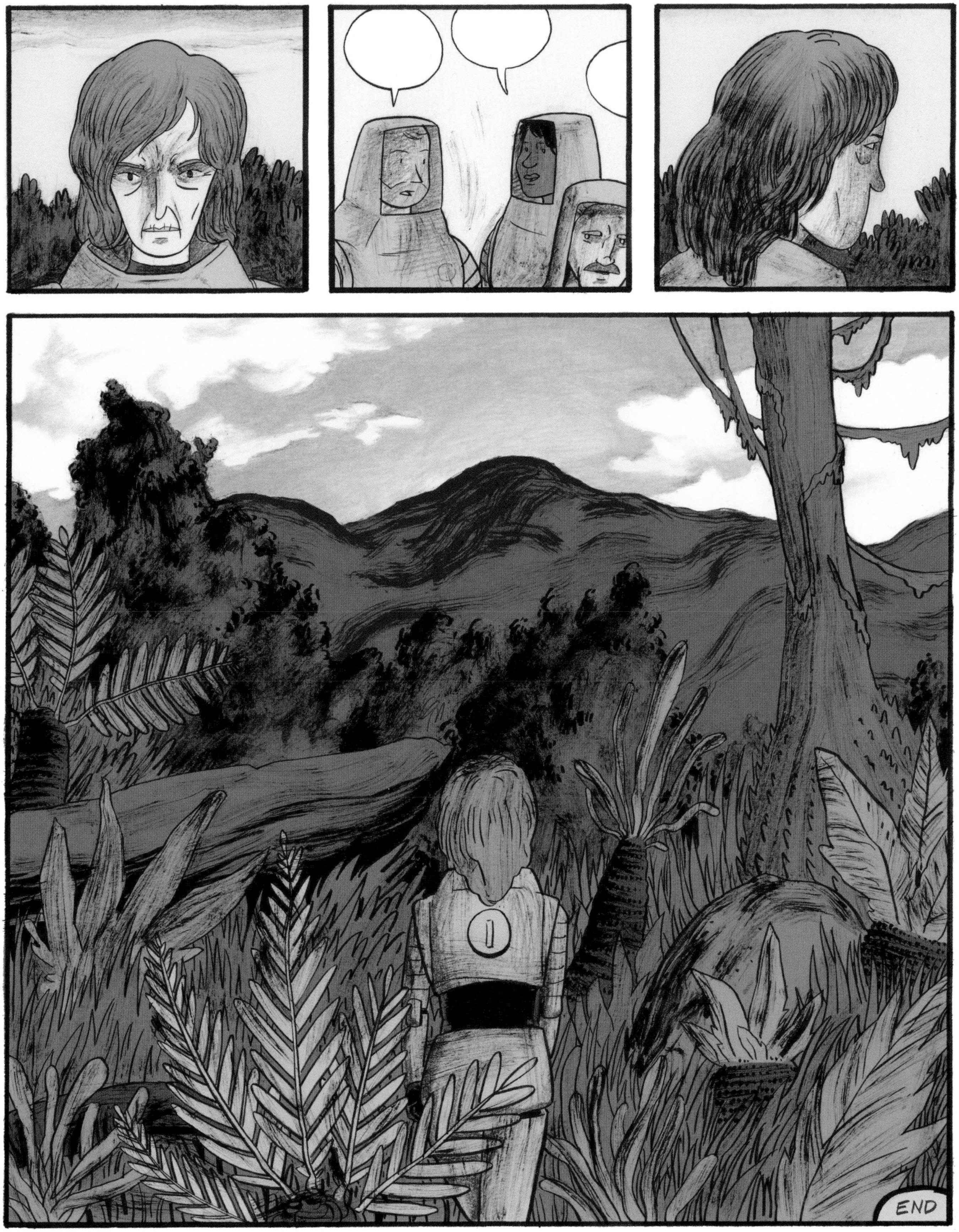
END

THE SCOUT
MALACHI WARD

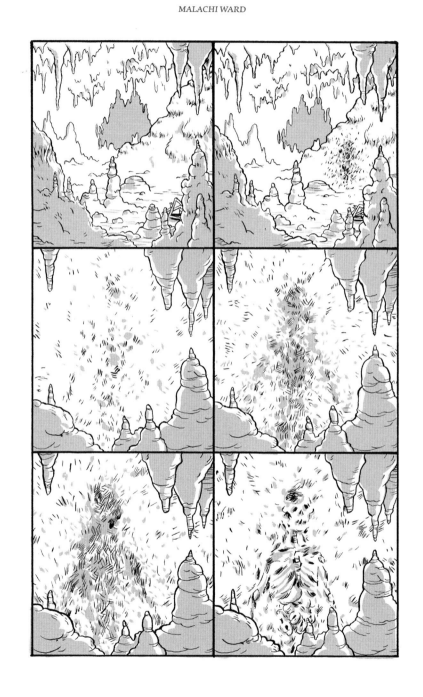

-IVATE

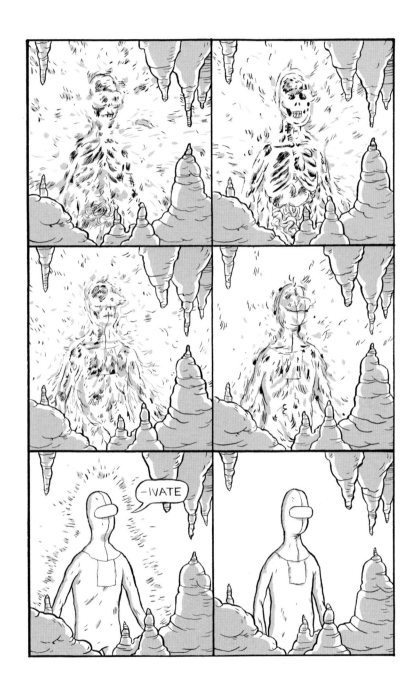

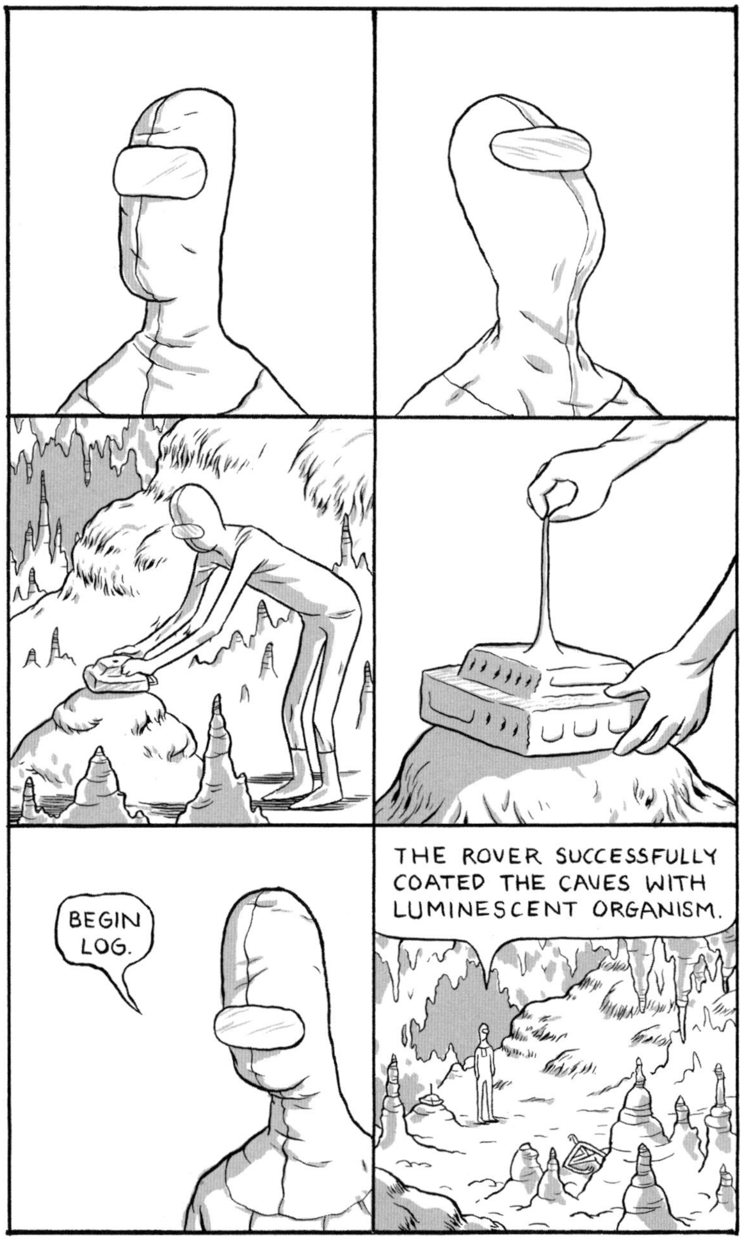
BEGIN LOG.
THE ROVER SUCCESSFULLY COATED THE CAVES WITH LUMINESCENT ORGANISM.

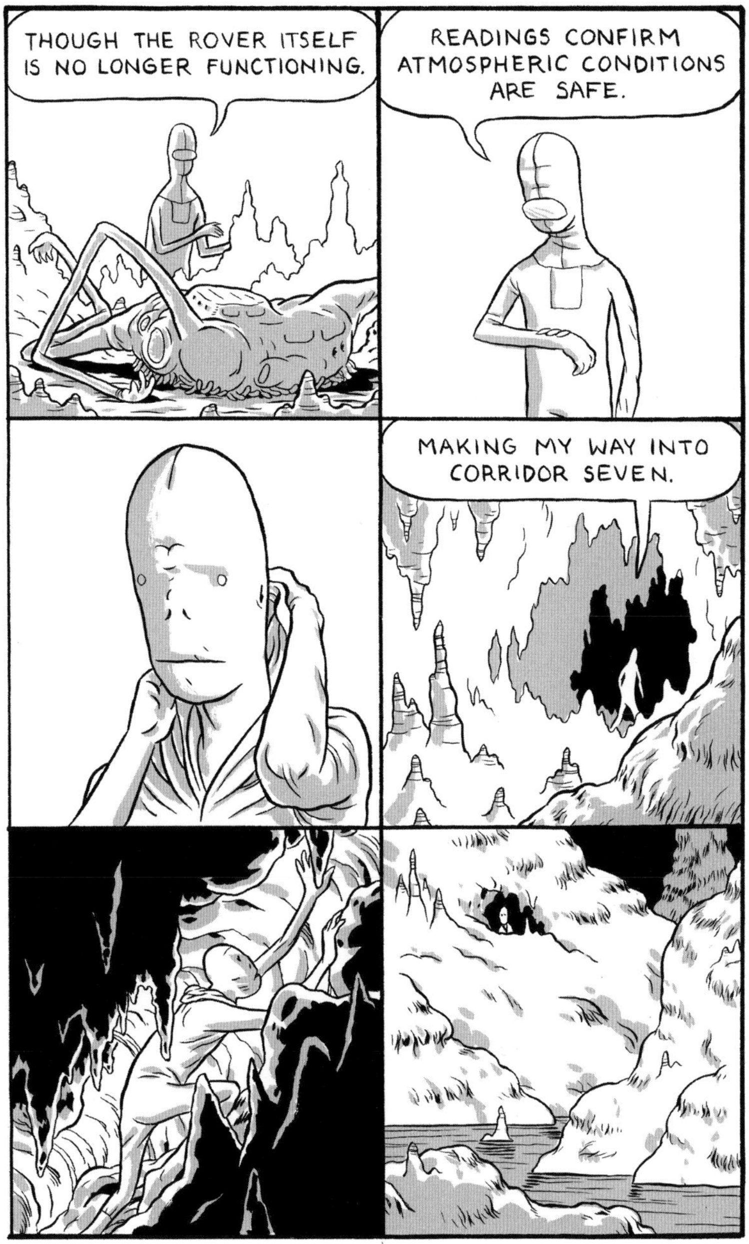
THOUGH THE ROVER ITSELF IS NO LONGER FUNCTIONING.
READINGS CONFIRM ATMOSPHERIC CONDITIONS ARE SAFE.
MAKING MY WAY INTO CORRIDOR SEVEN.

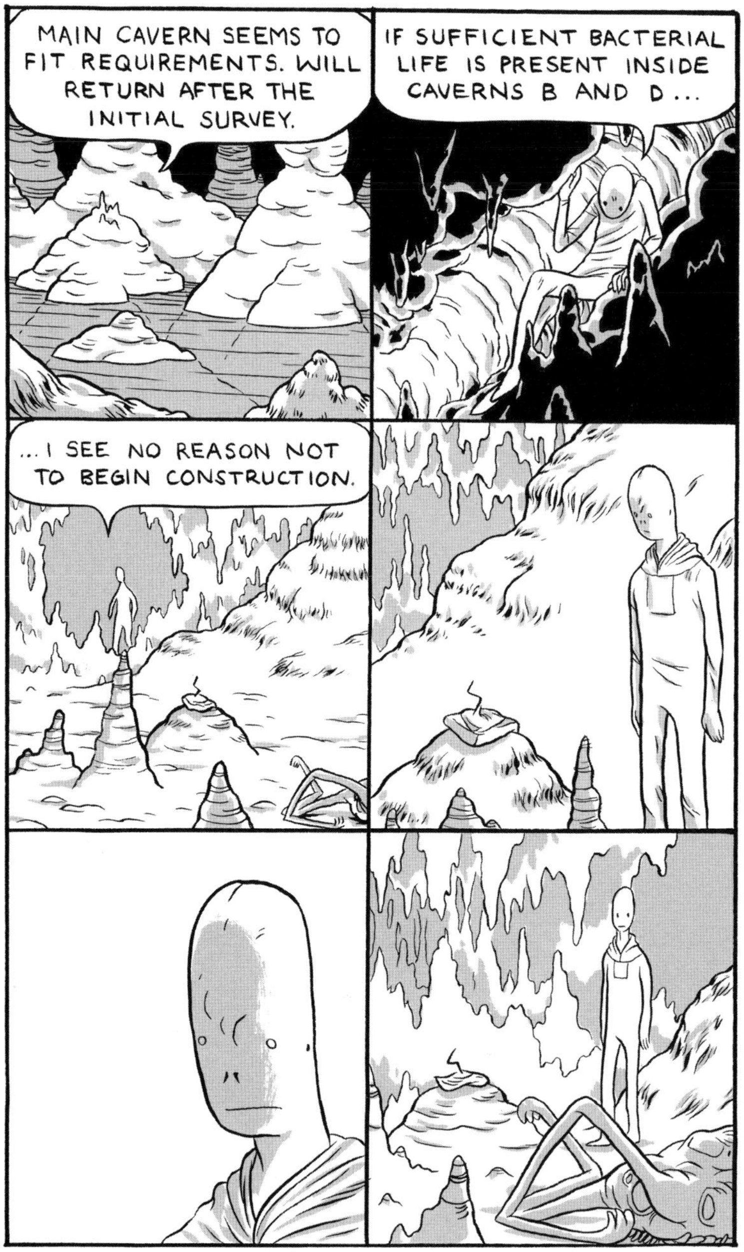
MAIN CAVERN SEEMS TO FIT REQUIREMENTS. WILL RETURN AFTER THE INITIAL SURVEY.
IF SUFFICIENT BACTERIAL LIFE IS PRESENT INSIDE CAVERNS B AND D...
...I SEE NO REASON NOT TO BEGIN CONSTRUCTION.

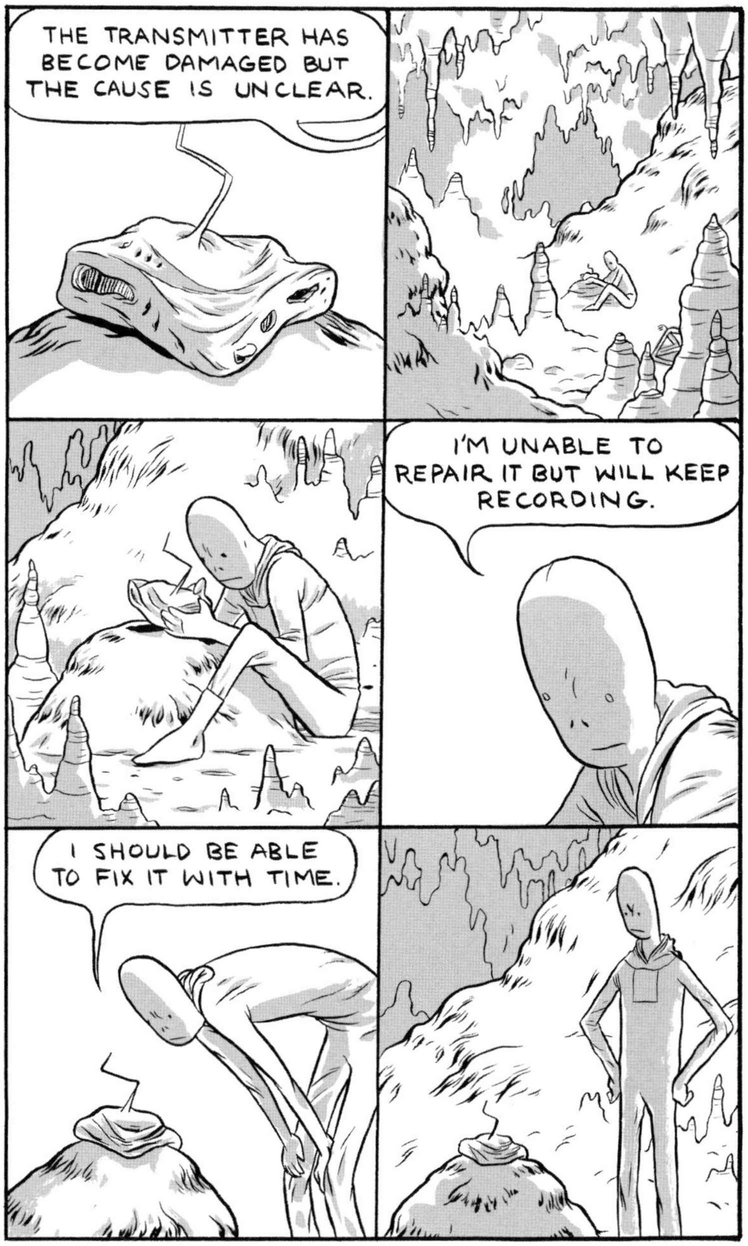
THE TRANSMITTER HAS BECOME DAMAGED BUT THE CAUSE IS UNCLEAR.
I'M UNABLE TO REPAIR IT BUT WILL KEEP RECORDING.
I SHOULD BE ABLE TO FIX IT WITH TIME.

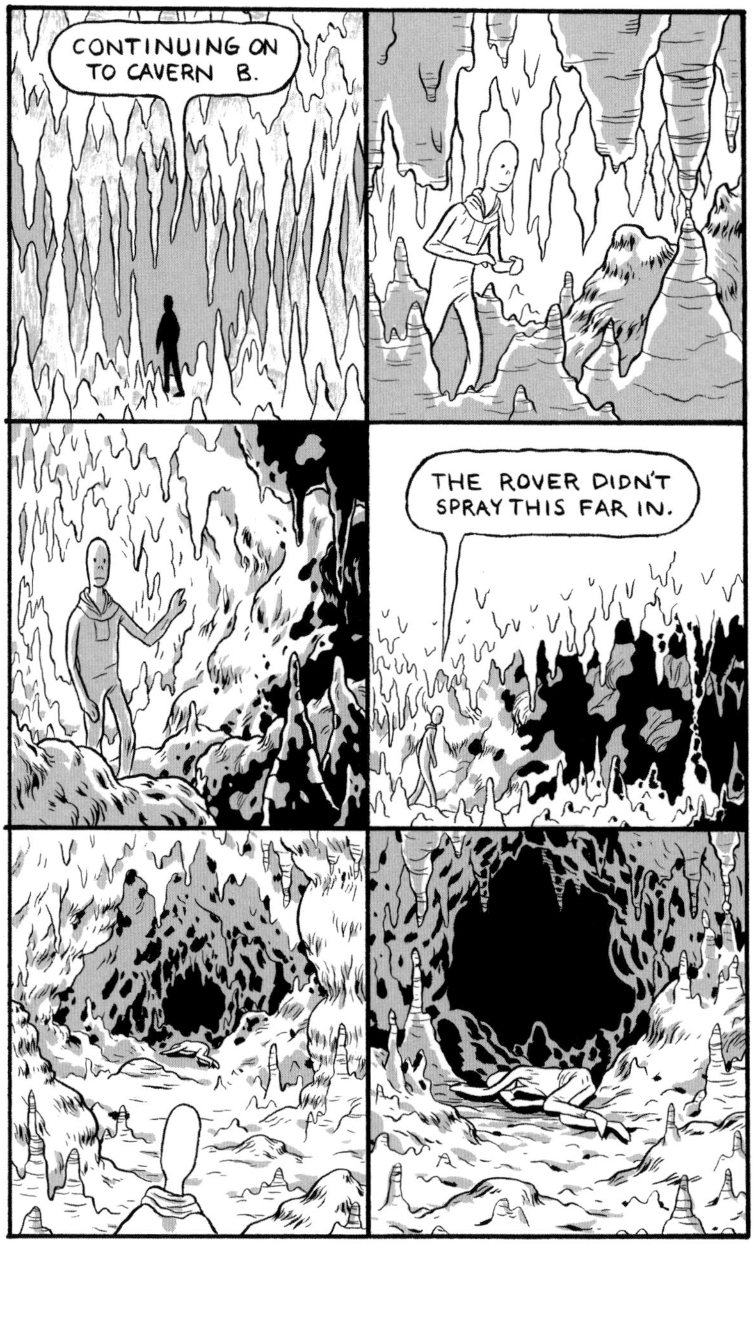
CONTINUING ON TO CAVERN B.
THE ROVER DIDN'T SPRAY THIS FAR IN.

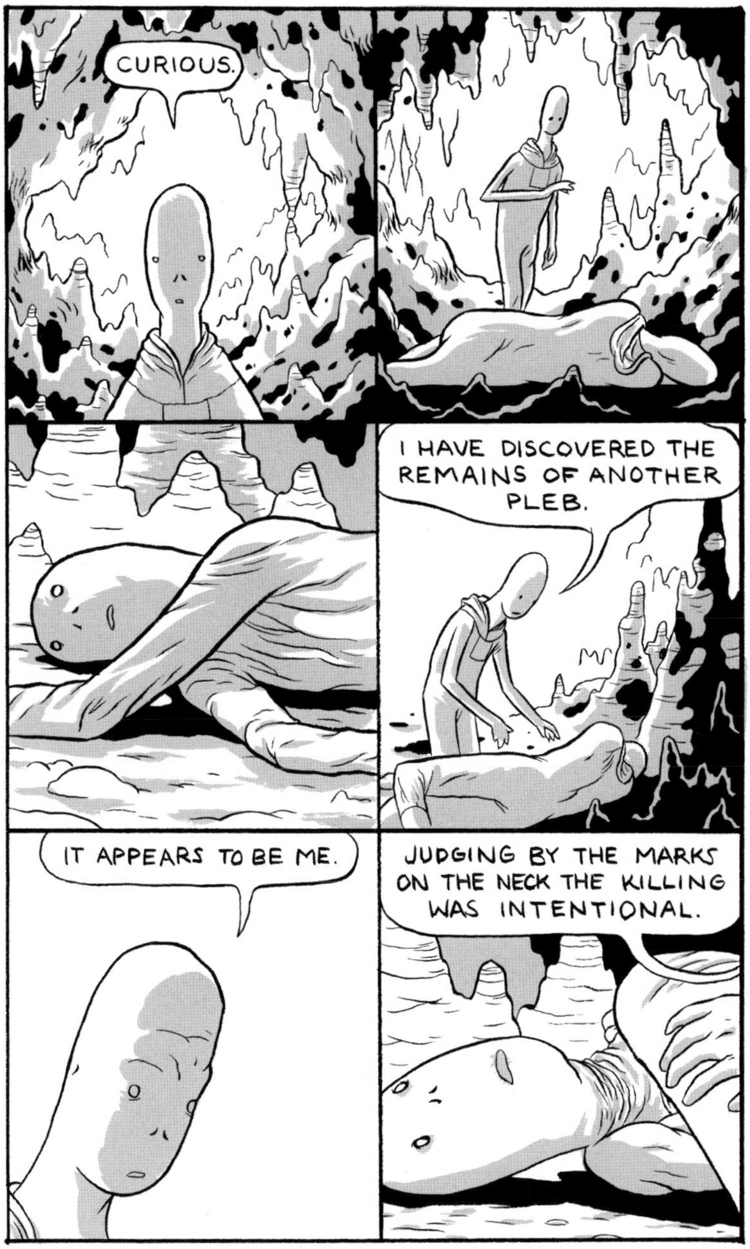
CURIOUS.
I HAVE DISCOVERED THE REMAINS OF ANOTHER PLEB.
IT APPEARS TO BE ME.
JUDGING BY THE MARKS ON THE NECK THE KILLING WAS INTENTIONAL.

I SUPPOSE MY INFORMATION HAS BEEN SENT MULTIPLE TIMES. THAT WOULD EXPLAIN THIS DUPLICATE.
HELLO.
WHO'S THERE?
COME IN.

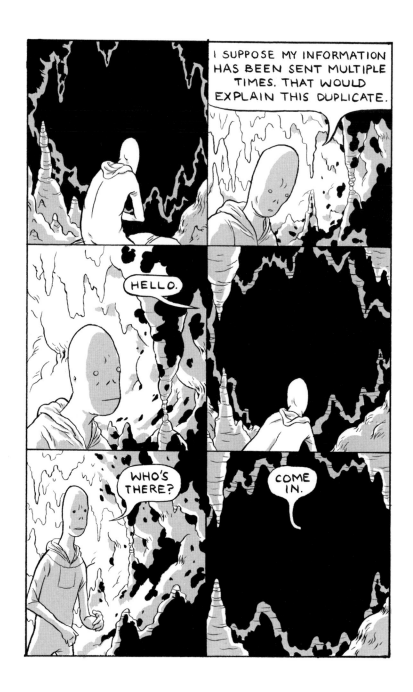

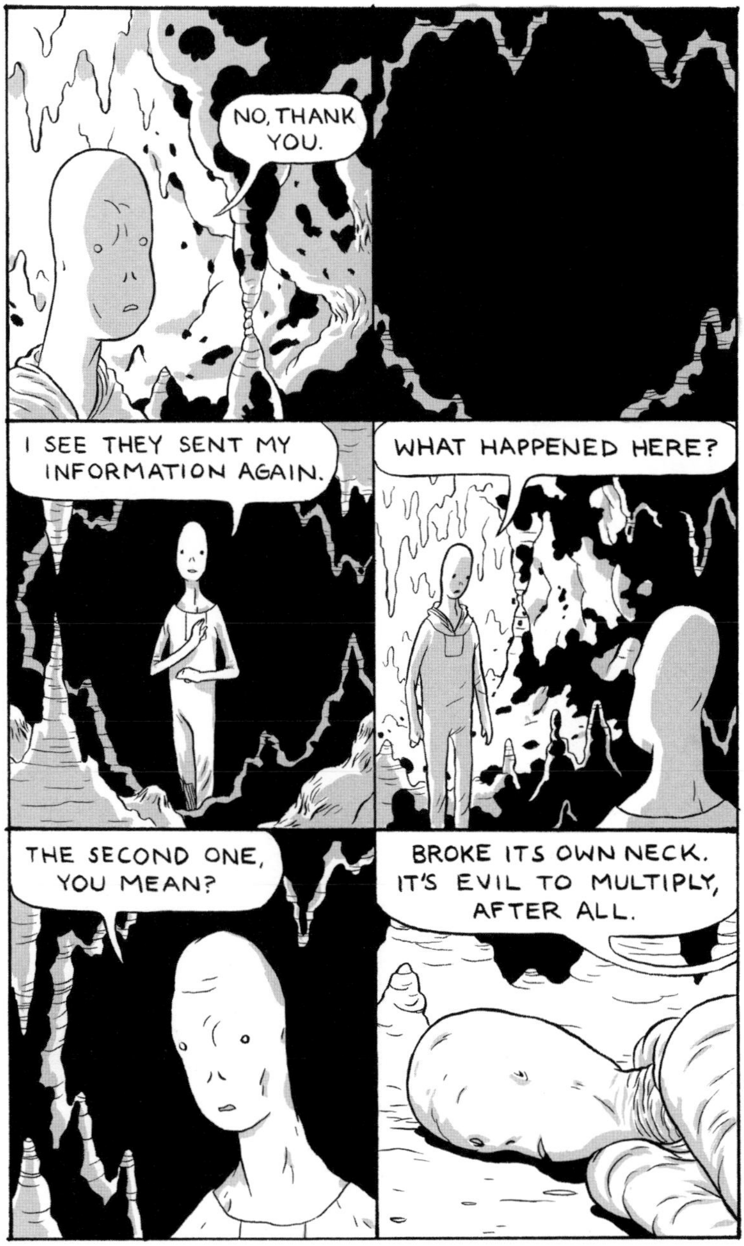
NO, THANK YOU.
I SEE THEY SENT MY INFORMATION AGAIN.
WHAT HAPPENED HERE?
THE SECOND ONE, YOU MEAN?
BROKE ITS OWN NECK. IT'S EVIL TO MULTIPLY, AFTER ALL.

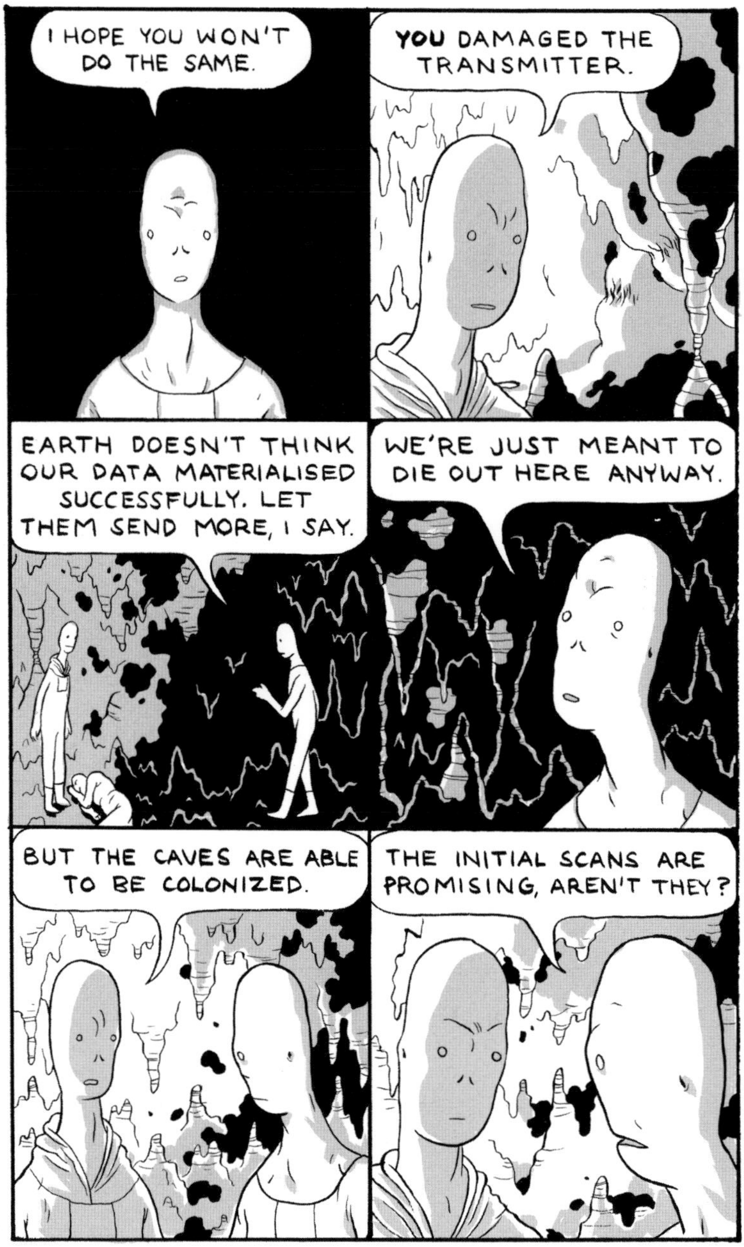
I HOPE YOU WON'T DO THE SAME.
YOU DAMAGED THE TRANSMITTER.
EARTH DOESN'T THINK OUR DATA MATERIALISED SUCCESSFULLY. LET THEM SEND MORE, I SAY.
WE'RE JUST MEANT TO DIE OUT HERE ANYWAY.
BUT THE CAVES ARE ABLE TO BE COLONIZED.
THE INITIAL SCANS ARE PROMISING, AREN'T THEY?

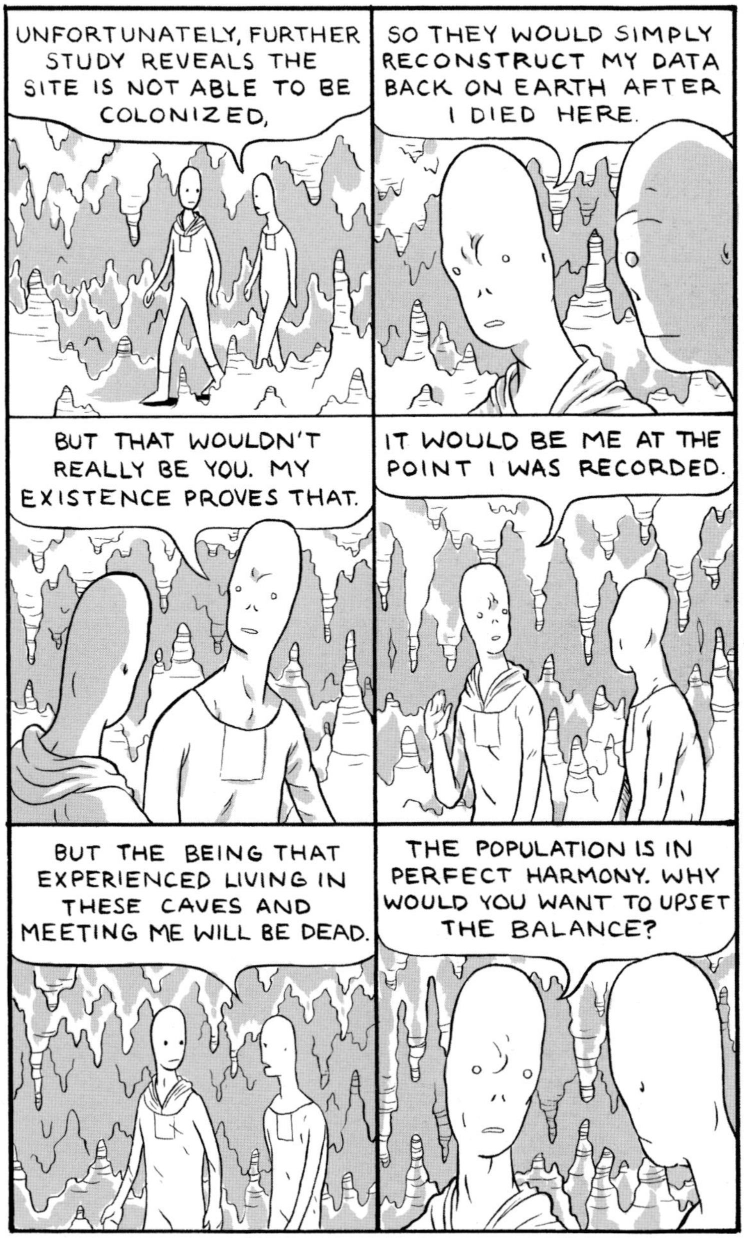
UNFORTUNATELY, FURTHER STUDY REVEALS THE SITE IS NOT ABLE TO BE COLONIZED,
SO THEY WOULD SIMPLY RECONSTRUCT MY DATA BACK ON EARTH AFTER I DIED HERE.
BUT THAT WOULDN'T REALLY BE YOU. MY EXISTENCE PROVES THAT.
IT WOULD BE ME AT THE POINT I WAS RECORDED.
BUT THE BEING THAT EXPERIENCED LIVING IN THESE CAVES AND MEETING ME WILL BE DEAD.
THE POPULATION IS IN PERFECT HARMONY. WHY WOULD YOU WANT TO UPSET THE BALANCE?

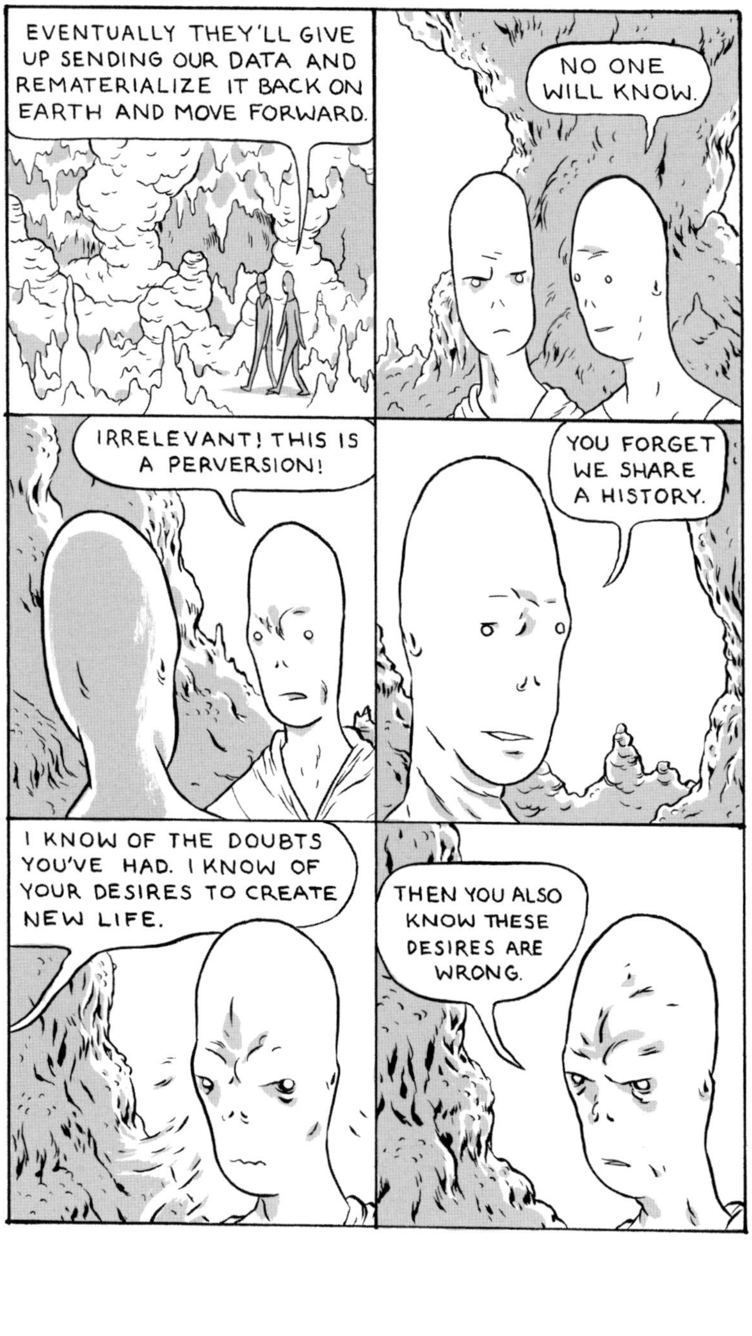
EVENTUALLY THEY'LL GIVE UP SENDING OUR DATA AND REMATERIALIZE IT BACK ON EARTH AND MOVE FORWARD.
NO ONE WILL KNOW.
IRRELEVANT! THIS IS A PERVERSION!
YOU FORGET WE SHARE A HISTORY.
I KNOW OF THE DOUBTS YOU'VE HAD. I KNOW OF YOUR DESIRES TO CREATE NEW LIFE.
THEN YOU ALSO KNOW THESE DESIRES ARE WRONG.

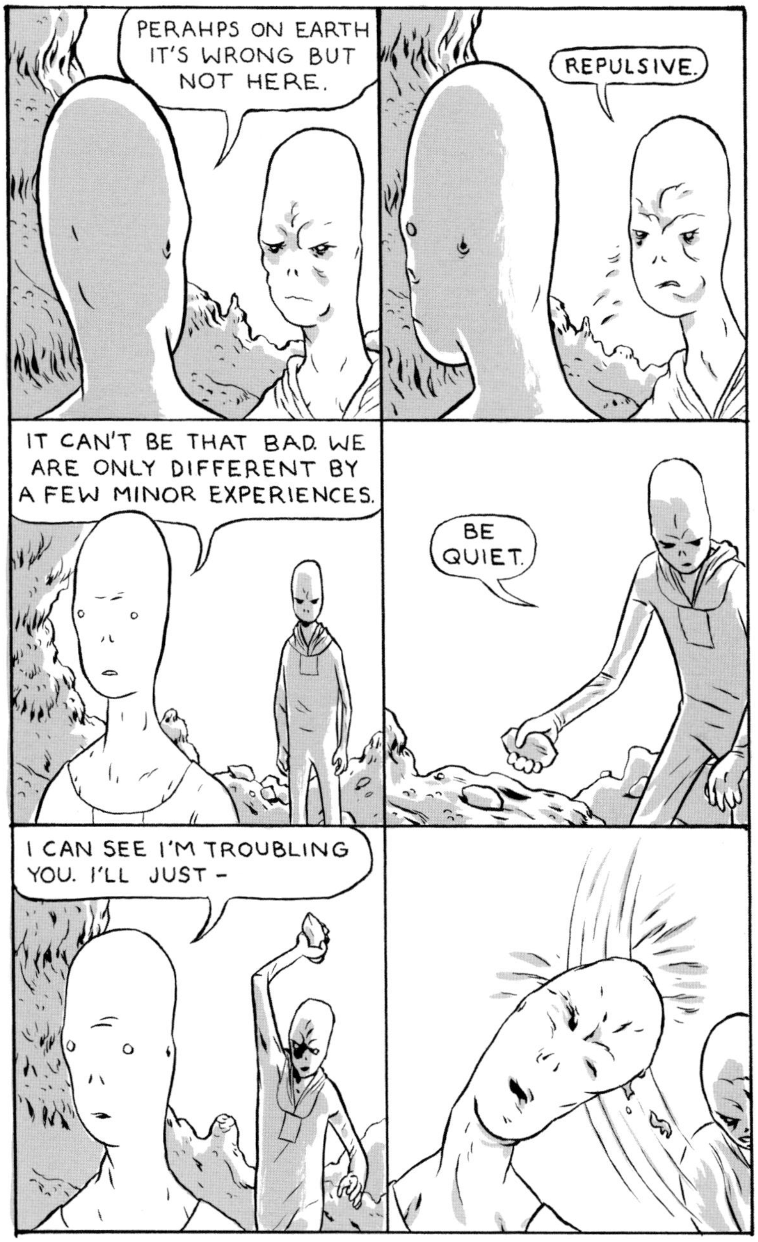
PERAHPS ON EARTH IT'S WRONG BUT NOT HERE.
REPULSIVE.
IT CAN'T BE THAT BAD. WE ARE ONLY DIFFERENT BY A FEW MINOR EXPERIENCES.
BE QUIET.
I CAN SEE I'M TROUBLING YOU. I'LL JUST -

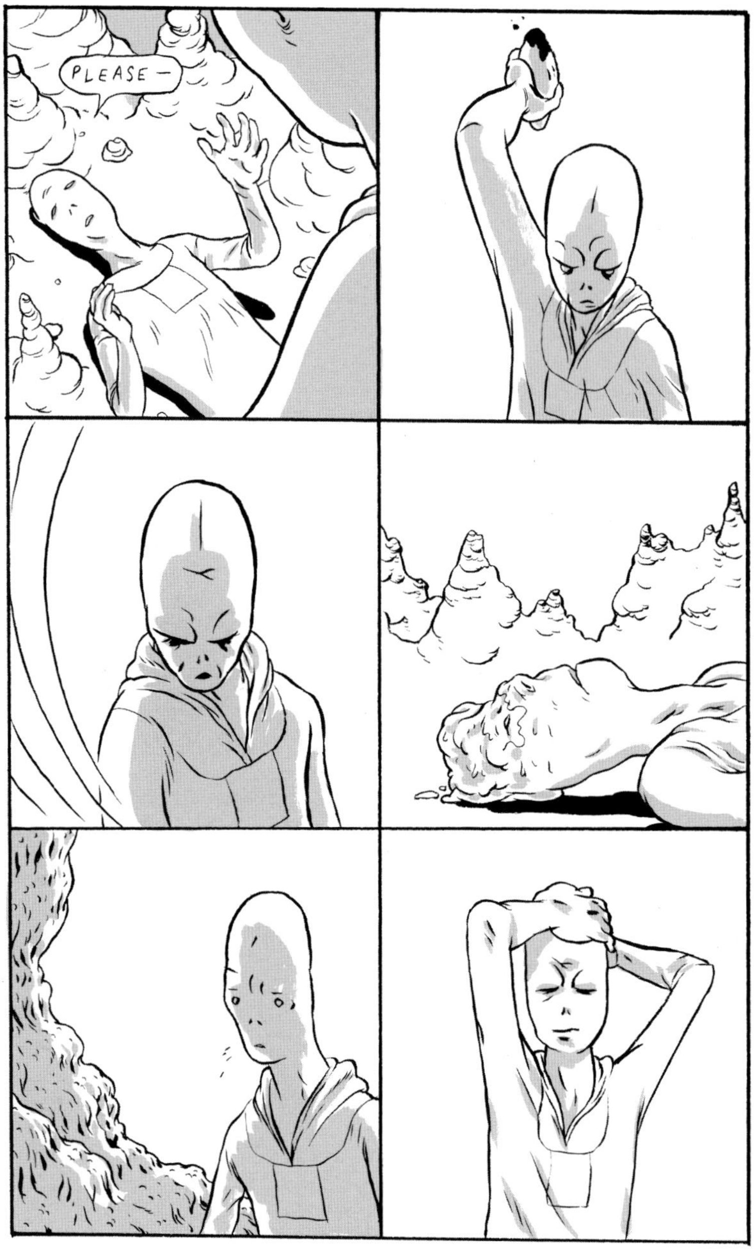
PLEASE —

-IVATE
THE END

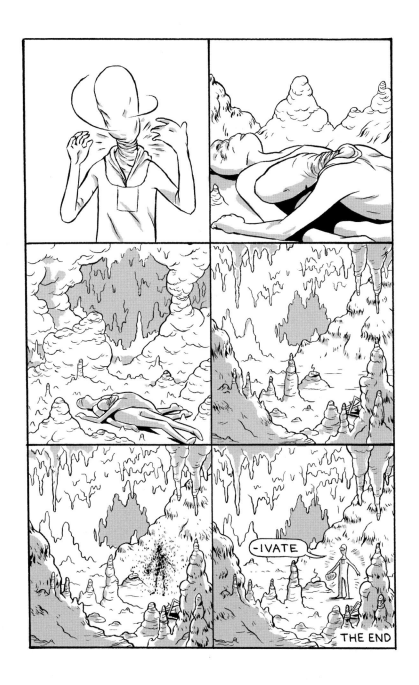

SWEET DREAMS

I HAD A DREAM THAT I WAS AN ALIEN
I WAS ABDUCTING PEOPLE...

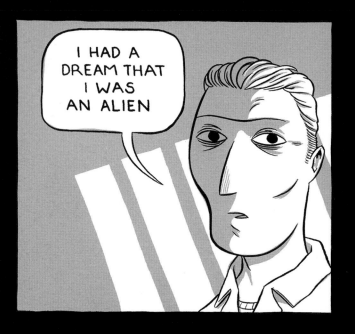

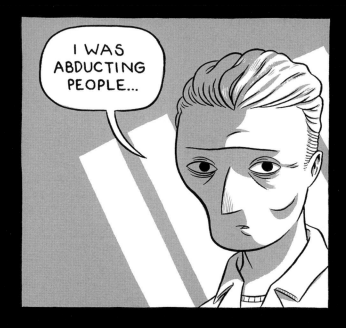

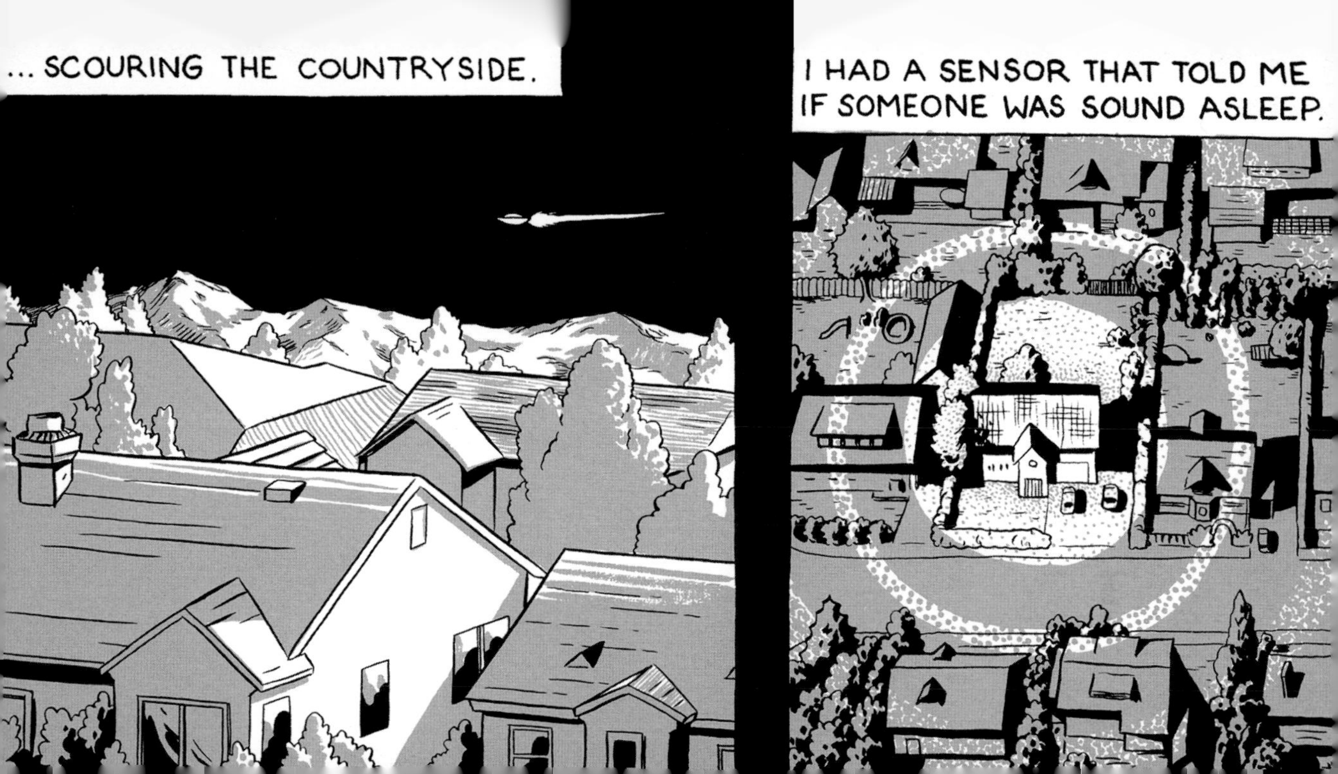
... SCOURING THE COUNTRYSIDE.
I HAD A SENSOR THAT TOLD ME IF SOMEONE WAS SOUND ASLEEP.

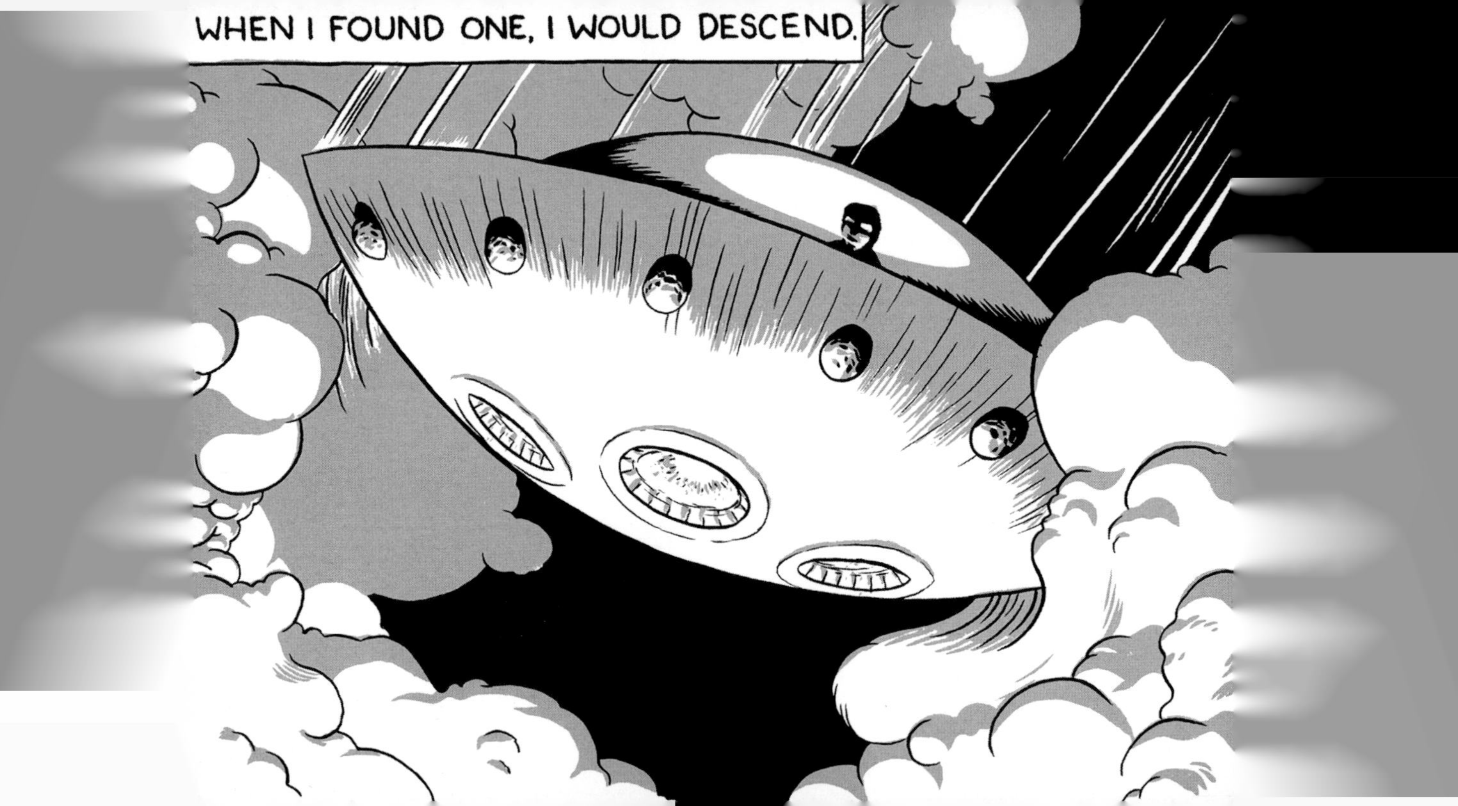
WHEN I FOUND ONE, I WOULD DESCEND.

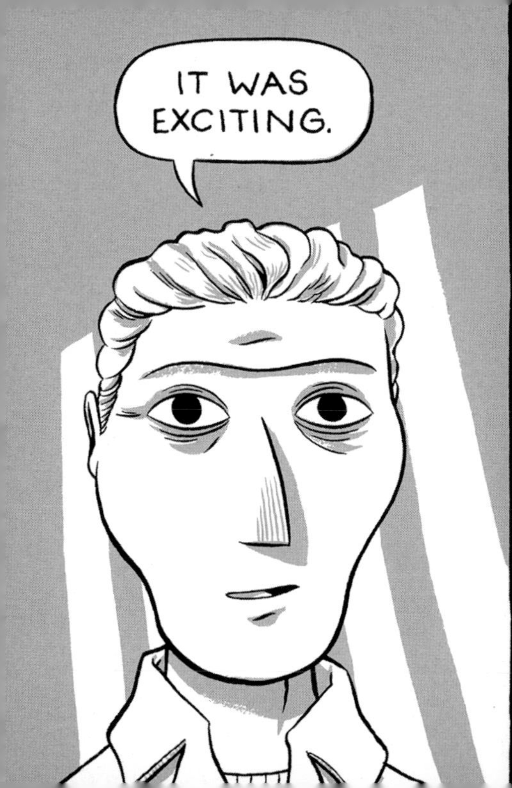
IT WAS EXCITING.

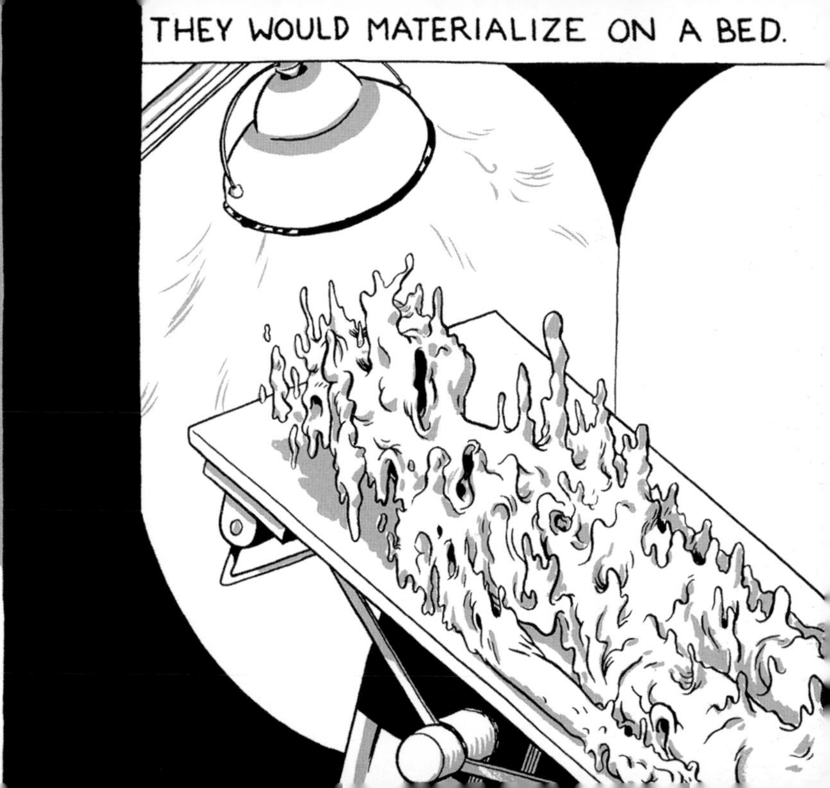
THEY WOULD MATERIALIZE ON A BED.

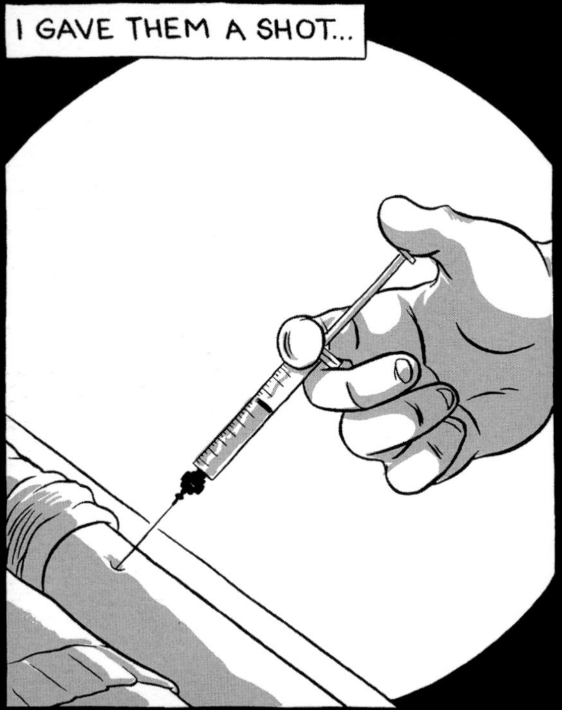
I GAVE THEM A SHOT...

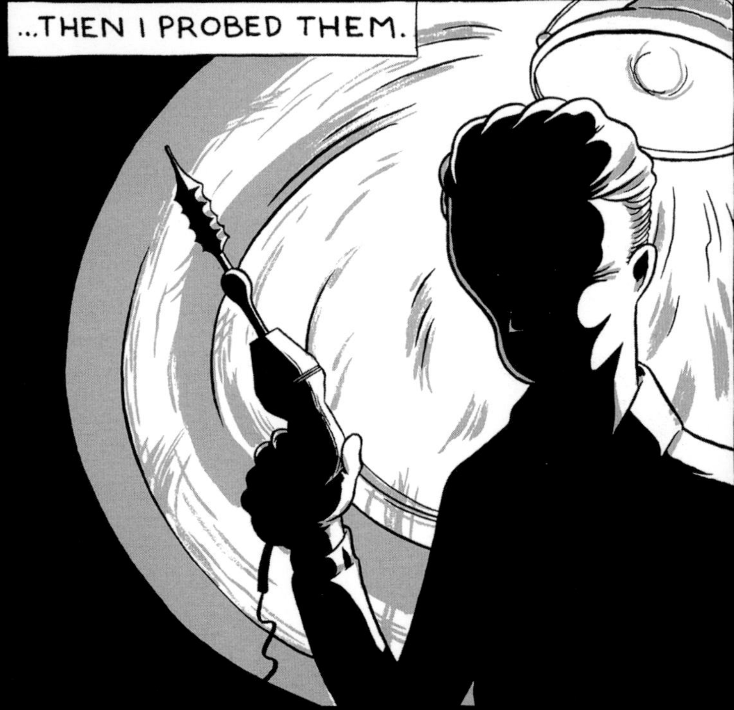
...THEN I PROBED THEM.

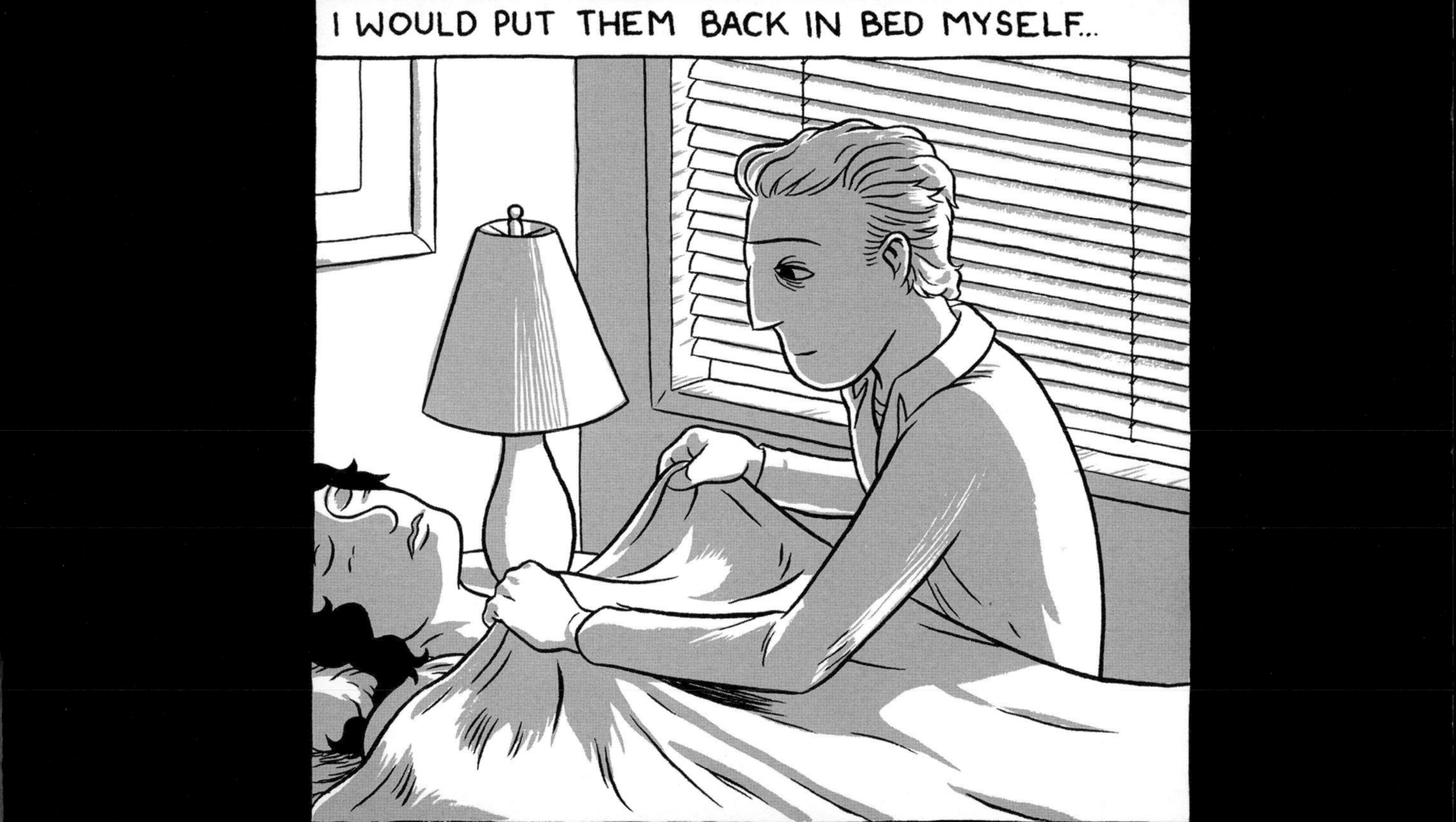
I WOULD PUT THEM BACK IN BED MYSELF...

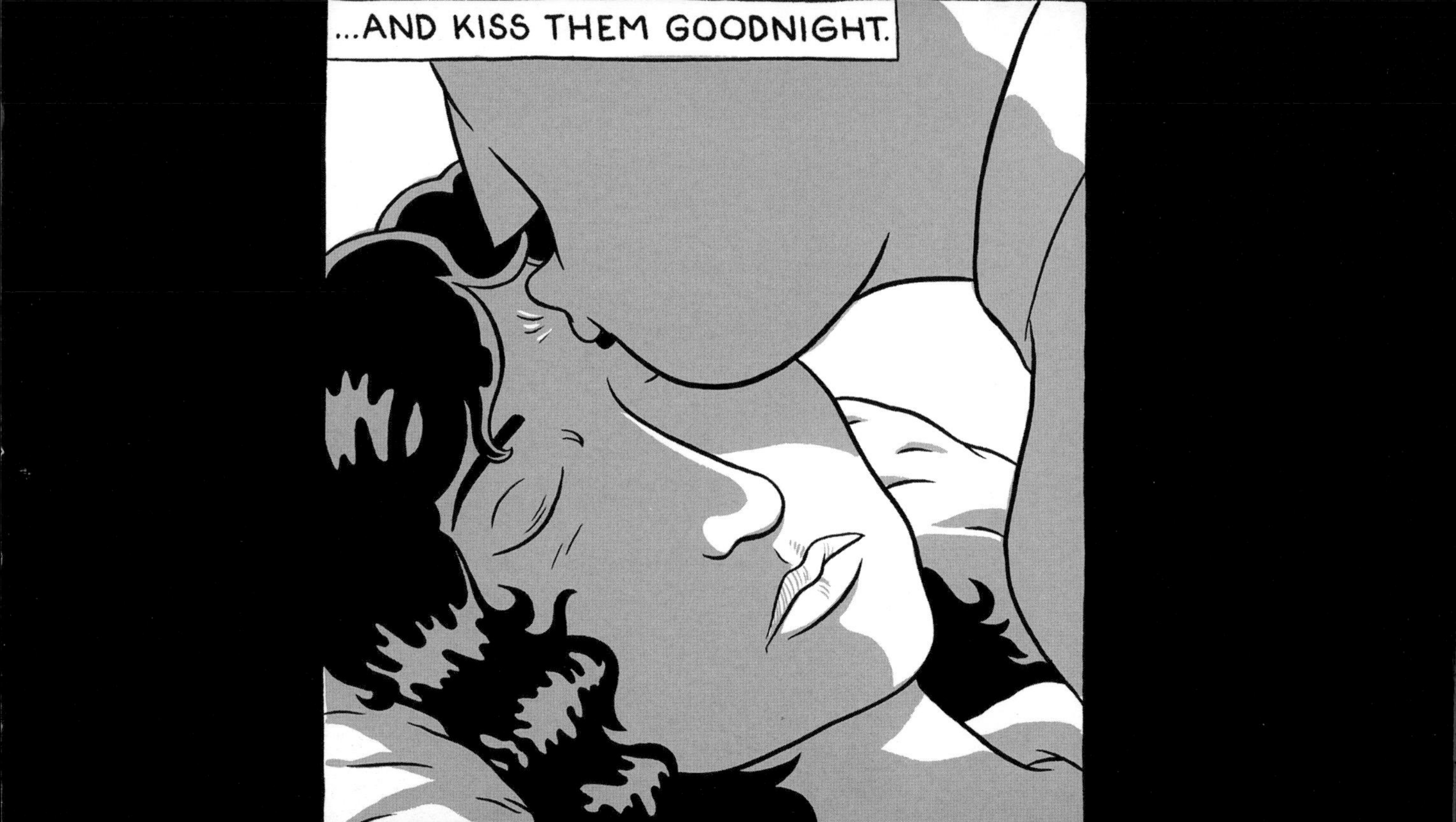
...AND KISS THEM GOODNIGHT.

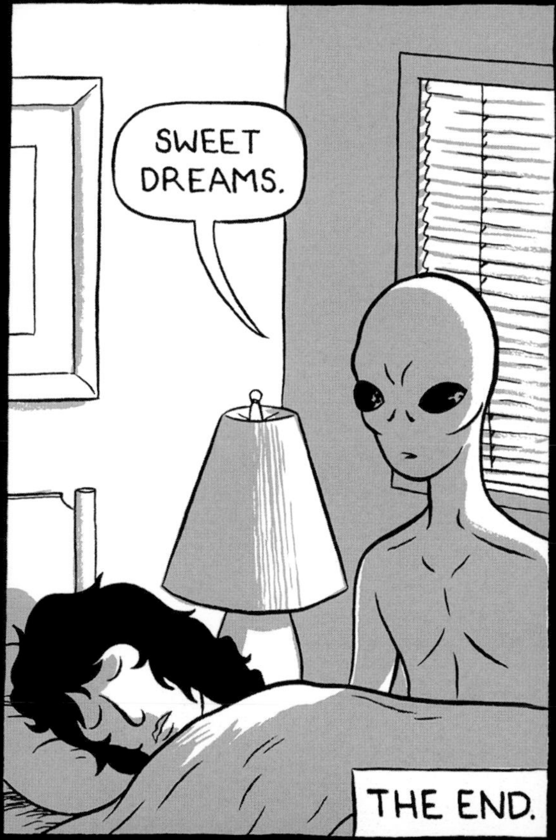
SWEET DREAMS.
THE END.

Malachi Ward is the creator of the *Ritual* comic book series for Revival House Press, The *Expansion* series with Matt Sheean, *The Scout, Utu,* and *Top Five*, which is included in the 2013 edition of *Best American Comics*. Malachi has done work for Brandon Graham's *Prophet*, *Mome*, *NoBrow*, *Island*, and *Study Group Magazine*.